PENGUIN
COMPASS

SHAMANIC VOICES

JOAN HALIFAX, Ph.D., is a medical anthropologist specializing in psychiatry and religion. She has done fieldwork in the Caribbean, North and Central Africa; North America, and Mexico and has been a researcher at Columbia University, the Musée de l'Homme, the University of Miami School of Medicine, and the Maryland Psychiatric Research Center, where she participated in a project utilizing LSD-assisted psychotherapy with individuals dying of cancer. Halifax is the author of many scholarly articles and coauthor with Stanislav Grof, M.D., of *The Human Encounter with Death.* A lecturer in Europe as well as the United States, she is on the faculty of the New School for Social Research and is a consulting editor for McGraw-Hill Publishers.

Shamanic Voices

Shamanic

A Survey of Visionary Narratives

PENGUIN COMPASS

Joan Halifax, Ph.D.

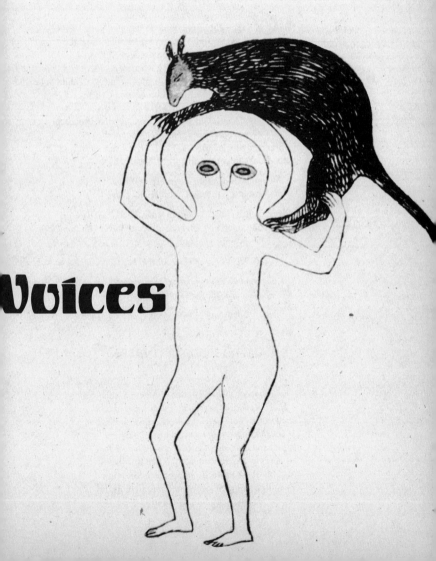

Voices

Title page illustration. This is a totemic ancestor who emerged from the earth's depths at the beginning of the Dreamtime and returned to the chthonic regions at the voyage's end. The Northwest Australian rock painting figure was discovered in the late 1800s. (From: *Journal of the Royal Anthropological Institute of Great Britain, 1890.*)

COMPASS
Published by the Penguin Group
Penguin Group (USA), 375 Hudson Street, New York, New York 10014, U.S.A.
Penguin Books Ltd, 80 Strand, London WC2R 0RL, England
Penguin Books Australia Ltd, 250 Camberwell Road,
Camberwell, Victoria 3124, Australia
Penguin Books Canada Ltd, 10 Alcorn Avenue, Toronto, Ontario, Canada M4V 3B2
Penguin Books India (P) Ltd, 11 Community Centre,
Panchsheel Park, New Delhi – 110 017, India
Penguin Books (N.Z.) Ltd, Cnr Rosedale and Airborne Roads,
Albany, Auckland, New Zealand
Penguin Books (South Africa) (Pty) Ltd, 24 Sturdee Avenue,
Rosebank, Johannesburg 2196, South Africa

Penguin Books Ltd, Registered Offices:
80 Strand, London WC2R 0RL, England

First published in the United States of America by E. P. Dutton
Published simultaneously in Canada by Fitzhenry and Whiteside Limited, Toronto
Published in Arkana Books 1991

11 13 15 17 19 20 18 16 14 12 10

Printed in the United States of America
Designed by Ernie Haim

To Joseph Campbell
    Matsúwa (Don José Ríos)
    Prem Das

Contents

Acknowledgments

I wish to acknowledge the generous contributions to this volume made by these friends and scholars: Marguerite Anne Biesele, John Brockman, William Burns, Joseph Campbell, Edmund Carpenter, Diana Clark, Leonard Crow Dog, Marlene Dobkin de Rios, Mircea Eliade, Richard Erdoes, Alvaro Estrada and his family, Verona Fonte, Peter Furst, Stanislav Grof, John and Eunice Halifax, Michael Harner, Wernher Krutein, Bruce Lamb, Stephen Larsen, John and Toni Lilly, Matsúwa (Don José Ríos), Brooke Medicine Eagle, Henry and Nati Munn, Barbara Myerhoff, John Perry, Prem Das, Gerardo Reichel-Dolmatoff, Ilana Rubenfeld, Carol Rubenstein, Ruturi (Elijio Carillos), María Sabina, Alan Strachan, R. Gordon Wasson, John Watts, Bill Whitehead, Johannes Wilbert, Peter Young, and deLynn Zorilla.

The wizard of the cavern of Les Trois Frères does
a ritual dance high above a medley of animals of
ancient times. His head is crowned with reindeer
antlers; his ears are those of the wolf, and his face
is bearded like a lion's. He has a horse's tail and
bear paws. The wide and startling eyes appear to
see not only the creatures gambolling beneath
him but through the timeless space separating us
from this paleolithic vision. *(After Breuil.)*

Author's Note

This volume in no way attempts to encompass the totality of the phenomenon of shamanism, a lifeway that
spans millennia and the entire planet. It represents one
view, the author's, through the many voices of the
shaman-narrators whose material is herein reproduced.
Behind and around these thirty-six narratives stands a
host of seers and healers whose voices could not be
included in this volume because of the limitations of
space and, in some cases, the unfortunate unavailabil-
ity of material. To the silent ones, I owe a great apology
because my desire was to include all. Yet, a story un-
folds through those who speak in the pages of this
book. It is intended to be read in sequence, from beginning to end. One voice illuminates the next.

Shamanic Voices

1 Into the Nieríka

"There is a doorway within our minds that usually remains hidden and secret until the time of death. The Huichol word for it is nieríka. Nieríka is a cosmic portway or interface between so-called ordinary and nonordinary realities. It is a passageway and at the same time a barrier between worlds."[1] Nieríka, a decorated ceremonial disc, is also said to mean mirror as well as face of the deity.

This Nierka is from a yarn painting done by the Huichol artist Ruturi and lent to the author by Prem Das. It is the threshold through which one passes on the voyage to the world of death and visions.

The Shaman

I am he who puts together, he who speaks, he who searches, says. I am he who looks for the spirit of the day, says. I search where there is fright and terror. I am he who fixes, he who cures the person that is sick. Herbal medicine. Remedy of the spirit. Remedy of the atmosphere of the day, says. I am he who resolves all, says. Truly you are man enough to resolve the truth. You are he who puts together and resolves. You are he who speaks with the light of day. You are he who speaks with terror. [2]

Shamanism is an ecstatic religious complex of particular and fixed elements with a specific ideology that has persisted through millennia and is found in many different cultural settings. The term *shaman,* derived from the Vedic *śram,* meaning "to heat oneself or practice austerities,"[3] indicates influences by Paleo-Oriental civilizations. But the complex of shamanism is more archaic, being part of the prehistoric cultures of Siberian hunters and occurring among protohistorical peoples in other areas of the world. Although shamans are mainly associated with the geographies of northern and central Asia, they can be found in Africa, Oceania, Australia, the Americas, and northern and eastern Europe, wherever hunting-gathering peoples still exist and wherever this ancient sacred tradition has maintained its shape in spite of the shifting of cultural ground.

The shaman, a mystical, priestly, and political figure emerging during the Upper Paleolithic period and perhaps going back to Neanderthal times, can be described not only as a specialist in the human soul but also as a generalist whose sacred and social functions can cover an extraordinarily wide range of activities. Shamans are healers, seers, and visionaries who have mastered death.

They are in communication with the world of gods and spirits. Their bodies can be left behind while they fly to unearthly realms. They are poets and singers. They dance and create works of art. They are not only spiritual leaders but also judges and politicians, the repositories of the knowledge of the culture's history, both sacred and secular. They are familiar with cosmic as well as physical geography; the ways of plants, animals, and the elements are known to them. They are psychologists, entertainers, and food finders. Above all, however, shamans are technicians of the sacred[4] and masters of ecstasy.

The Crisis Journey

*I am not a shaman, as I have
neither had dreams nor been ill.*[5]
—Ikinilik

The shaman's initiation—whether in a cave, on a mountain, atop a tree, or on the terrain of the psyche—embraces the experience of death, resurrection, and realization or illumination. Variations on the fundamental theme of death and rebirth are found in all mythological traditions, and an encounter with death and release into rebirth are immutable dimensions of most personal religious experiences. The initiatory crisis of the shaman must therefore be designated as a religious experience, one that has persisted since at least Paleolithic times and is probably as old as human consciousness, when the first feelings of awe and wonder were awakened in primates.

From this perspective, the initiation of the shaman is an ahistorical event, transcending the confines of culture and bringing into focus ontological concerns that have existed within the human mind for aeons. Furthermore, in many societies, the shaman is the focus of basic human values that define relationships between human beings, the culture's relationship to the cosmos, and the society's relationship to the environment. The shaman is one who has traversed and explored the thresholds as well as the territories of these domains of human, natural, and supernatural interaction. This complete vision of the society is the fruit born of a profound life crisis.

When certain signs have appeared at birth indicating the sacred and special condition of the neonate, the people of a culture are sometimes made aware of a newborn's destiny as a shaman. The shaman's vocation may also be passed from generation to generation, creating a shamanic lineage. In other cases, an individual will begin to show a proclivity for the sacred: For example, certain young children have been powerfully attracted to follow the way of the healer, the priest, the metaphysician. For others, the role has been revealed during dreams or other visionary states, such as an experience with hallucinogenic substances. Or in the course of a traditional vision quest associated with a rite of passage, such as we find among many Native American peoples, the neophyte learns that the life he or she is to follow is that of the Holy One.

Those who, in visions and dreams, have seen the road to what one Eskimo shaman has called "the great task" have often experienced the ordeal of entering the realm of death. Those who have nearly died, through an accident or severe illness, or who have suffered a psychological or spiritual trauma of such proportions that they are catapulted into the territory of death will come to know the inner workings of crisis. The shaman learns to integrate the experiences of sickness, suffering, dying, and death, as well as to share the special knowledge of these powerful events with those who face disease or death for the first time. Shamanhood implies something more than prescribed sacred action. It is an intimate, mystical encounter with the fields of life and death and the forces that fuse these realms.

The encounter with dying and death and the subsequent experience of rebirth and illumination are the authentic initiation for the shaman. Although this process frequently takes the form of an inner experience, the symbolism and feelings have many unusual parallels in the experience of actual biological birth.[6] Furthermore, it provides a very different perspective on so-called psychopathological states, whether they be "culture-bound reactive syndromes" such as "Arctic hysteria" or "acute schizophrenia" in the West.

What follows is an exploration of the various inflections of shamanic initiation by crisis and of the value of these experiences in the lives of those who have gone through them.

The Wilderness Solitude

The call to shamanhood often sends the neophyte into the wildest of terrains, into a world inhabited only by beasts and spirits. It is in these lonely places that the sacred mysteries, which infuse all yet are visible to none, can find their way to the human mind. For the shaman, as for the Tibetan anchorite and most seers and visionaries, nature's wilderness is the locus for the elicitation of the individual's inner wilderness, "the great plain in the spirit," and it is only here that the inner voices awaken into song. The inanimate sermon of pristine deserts, mountains, high plains, and forests instructs from a place beyond idea, concept, or construct.

Many years ago, the Caribou shaman Igjugarjuk told the Arctic explorer Knud Rasmussen that "all true wisdom is only to be learned far from the dwellings of men, out in the great solitudes; and is only to be attained through suffering. Privation and suffering are the only things that can open the mind of man to those things which are hidden from others."[7] (See Igjugarjuk's narrative, pp. 68–70.) Najagneg, another Eskimo shaman, said, "I have searched in the darkness, being silent in the great lonely stillness of the dark. So I became an *angakoq*, through visions and dreams and encounters with flying spirits."[8] And the Mexican Huichol *mara'akáme* (shaman) Matsúwa told me that "I have pursued my apprenticeship for sixty-four years. During these years, many, many times I have gone to the mountains alone. Yes, I have endured much suffering during my life. Yet to learn to see, to learn to hear, you must do this—go into the wilderness alone. For it is not I who can teach you the ways of the gods. Such things are learned only in solitude." (See Matsúwa's narrative, pp. 249–252.)

The Quest for Vision

Certain potential shamans are given explicit instructions that, if properly carried out, will surely transform his or her awareness so dramatically that an experience of death and rebirth is inevitable. Gustav Holm describes an experience of mystical rebirth among the Angmagsalik Eskimos: "The first thing the disciple has to do is to go to a certain lonely spot, an abyss or a cave, and there, having taken a small stone, to rub it on the top of a large one the way of the sun. When they have done this for three days on end, they say, a spirit comes out from the rock. It turns its face toward the rising sun and asks what the disciple will. The disciple then dies in the most horrible torments, partly from fear, partly from overstrain; but he comes to life again later in the day."[9] (See Sanimuinak's narrative, pp. 110–113.)

The spontaneous experience of death and rebirth is also found among the Plains Indians of North America. It can occur during the Sun Dance, in which flesh is given or pierced, or on the occasion of a vision quest associated with puberty or other important passages in a person's life. All such events include a period of purification, isolation, and frequently, body mortification.

Plenty-coups, the Crow chief, told Frank Linderman about his friend The-Fringe's initiation into the role of medicine man. In his quest for knowledge, The-Fringe crossed over to an island by means of a precariously placed pole. However, the water over which he had passed was not ordinary spring water. Not only did the water have healing properties, but its heat was tremendous. The-Fringe then ascended to the top of the mountain and remained alone for three days. On the third morning, his friends could no longer see him, and they knew that the Medicine Water had taken him. As Plenty-coups said, "Nothing could live in the Medicine Water, and there was no way The-Fringe could reach the shore and live."

Finally, on the fourth day, his friends approached the shore of the boiling spring and found The-Fringe, who commanded that they return to the village and make sacred preparations for him. When all was ready, The-Fringe told his dream to eleven Wise

Ones: On the first and second nights on the island, the scalding Medicine Water had washed his body and burned his skin, but he had not moved or cried out. Then an ill-tempered, rough-looking "Person" had led him beneath the boiling Medicine Water, but this time he felt no pain. In this watery abyss, they had come to a great lodge painted in black and red vertical stripes. He was to learn later that this indicated that he was to be a healer of wounds and would become a Wise One. The Otter and White Bear flanked the lodge. Although they spoke angrily to him, they would forever be his allies. Shortly before The-Fringe's departure, the handsome yet strange and silent woman inside the lodge asked the "Person" why he did not give his son something that he could use to help his people. An otter skin and picket pin were given to The-Fringe. The otter skin was his medicine, his power; the picket pin, his wealth. When he concluded his account of his experience, The-Fringe said, "When I awakened I was not on the island where I had made my bed, but on the shore bordering the Medicine Water."[10]

Chief Maza Blaska, of the Oglala Sioux, told ethnomusicologist Natalie Curtis, "To the Holy Man comes in youth the knowledge that he will be holy. The Great Mystery makes him know this. Sometimes it is the Spirits who tell him. When a Spirit comes, it would seem as though a man stood there, but when this man has spoken and goes forth again, none may see whither he goes. Thus the Spirits. With the Spirits the Holy Man may commune always, and they teach him holy things."[11] This knowledge, attained through communication with the world of spirits, sets the shaman apart. But unlike shamans in other parts of the world, those of the Sioux and their neighbors often discover this sacred role in the process of the quest for vision. A sign is given, as it was to The-Fringe, that the youth is one who is chosen by the Spirits to heal; he is designated as one who is holy. "The Holy Man goes apart to a lone tipi and fasts and prays. Or he goes into the hills in solitude. When he returns to men, he teaches them and tells them what the Great Mystery has bidden him to tell. He counsels, he heals, and he makes holy charms to protect the people from all evil. Great is his power and greatly is he revered; his place in the tipi is an honored one."[12]

Ordeals of the Threshold

The specific ordeals of neophyte shamans follow every imaginable form. For example, Igjugarjuk (see pp. 66–70) was compelled by the mysterious divine force Sila to become an *angakoq*. He told Rasmussen that as a young man he was beseiged by dreams that he did not understand: Strange beings spoke to him, and on waking, he saw his dream so clearly that he could recount it totally to his friends. Soon it became evident that he was destined to become a shaman, and the old man Perqánâq was chosen as his instructor. In the depth of winter, Igjugarjuk was put on a sledge just large enough for him to sit on and taken far from his home. When he reached the appointed spot, he remained on the sledge while Perqánâq built a snow hut so small that the neophyte could barely sit cross-legged in it. Not permitted to set foot on the snow, he was lifted from the sledge, carried into the hut, and placed on a small piece of skin. He was not allowed any food or drink and was exhorted to think only of the Great Spirit and of the helping spirit that should presently appear.

After five days, Perqánâq appeared with a drink of tepid water and then left him as before. After fasting for fifteen days, he was given another drink of water and a very small piece of meat, which had to last him ten more days. At the end of this period, Perquqnqoq brought him home. Igjugarjuk declared that the strain of those thirty days was so severe that he "sometimes died a little"[13] (see Igjugarjuk's narrative, pp. 65–70).

In *Across Arctic America*, Rasmussen gives two other accounts of shamanic initiation that illustrate the nature of the ordeals that a shaman can endure in the process of realization.

> Kinalik was still quite a young woman, very intelligent, kind-hearted, clean and good-looking, and spoke frankly, without reserve. Igjugarjuk was her brother-in-law, and had himself been her instructor in magic. Her own initiation had been severe; she was hung up to some tent poles planted in the snow and left there for five days. It was midwinter, with intense cold and frequent blizzards, but she did not feel the cold, for the spirit protected her. When the five days were at

an end, she was taken down and carried into the house, and Igjugarjuk was invited to shoot her, in order that she might attain to intimacy with the supernatural by visions of death. The gun was to be loaded with real powder but a stone was to be used instead of the leaden bullet, in order that she might still retain connection with earth. Igjugarjuk, in the presence of the assembled villagers, fired the shot, and Kinalik fell to the ground unconscious. On the following morning, just as Igjugarjuk was about to bring her to life again, she awakened from the swoon unaided. Igjugarjuk asserted that he had shot her through the heart, and that the stone had afterwards been removed and was in the possession of her old mother.

Another of the villagers, a young man named Aggjartoq, had also been initiated into the mysteries of the occult with Igjugarjuk as his teacher; and in his case, a third form of ordeal had been employed; to wit, that of drowning. He was lashed to a long pole and carried out on to a lake, a hole was cut in the ice, and the pole with its living burden thrust down through the hole, in such a fashion that Aggjartoq actually stood on the bottom of the lake with his head under water. He was left in this position for five days and when at last they hauled him up again, his clothes showed no sign of having been in the water at all and he himself had become a great wizard, having overcome death."[14]

A Caribou shaman summarizes that those who do no evil pass from one life to another, being born again and again in human form. Thus, human beings need not fear death. Those who do evil are reborn as beasts. As such, all life, all consciousness is for all times preserved and is in all ways replenished, "for no life once given can ever be lost or destroyed."[15]

The Underworld of Disease

The crisis of a powerful illness can also be the central experience of the shaman's initiation. It involves an encounter with forces that decay and destroy. The shaman not only survives the ordeal of a debilitating sickness or accident but is healed in the process.

Illness thus becomes the vehicle to a higher plane of consciousness. The evolution from a state of psychic and physical disintegration to shamanizing is effected through the experience of self-cure. The shaman—and only the shaman—is a healer who has healed himself or herself; and as a healed healer, only he or she can truly know the territory of disease and death.

The Tungus shaman Semyonov Semyon succinctly describes how sickness compelled him to become a shaman: "Before I commenced to shamanize, I lay sick for a whole year. I became a shaman at the age of fifteen. The sickness that forced me to this path showed itself in a swelling of my body and frequent spells of fainting. When I began to sing, however, the sickness usually disappeared."[16]

Although the shaman's illness is frequently ascribed to the intrusion of malign spirits, such an invasion usually has beneficial consequences. During the often dramatic and painful sequences of combat with evil spirits, neophyte shamans engage in a powerful struggle against the difficult physical and psychological forces that have previously afflicted their lives. That struggle also trains them for future encounters of a similar sort, which they will enact on behalf of others. In fact, the shaman's ability to subdue, control, appease, and direct spirits separates him or her from ordinary individuals, who are victims of these powerful forces.

Although the Huichol *mara'akáme,* Matsúwa had made many arduous pilgrimages on foot to *Wirikúta* (the Sacred Land of Peyote), although he had spent much time in the wilderness alone, he did not achieve his shamanhood until he had suffered the loss of his right hand and the maiming of his left, both accidents that occurred when he was in his thirties. After that, he began to recognize his own power, and his shamanizing became clear and strong (see pp. 249–252).

Ramón, Matsúwa's apprentice, also seems to have achieved his shamanic power through illness. Ramón recalled that he began to have strange and unusual dreams while he was still young: "It happened one night that *Tayaupá* [Our Father Sun] spoke to me. He said, 'Look, son, do not worry. You must grow a little more so you can go out and become wise, so that you can support yourself.' He said, 'Do not worry, son. It will be good with you one day.' I heard everything. I saw my life. And then I was very happy."[17]

When Ramón was eight years old, he was bitten by a poison-ous serpent. His grandfather, a *mara'akáme,* revealed that Ramón would himself one day be a great shaman if he survived this terrible ordeal. For six months, Ramón was paralyzed and in tre-mendous pain. During this long illness, the young boy, alone much of the time, reflected on what had been revealed to him. After his recovery, he began to accept the destiny that was unfold-ing before him, and he followed the will of the gods.[18] (See pp. 135–137, 169–173, and 233–237.)

An account by A. A. Popov of the initiation of an Avam-Samoyed shaman in the early 1900s gives some notion of the psychosymbolic context of shamanic illness: Stricken with small-pox, the future shaman remained unconscious for three days, so nearly dead that on the third day he was almost buried. He saw himself go down to hell, and, after many adventures, he was carried to an island in the middle of which stood a young birch tree that reached up to heaven. It was the Tree of the Lord of the Earth. And the Lord gave him a branch of it to make himself a drum. Next he came to a mountain. Passing through an opening, he met a naked man playing the bellows at an enormous fire beneath a kettle. The man caught him with a hook, cut off his head, and chopped his body to bits and put them all in the kettle. There he boiled the body for three years, and then forged him a head on an anvil. Finally, he fished out the bones, which were floating in a river, put them together, and covered them with flesh. During his adventures in the Other World, the future shaman met several semidivine personages, and each revealed doctrines to him or taught him secrets of the healing art. When he awoke in his hut, he was initiated and could begin to shamanize.[19]

The often terrifying descent by the shaman initiate into the underworld of suffering and death may be represented by figura-tive dismemberment, disposal of all bodily fluids, scraping of the flesh from the bones, and removal of the eyes. Once the novice has been reduced to a skeleton and the bones cleansed and purified, the flesh may be distributed among the spirits of the various diseases that afflict those in the human community. The bones are all that remain of the shaman, but like seeds, the bones have the potential for rebirth within them. These bone-seeds are covered with new flesh, and the shaman is given new blood. In this transformed condition, the resurrected one receives knowledge of a special and sacred nature and acquires the power of healing, most often from spirit allies. The intense suffering of the neophyte and the subsequent experience of transcendence and knowledge render sacred the condition of this individual, and recovery from the crisis that has immobilized his or her body during this terrifying journey establishes the shaman as one who has met death and been reborn.

Matsúwa was terribly maimed in accidents. Ramón came near death when he was poisoned with snake venom. The Tungus shaman was dying of smallpox and fever. Uvavnuk, a Netsilik Eskimo woman, achieved her great power in one extraordinarily dramatic instant. According to Rasmussen, a ball of fire came down from the sky and struck Uvavnuk senseless. When she regained consciousness, the spirit of light was within her. Her great power was used only to help her people. And when she sang, "all those present were loosed from their burden of sin and wrong; evil and deceit vanished as a speck of dust blown from the hand.

"And this was her song:"

> *The great sea has set me in motion*
> *Set me adrift,*
> *Moving me as the weed moves in a river.*
> *The arch of sky and mightiness of storms*
> *Have moved the spirit within me,*
> *Till I am carried away*
> *Trembling with joy.* [20]

The Bone-Seed

Shamanic initiation demands a rending of the individual from all that constitutes his or her past. Among the Siberian Yakut, the shaman is an observer of his or her own dismemberment. In that state of awareness, he or she learns the territory of death. Here is another account of the shaman's sacrifice of self to the spiritual forces that will guide as they consume: "They cut off the head and place it on the uppermost plank of the *yurta*, from where it watches the chopping up of its body. They hook an iron hook into the body and tear up and distribute all the joints; they clean the bones, by scratching off the flesh and removing all the fluid. They take the two eyes out of the sockets and put them on one side. The flesh removed from the bones is scattered on all the paths of the underworld; they also say that it is distributed among the nine or three times nine generations of the spirits that cause sickness, whose roads and paths the shaman will in future know. He will be able to help with ailments caused by them; but he will not be able to cure those maladies caused by spirits that did not eat of his flesh."[21]

The shamans who have sacrificed themselves to the "great task" and become the sacrament for spirit forces learn the art of dying and acquire the knowledge of healing particular illnesses from the spirits that have consumed their flesh. Through knowledge of those illnesses that have beseiged them, they are able to cure others who find themselves in similar situations. The territory of disease has been revealed to them, and they can now guide the suffering across the terrain of sickness and even death.

For hunting and gathering peoples, bone, like seed, represents the very source of life. To divest oneself of flesh and be reduced to a skeleton is a process of reentering what Mircea Eliade has called the "womb of primordial life" in order to be born anew into a mystical condition.[22] Furthermore, bone, like a quartz crystal or seed, is the enduring source from which light and life spring anew. Shamans, like other religious ascetics, divest themselves of flesh, reduce their bodies to that mysterious yet durable matter which, like the liquid crystal of semen, is the fertile source, ever capable of reproducing itself, and, like the sacred quartz crystal, is the clear body, the diamond body, the bone of emanant light.* Bone, like

---

*Shamans the world over have a special relation to fire, heat, and light. The Vedic term *śram* means "to heat oneself," and the shaman is one who is not only the supreme master of fire but also the embodiment of a heat so fierce that its spiritual luminescence is associated both with purity and with knowledge. An Eskimo shaman explained this to Knud Rasmussen: "Every real shaman has to feel an illumination in his body, in the inside of his head or in his brain, something that gleams like fire, that gives him the power to see with closed eyes into the darkness, into the hidden things or into the future, or into the secrets of another man. I felt that I was in possession of this marvelous ability." (Andreas Lommel, *Shamanism*, p. 60.)

a crystal or a seed, has a dual aspect and represents both the repository of the very source of life and that which is not perishable.[23] Rasmussen suggests that it is bone that will longest withstand the action of sun, wind, and weather after an individual has died. Thus freed from the decaying and evanescent flesh, the shaman has access to the eternal being, ever capable of rebirth from his or her own bones.[24]

The shaman's dismemberment and reconstitution is, then, an essential act of the creation that occurred in primordial times. In *The Two Hands of God,* Alan Watts summarized the process succinctly: "Where there is dismemberment in the beginning there is remembrance at the end—that the fulfillment or consummation of the cosmic game is the discovery of what was covered and the recollection of what was scattered."[25]

The Sacred Tree

The mortal and finite dimensions of existence are transcended by the shaman's rebirth from bones. The vehicle of ascension to the sky realm of the sun, to the territory of illumination, can be the drum. The Yakut says, "The drum is our horse."[26] The pulse of the drum frequently carries the shaman from the underworld, through the roots of the World Tree, up the body of the tree that transects the middle world or earthly plane, and finally, to the glorious summit of the Sacred Tree whose crown embraces the shining heavens.

This Sacred Tree, path to rebirth, symbol of the place of confluence of the human collective, draws the society together by directing its energy toward its powerful center. It is also the means of achieving a transcendent vision of the culture by directing the spirit heavenward. As the shaman is one who is in dynamic relationship to this "axis of the world," the shaman is also the one who balances and centers the society, creating the harmony from which life springs. When this precious equilibrium is lost, the symbolic expressions of the culture's deepest structures are also lost, as though the skeleton were to turn to dust and the primordial forms were no more.

The great North American Indian visionary Black Elk, an Oglala Sioux, was given a bright red stick in a vision. The stick was alive, and as he looked at it, it "sprouted at the top and sent forth branches, and on the branches many leaves came out and murmured and in the leaves the birds began to sing. And then for just a little while [he] thought [he] saw beneath it in the shade the circled villages of people and every living thing with roots or legs or wings, and all were happy."[27] Later, Black Elk mourned, "There is no center any longer and the sacred tree is dead."[28]

The Spirit flight

The shaman's spirit ascends, breaking the plane of death, soaring to a timeless place. The winglike rhythms of the drum and the dance and the pitch of the song transport the ecstatic's spirit to realms far beyond the ordinary, a messenger in flight across the perilous threshold of the two-light world, where the illumination of the dream world of night and the light of the day's sun transect and fuse into the field of twilight, where transcendent vision is awakened. The wizard's soul is transformed into a bird, the wings and body of the spirit-bird and the shaman's soul are one body, and the distinction between the shaman and the animal ally dissolves. Nature, culture, and supernature merge into the field of transcendent consciousness.

The feathers that are so often associated with shamanistic performance—prayer arrows, healing wands, bird staffs, feathered capes and headdresses—are symbolic not only of the ascension of the shaman's soul into the sky realm but also of the golden rays of the spiritual sun, the light of awakened consciousness unfettered by gravity, the boundaries of space, materiality, and the strictures of time.

The shaman's flight is also facilitated by song, the birdsong of animal familiars. The shaman is one who is enchanted (sung into), the very breath of the song metamorphosing the wizard into a sky being or soul-bird. Among the Siberian Yakut, "Mysterious noises are audible, sometimes from above, sometimes from

below, sometimes in front of, sometimes behind the shaman.
... You seem to hear the plaintive call of the lapwing mingled with
the croaking of the falcon interrupted by the whistle of the woodcock, all that is the voice of the shaman, varying the intonation of
his voice—you hear the screaming of eagles mingled with the
plaints of the lapwing, the sharp tones of the woodcock and the
refrain of the cuckoo."[29] And Richard Erdoes has described the
sacred songs of his Sioux friends as the crying of flocks of birds,
a sound that transports the listener into flight.

During their initiatory trances, some fledgling Siberian shamans find themselves being nurtured in nests high in the World
Tree. The higher the nest, the more powerful the shaman will be.
Here is a description of one such experience: "Up and above there
is a certain tree. There the souls of the shamans are raised before
they attain their powers. On the boughs of this tree are nests in
which the souls of the shamans lie and are attended. The name of
the tree is 'Tuuru.' The higher the nest is placed in this tree, the
stronger will the shaman be who is raised in it, the more will he
know, and the further will he see."[30]

The bird-shaman, appearing at least as early as the Old Stone
Age and still found today from the Arctic to the southern reaches
of the Americas, is vividly portrayed in several Magdalenian caves
of central France. Deep in a crypt at the back of the great labyrinthian Lascaux Cave is a mysterious and uncanny painting from
Paleolithic times. To the right is a bison bull, his bowels unfurling
from a wound in his belly, a spear transecting his hindside from
anus to sexual organs. The head of this eviscerated beast is turned
as though to gaze at his uncoiling innards. On the left side of this
tableau, a rhinoceros with feces dabbed beneath his tail seems to
be walking away. And between these two carefully rendered
figures lies a crudely drawn man; he wears a bird mask, his hands
are claws, and his erect penis points toward the wounded bull. To
the prostrate man's right is a staff surmounted by a bird. The
human figure is undoubtedly that of a shaman, an entranced wizard whose spirit is in mystical flight. This we can surmise not only
by the fact that his penis is erect, a condition that is not infrequent
during dreams or trance states, but also by the bird mask adorning
his face, his claws, and the bird staff, similar to shamans' staffs the
world over and denoting the flight of the spirit.[31] This image of

the flight of the spirit as a bird, as depicted some 15,000 years ago in this initiatory chamber, has persisted over time and across many cultures: the Indian gander; the Amerindian parrot, hawk, and eagle; the Siberian goose; and the dove. The rapture induced by trance, when the soul of the ecstatic leaves the body and flies into the realm of spirits and gods, is indeed an act of transcendence.

In the experience of initiation through which the shaman passes, the mythic images woven into a society's fabric suddenly become not only apparent but often enacted and made boldly visible and relevant for all. The initiatory crisis and the experience of death and resurrection, then, do not represent a rending of the individual from his or her social ground. Rather, they are a deepening of the patterns that compose the sacred, ahistorical territory that supports the more superficial and transient aspects of human culture. The direction that the psyche takes as a result of the crisis is not circumscribed or curtailed by society. Rather, the human spirit is oriented toward the cosmos, the ground of being is the universe, and the life field is therefore amplified to include *all* dimensions of "Unconcealed Being."

Balanced between worlds, the shaman teaches by powerful example that illness can be a passageway to a greater life where there is access to great power at great risk. The healing image that the shaman projects is of disease as a manifestation of the transformative impulse in the human organism.

Shamanic Balance

The shaman is a healed healer who has retrieved the broken pieces of his or her body and psyche and, through a personal rite of transformation, has integrated many planes of life experience: the body and the spirit, the ordinary and the nonordinary, the individual and the community, nature and supernature, the mythic and the historical, the past, the present and the future. The threshold place of the initiatory experience is the two-light world.

The shaman, lord of the three realms of sky, earth, and the

underworld, is an individual endowed with the ability to enter profound trance states, a "technician of ecstasy," as Mircea Eliade has so aptly termed this religious specialist.[32] In these visionary states, the shaman is open to contact with animal allies and spirit helpers. Or the wizard may leave his or her body behind like a husk while the disincarnate soul journeys to the celestial realms above or the underworld of disease and death. The knowledge of these domains makes it possible for the shaman to retrieve the souls of those who are sick, to guide the souls of those who have died, and to have direct relations with a celestial supreme being. On other occasions, the shaman's body can become a vessel for entities that possess and communicate through the physical human form, making the world of spirits present, living, and accessible.

As intermediary between the realms of the divine, the nether world, and the middle world, the shaman becomes a master of thresholds, putting his or her body on the line to make manifest a process that is intrinsic to all of shamanism: shamanic balance. Just as twilight is the temporal threshold, shamanic equilibrium is the process occurring at that threshold, where the shaman-wizard becomes the guide, the path, the vision, the image and personification of both the transfigured and the field of transfiguration.

Anthropologist Barbara Myerhoff, a keen and sensitive observer of human behavior, recounts an important episode of a demonstration of shamanic equilibrium by her close friend Ramón Medina Silva, the Huichol shaman:

> I first became aware of the significance of the shaman's need for exquisite balance in my contact with the Huichol Indians of North Central Mexico several years ago. For some time I had been working with a Huichol *mara'akáme,* or shaman priest, named Ramón Medina Silva. One afternoon, without explanation, he interrupted our sessions of taping mythology to take a party of Huichol friends and myself, to an area outside his home. It was a region of steep barrancas cut by a rapid waterfall cascading perhaps a thousand feet over jagged, slippery rocks. At the edge of the fall, Ramón removed his sandals and announced that this was a special place for shamans. He proceeded to leap across the waterfall, from rock to rock, frequently pausing, his body bent forward, his arms

outspread, head thrown back, entirely bird-like poised motionlessly on one foot. He disappeared, reemerged, leaped about, and finally achieved the other side. I was frightened and puzzled by the performance, but none of the Huichols there seemed at all worried. The wife of one of the older Huichol men told me that her husband had started to become a *mara'akáme* but had failed because he lacked balance. I assumed that she referred to his social and personal unsteadiness, for he was an alcoholic and something of a deviant. I knew I had witnessed a virtuoso display of balance, but it was not until the next day when discussing this event with Ramón that I began to understand more clearly what had occurred. "The *mara'akáme* must have superb equilibrium," he said and demonstrated the point by using his fingers to march up his violin bow. "Otherwise he will not reach his destination and will fall this way or that." And his fingers plunged into an imaginary abyss. "One crosses over; it is very narrow and without balance, one is eaten by those animals waiting below."[33]

The shaman's journey, as Myerhoff describes it, signifies that a connection still exists between the familiar world of ordinary human existence and a paradisical realm free of suffering, a mythological world that existed before the primordial divisions emerged, destroying a harmonious and divine past. Since that rupture, mortality is a condition characterized by separation and loss. This situation is symbolically mended when the shaman undertakes magical flights.[34]

The shaman, having ascended the *Axis Mundi,* the World Tree, has come to know the very hub of life and death, heaven and earth, the still point between the pairs of opposites, and has experienced the dissolution of separateness and the attainment of balance in the field of the infinite. The whirling of the wizard's dance transports the mage to the utter stillness of the timeless center. Here the Kwakiutl Indian chants, "I am the center of the world!"

As the holy man and visionary Black Elk stood on the summit of Harney Peak, he had a mystical perception of the universe, a cosmos of harmony and balance transcending all polarities: "Then I was standing on the highest mountain of them all, and round about beneath me was the whole hoop of the world and while I stood there I saw more than I can tell and I understood more than I saw, for I was seeing in a sacred manner the shapes of things in the spirit, and the shape of all shapes as they must live together like one being. And I saw that the sacred hoop of my people was one of many hoops that made one circle, wide as daylight and as starlight, and in the center grew one mighty flowering tree to shelter all the children of one mother and one father. And I saw that it was holy."[35]

The Sacred Politician

The shaman's work entails maintaining balance in the human community as well as in the relationships between the community and the gods or divine forces that direct the life of the culture. When these various domains of existence are out of balance, it is the shaman's responsibility to restore the lost harmony.

When I was in Huichol country in Mexico, I came to realize that Matsúwa was not only a shaman-priest but also a politician —a sacred politician. His political action was effected not only through ceremony, when the community gathered to celebrate the gods that guide them on their way, but also individually, whenever the need arose. However, the ancient rituals that have persisted through millennia are the true heart of the community, linking it to an inexhaustible and sacred past. When there is social strife and disharmony, resolution is frequently achieved through these timeless events.

I remember Matsúwa, at the end of the second night of the *Wima'kwari* (drum ceremony), fiercely beckoning individuals from disparate social factions to the sacralized ground before him. He touched his prayer feathers *(muviéri)* to objects that had become infused with life energy force *(kupúri)* and transferred the precious substance to those who were in need of it, a transmission similar to the communication of shakti between Hindu guru and disciple. By doing this, Matsúwa was equalizing or balancing a social situation that was obviously a problem in the community. He also brought his people into the real field of power, a power that would enable them to see and understand the true meaning of their own lives.

The Androgyne Shaman

The dissolution of the contraries—life and death, light and dark, male and female—and reconstitution of the fractured forms is one of the most consistent impulses in the initiation and transformation process as experienced by the shaman. To bring back to an original state that which was in primordial times whole and is now broken and dismembered is not only an act of unification but also a divine remembrance of a time when a complete reality existed. In many instances, shamanic rituals of initiation put the neophyte or apprentice in relation to a mythological origin, connecting the individual with a continuum that transcends the confines of the human condition. The neophyte ultimately embraces the mystery of the totality that existed in *illo tempore,* becoming that totality, a process of profound recollection. The occasional androgyny of the shaman is one inflection of paradise, where the two become one. The death of separation dissolves all worldly distinctions, and balance is attained.

The situation that reconciles the paradox in the sexual domain, androgyny, has an archaic history, and its manifestations in the realms of sacred behavior are manifold. During mysteries of initiation such as those of shamanic election, androgyny can appear at two very significant moments in this sacred continuum: at its inception and at its termination. Initiation relieves the *oppositorum* and the errant polarities from their painful exile. It provides the ground for the reenactment of creation, for the death of alienation, and for the rebirth of unity, reconciling, if only for an instant, all contraries and making known to the initiated the paradox of divine reality.

The shaman must have access to the totality and ultimately must incorporate it. Just as those spirits of disease that consume the body in the process of initiatory crisis lend power to cure illness by allowing the neophyte shaman direct knowledge of the state, the direct experience of sexual totality by assuming the role of the opposite sex gives the shaman the opportunity to recognize and understand the condition of femaleness or maleness and ultimately to become total.

Soft Men

Among Siberian peoples, androgynous shamans appear to be unusually prevalent. Waldemar Bogoras recounts the sexual transformation of the young Chuckchee neophyte. The spirit ally, or *ke'let*, demands that the young man become "a soft man being." Many instances of suicide among adolescent shamans occurred as a result of their refusal to meet this requirement. Nonetheless, most neophytes complied in spite of their profound social and psychological ambivalence. The transformation process is heralded by the spirits guiding the young man to braid his hair like a woman's. Next, the spirits, through dreams, prescribe women's clothing for the young man. (Shaman healers also occasionally braid the hair of a sick man or dress him in woman's clothing to disguise him from the spirits of illness as well as to effect further the healing rituals.)[36]

The third stage of this initiation entails a more total feminization of the male shaman. The youth who is undergoing the process relinquishes his former male behaviors and activities and adopts the female role. According to Bogoras, "He throws down the lasso of the reindeer herdsman and the harpoon of the seal hunter, and takes to the needle and the skin scraper." His spirits are guiding and teaching him in the woman's way. His mode of speech changes as well as his behavior, and on certain occasions, so does his body: "He loses his masculine strength, fleetness of foot in the race, endurance in wrestling, and acquires instead the helplessness of a woman. Even his physical character changes. The transformed person loses his brute courage and fighting spirit, and becomes shy of strangers, even fond of small talk and of nursing small children. Generally speaking, he becomes a woman with the appearance of a man. . . ."[37]

The transformative process can also involve an actual change in sex role. The "soft man" comes to experience himself sexually as a female. With the help of his spirit allies, he is able to attract the attention of eligible men, one of whom he chooses to be his husband. The two marry and live as a man and wife, often until death, performing their appropriate social and sexual roles. Certain Siberian shamans tell of transformed shamans giving birth to animals as well as human beings.[38]

Androgyny as union of the opposites is also found among the Ngadja Dyak. These people refer to the class of shamans as *basir* (unable to procreate, impotent). The *basir* dress in female garb and assume a female social role. Mircea Eliade believes that the bisexuality and impotence of the *basir* arise because these priest-shamans are regarded as the intermediaries between two cosmological planes, earth and sky, and because they combine in their own person the feminine element (earth) and the masculine element (sky).[39]

In an earlier time, the Sea Dyak shaman, at the completion of the initiatory process, donned female clothing, which he wore for the rest of his life. Today, this practice occurs under special circumstances. If the shaman is commanded on three occasions in his dreams to dress as a woman, he assumes this role in spite of village ridicule. Not to do so would invite death. It is not unusual for individuals undergoing this transformative process to encounter profound feelings of dread.[40] Bogoras recounts the horror experienced by those shamans undergoing a transformation from male to female.[41] Yet, among the Koryak, androgynous shamans were believed to be the most potent of all wizards.[42] And Bogoras noted that the Chuckchee jested only in whispers because the people were terrified of those shamans who were transformed.[43]

Warrior-Women

Women shamans can undergo similar transformations, although the accounts of such instances are indeed few. After an intense religious retreat in the woods, Liomkee, a Toradja woman, dressed as a male warrior and became a medium for the ancestral spirit who told her people it would no longer be necessary to plant their fields or tend their livestock. Headhunting had been outlawed, and the people feared that the spirits would consume them because they were not able to feed the hungry spirits the heads of slain enemies. So cultists proceeded to construct a large canoe on stilts, a shaman's boat, that would bear them heavenward to the upperworld, where they would join their ancestral spirits without dying.[44]

There is also an extraordinary account of a Kutenai woman, a prophetess, who adorned herself in male clothing and joined a war party. Manlike Woman had been residing at the North West Company's post on the Columbia River with her husband, who was a servant there. After her transformation, she left her husband and married another woman as a result of her visions. Later, around 1812, she began to prophesy the end of the Indian way and the devastation of the world by two gigantic supernatural beings. After this catastrophy, there would be a new dawning of Indian life.[45] Both of these women had messianic personalities and were involved not only with psychic and sexual transformation but also with cultural transformation and social change.

What follows is a story, told by the Eskimo Manelaq, of an old wizard, a woman, who transformed herself into a man. This tale gives some notion of the androgyne shaman's power to manipulate the elements from the position of balance attained at the threshold.

There was once an old foster mother and her adoptive daughter. Nobody cared about them, and when people were moving to new hunting places they left them behind in the empty snow huts.

Hunting was bad, and people were hungry and in distress, and no one would have the old woman and her adoptive daughter with them. It mattered nothing if they stayed behind and died of hunger.

But the old foster mother was a great shaman and, when they had been left alone, and all her neighbors had gone their way, she turned herself into the form of a man and married her adoptive daughter. With a willow branch she made herself a penis so that she might be like a man, but her own genitals she took out and made magic over them and turned them into wood, she made them big and made a sledge of them. Then she wanted a dog, and that she made out of a lump of snow she had used for wiping her end; it became a white dog with a black head; it became white because the snow was white, but it got the black head because there was shit on one end of the lump of snow. Such a great shaman was she that she herself became a man, she made a sledge and a dog for hunting at the breathing holes.

At first they suffered want. The old foster mother did not yet know how to hunt properly, but then it occurred to her to utter powerful magic words: *nacermik:* she began to entice seals to the house. It was early in the morning, and it was not long before they heard a seal scraping down in the floor of the snow hut. As soon as it had made a hole up through the floor the old foster mother seized it and caught it with her very hands; still, she was badly scratched and bitten on the hands.

After that they lived on the seal, but as soon as it was all eaten up the old foster mother uttered magic words intended to entice foxes to the house. It was early in the morning, and it was not long before they could hear a fox scraping at the door of the snow hut. At last the block fell right over and a little fox came into the house. After the first one came still another fox, and so it went on. The old woman and her adoptive child lived in a double house and only when one half of the house was quite full of foxes did the old foster mother stop the flocking of the animals; but indeed by that time there were so many foxes that they entirely filled the house from floor to roof. After that they lived on all these foxes, skinning them and eating the meat. Of all the pads of the many small fox feet they made platform mats for their sleeping rugs; and they got clothing and sleeping rugs out of the fox skins.

Some time afterwards they were visited by a man, and he told later, when he got home, that the old woman and her adoptive daughter were soiled all over clothing and hair with fox fat, so much had they been revelling in fat foxes.

As soon as there was no more fox meat the old foster mother uttered magic words to entice caribou to the house.

Caribou flocked up, as many as the big double house could hold, and even more; they killed the caribou and as there were so many that they were quite unable to eat them up themselves, they sent word to their old neighbours, but only to those who had been good to them, not those who had wanted to starve them to death; and summer came, and still the caribou meat had not been all eaten.

The old foster mother was in the habit of being a woman when there were callers, and only when they were alone was she a man. But so it happened once that a young man came on a visit while the old foster mother was out hunting. And when she was a man she was always a young, handsome man, for she was a great shaman.

The young guest came into the house and saw that the young girl was sitting sewing a man's inner coat; she sewed with small, fine stitches. He had not been long in the house before the old foster mother came home without knowing that a stranger was present, and the visitor distinctly saw a man's coat flap outside the window. But when the man came in through the passage and into the house, and found the young visitor, he suddenly sank on his knees and became an old woman. This was because she was ashamed. The young adoptive daughter burst into tears when she saw this; she cried with sorrow because she had lost her husband, who hunted so well for her.

But it is said that when the young man went away again, the old foster mother turned back into a man, a young, agile and skillful hunter, and thus she lived afterwards until her death.[46]

Beyond the Paradox

Androgyny then can be seen as the outcome of transcending the pairs of opposites, the attaining of equilibrium between two polar forces in a relationship of dynamic tension, and the unification of planes of being, earth and sky, female and male, the intuitive and the rational, the visionary and the ordinary, the Dionysian and Appollonian, and the lunar and the solar. Although there are numerous instances of shamans becoming, to greater or lesser degrees, androgynous, the process of uniting and/or transcending the pairs of opposites sometimes occurs on a symbolic level. For example, Johannes Wilbert has reported that among the Warao of Venezuela, the *hebumataro,* or fire gourd, is the primary object of power after the sacred stone. The first rattle was obtained when an ancestral shaman ascended to the place of the spirit of the South. During his visit, he received the sacred fire rattle and was given instructions about the creation of channels of communication with the supernatural so that he and his kind might never lose contact with the gods of the cardinal directions and the sacred center.

The construction of the rattle is a deeply sacred process. After the proper fruit has been carefully selected and prepared by the shaman, four mouth slits are cut into the body of the gourd. At times, these are decorated with incised teeth. Then small quartz crystals, each one an ancestral spirit, are consecrated and, one by one, placed inside the belly of the gourd. The shaman refers to these tiny crystals as his family, for they will assist him in his ministration to the sick. When his spirit family is collected inside the rattle's head, the shaman inserts a central shaft through the vaginalike openings at either end of the gourd's body. The handle is referred to as the rattle's *leg*, but this act is actually a ritual symbolic union of male and female and is related to the fertilizing power felt to be part of the completed instrument. The Warao shaman also believes the rattle to be the world axis. In his journey after death, he carries the rattle in a vertical position in front of himself, ascending along its fiery path to the house of his patron deity. The rattle, itself a union of opposites, becomes the instrument of balance, transformation, and flight.[47]

The Double Being

The shaman's quest is the acquisition of metaphysical knowledge. The shaman's efforts to incorporate or embrace the paradox involve him or her in the constant practice of transformation, as if moving from one point of view to another provides the experiential ground of understanding, of wisdom, of true perspective. These viewpoints are generally attained through metaphysical vision. They can be termed initiatory because it is precisely the focus of the initiation to open the mystery by becoming it, to transcend death by dying in life, to pierce duality by embracing the opposites, to reunite the fractured forms. The androgynization of the shaman represents the biunity of earth and sky; the shaman becomes a bridge between the lower and middle worlds and the sky realm. The shaman thus becomes a double being that like the philosopher's stone, the Rebis, has the potential of transmutation as an intrinsic condition.

Shaman Song

The Dakota holy man Good-Eagle told the story of another holy man, one of the ancient times, who through the power of song made the World Tree yield its precious waters so that all could drink from this sacred and inexhaustible source and be healed. Here is his story:

> After giving offerings to this holy man of long ago, the people prepared for him a sweat lodge, where he went to purify himself and be renewed in solitude. Then, into the earth he erected a pole on which he bound a painted scarlet buffalo calf hide. The sick and suffering people, gathering around the pole, cut from their own arms pieces of flesh that they laid at the base of the pole. The holy man placed a wooden cup next to the offered strips of flesh and began to sing a song of power:
>
> *O ye people, be ye healed*
> *Life anew I bring ye.*
> *O ye people, be ye healed*
> *Life anew I bring ye.*
> *Through the Father over all*
> *Do I thus*
> *Life anew I bring ye.*
>
> As he was singing, sacred water trickled down the pole until the cup was filled to the brim. All the suffering people drank from this divine source, and their sickness left them.
>
> The holy man sent the healed ones to their tipis to rest until night. Then the people returned to the sacred pole, the center, where the holy man drew signs on the ground. None of the gathered understood the meaning of what had been inscribed until the holy man, holding his hands above the ground, said, "The spirits of the fathers tell me tomorrow that you shall see buffalo in plenty, and every man of you shall kill three." He went on to say, "You shall cut off the legs and cut out the tongues and hearts of all those that you kill and

leave them for an offering to the Great Mystery, but you shall bring me forty hides."

The people found it to be as the holy man said it would be. They brought him the hides, and he made special shirts for them. He also made gunpowder, caps, and wads from clay, straw, and charcoal. These he presented to the men. Then he arranged all his people into a line, placing himself at the end. He lit his pipe from the rays of the sun, and each man drew a few whiffs to symbolize the breath of life.

The holy man then said, "This, people, is good. I have healed their sickness. I have renewed their life. Now I shall go back to my own place." After this, he was never seen again.[48]

As the World Tree stands at the center of the vast planes of the cosmos, song stands at the intimate center of the cosmos of the individual. At that moment when the shaman song emerges, when the sacred breath rises up from the depths of the heart, the center is found, and the source of all that is divine has been tapped.

On the Alaskan island called Little Diomede, Knud Rasmussen encountered an old woman living among the shreds of her life in a cold, dark cave. A diviner, she had seen many seasons come and go and many lives pass as the seasons do. She spoke to the Greenlander of her own life and imminent passing. Her final words to him concerned the genesis of song. With eloquent and profound insight, she described the source of the sacred sounds that are the most important of the shaman's voices, those voices that awaken during threshold experiences: "For our forefathers believed that the songs were born in stillness while all endeavored to think of nothing but beautiful things. Then they take shape in the minds of men and rise up like bubbles from the depths of the sea, bubbles seeking the air in order to burst. This is how sacred songs are made."[49]

Like seeds buried in the earth or bubbles in the sea's depths, song seems to emerge for the shaman only in a special season. The pain of the body and loneliness of the soul can decay the husk protecting the song within the singer. At that moment when the shaman is most profoundly enmeshed in the experience of suffering or joy, at the moment of ecstasy when he or she is transported to a place that is beyond mortality, the poetry breaks forth to overwhelm, a potent and aesthetic resolution.

This is an emotion-filled process and one that is difficult, at best, for the prose writer, to describe, for it occurs in the realm of the spirit. Yet, a few shaman-poets, such as Isaac Tens, Aua, and Orpingalik, have described this moment when the seed of song breaks open. To Rasmussen, Orpingalik explained that "man is moved just like the ice floe sailing here and there out in the current. His thoughts are driven by a flowing force when he feels joy, when he feels sorrow. Thoughts can wash over him like a flood, making his blood come in gasps, and his heart throb. Something, like an abatement in the weather, will keep him thawed up, and then it will happen that we, who always think we are small, will feel still smaller. And we will fear to use words. But it will happen that the words that we need will come of themselves. When the words we want to use shoot up of themselves—we get a new song."[50]

The songs and chants of the shaman are in and of themselves manifestations of power achieved in the course of a painful ordeal that puts the one who has quested in contact with the supernatural. The Papago of the American southwestern desert say that vision comes not to those who are unworthy. Only to one who is humble does the dream come, and contained within the dream, there is always the song.[51]

These great poetries, emerging from the limitless depths of the human spirit that have been opened to the territory of the sacred through the experience of crisis and suffering, mark the very moment of creative illumination; each subsequent singing then becomes a reenactment or remembering of that powerful transforming event. The singer brings into play his or her past experience of affliction and transcendent realization in relation to one who is now suffering. From the field of primary inspiration, he or she "sings into life"[52] those who are plagued with disease and those who are facing death.

Orpingalik once exclaimed that songs were "comrades in loneliness."[53] As personified comrades, songs are living as men are living and as the world of spirit is also living. Indeed, the shaman's song is the sound of the gods coming through the human being, as the high, whining voice of the bull-roarer is the sound of spirits.

Geronimo, the Apache chief and holy man, told ethnomusicologist Natalie Curtis that the song he was about to sing was holy and had great power: "As I sing, I go through the air to a holy place where Yusun [the Supreme Being] will give me power to do wonderful things. I am surrounded by little clouds, and as I go through the air I change, becoming spirit only."[54] Here song is felt to be not only the vehicle of flight but also the means of transformation.

Shaman song, therefore, represents a profound relationship between spirit and matter. The spirit of breath, emerging from within the human organism in the form of song, can be likened to the illumined soul shining through human eyes. Orpingalik told Rasmussen: "Songs are thoughts, sung with the breath when people are moved by great forces and ordinary speech no longer suffices."[55] And he continued, "How many songs I have I cannot tell you. I keep no count of such things. There are so many occasions in one's life when a joy or sorrow is felt in such a way that the desire comes to sing; and so I only know that I have many songs. All my being is song. I sing as I draw my breath."[56]

Song is often a signal, too, of the communion of the shaman with a spirit entity. The English word *spirit* is derived from the Latin word *spirare,* "to breathe," which is indeed the source (inspiration) and manifestation of song. Among the Klamath Indians, spirit and song are one thing; the same word indicates both, song being the embodiment of spirit and the spirit awakening in song.[57] Of one of his songs, Orpingalik exclaimed, "My breath—this is what I call this song, for it is just as necessary for me to sing as it is to breathe."[58]

The shaman who desires a song does not fix his or her mind on particular words nor sing a known tune. In dreams or other dreamlike states, the song comes through the barrier that separates the human being from the spirit world. For the Papago, the shaman could hear a song, " 'and he knows it is the hawk singing to him or the great white birds that fly from the ocean.' Perhaps, the clouds sing, or the wind, or the feathery red spider, swinging on its invisible rope."[59] Perhaps, as among the Huichol Indians, it is the fire's song that is translated into language, or the wind in dry brush or the rain falling on thatching. Or perhaps it is the mind of the shaman that is now ready to receive the sacred sounds that come from within or without and are rendered into a poetic chant.

These poetries, arising at a moment of divine inspiration in the crucible of the soul, are often felt to be medicine. Isaac Tens, a Gitksan Indian, recalled that his first encounter with the spirit was heralded by a loss of consciousness. His body was quivering: "While I remained in this state, I began to sing. A chant was coming out of me without my being able to do anything to stop it. Many things appeared to me presently: huge birds and animals . . . these were visible only to me, not to others in my house. Such visions happen when a man is about to become a shaman; they occur of their own accord. The songs force themselves out complete without any attempt to compose them."[60]

The sung word is powerful; it names a thing, it stands at the sacred center, drawing all toward it. The word exists and does not exist. It both awakens an image and is an awakened image. The word disappears, the poetry is gone, but the imaginal form persists within the mind and works on the soul. *Poesis*, then, an action and an interaction in its primary sense, is the process of creation.

The power of song to heal the singer as well as the listener is a persistent and remarkable feature of shamanic songs. Tungus shaman Semyonov Semyon confided that when he sang, his sickness usually disappeared.[61] And Aua, a Netsilik Eskimo, during his painful, tireless efforts to become a shaman, discovered that the spontaneous emergence of song accompanied the alleviation of suffering. "Then I sought solitude, and here I soon became very melancholy. I would sometimes fall to weeping, and feel unhappy without knowing why. Then, for no reason, all would suddenly be changed, and I felt a great, inexplicable joy, a joy so powerful that I could not restrain it, but had to break into song, a mighty song, with only room for the one word: joy, joy! And I had to use the full strength of my voice. And then in the midst of such a fit of mysterious and overwhelming delight I became a shaman, not knowing myself how it came about. But I was a shaman. I could see and hear in a totally different way."[62]

Song becomes the manifestation of the shaman's transformed psyche and spirit, a soul that at one time has found itself vulnerable and wounded and is now healed and powerful. The sign of the human spirit's wholeness is its song.

The Shaman's Voice

The shaman's voice, whether raised in song or chant, echoing the ancient stories of a mythological past, or narrating a personal account of trance, initiation, or healing, is the carrying frequency for the timeless symbols that characterize this most archaic of sacred manifestations. In the process of shaping this book, I came to realize that shamans communicate about their world in an elegant metaphorical style that could awaken a particular kind of experience in the reader. And in the voice of the shaman-narrator, other voices can frequently be heard, the voices of gods and ancestors or the shadowy spirits of the dead, the voice of the mushroom, the songs of creatures and the elements, the numinous sounds of far-off stars, or echoes from the underworld. It is only these visionaries who can transmit to us the totality of their ecstatic lifeway. The Western scholar must, of necessity, bring his or her bias into play when interpreting what shamans have told them or what they have observed. My own particular bias is evident; the preceding discussion reflects my research interest in song, myth, and psychological transformation, including the phenomena of death and rebirth and the process of androgyny.

Ultimately, to understand shamanism in even the most rudimentary way, it is necessary to listen closely to shamans as they communicate about their lives. It is the shaman who weaves together the ordinary world that is lived in and the philosophical image of the cosmos that is thought of. Human existence, suffering, and death are rendered by shamans into a system of philosophical, psychological, spiritual, and sociological symbols that institutes a moral order by resolving ontological paradoxes and dissolving existential barriers, thus eliminating the most painful and unpleasant aspects of human life. The perfection of the timeless past, the paradise of a mythological era, is an existential potential in the present. And the shaman, through sacred action, communicates this potential to all.

2 Journeys to Other Worlds

These figures are redrawn from a larger group of antelope men painted on the walls of the Procession Shelter in the Ndedema Gorge, South Africa. Above these shamans hovers an ales, a mythical spirit creature associated with the mysteries of transformation. *(From: Harald Pagar, Ndedema Akademische Druck-u. Verlagsanstaat. Gràz, Austria, 1971, p. 340.)*

Sereptie

SIBERIA/TAVGI SAMOYED

Twenty years after becoming a shaman, Sereptie, a Nganasani or Tavgi Samoyed of Siberia, told the story of his initiation. Among Samoyeds and many other Siberian peoples, the election of the future *nga* (shaman) involved not only his shaman ancestors but also many deities and spirits, malevolent and benevolent, that were associated with elements in nature as well as powerful diseases. The future *nga* was chosen by these entities to pursue his profession, but the central event directing the novice was, inevitably, a severe physical illness or psychological crisis that opened the gate to worlds of nonordinary experience.

Siberian shamans are generally guided and taught by one or more spirits that reveal both the road they are to follow and the significance of what they encounter on their inner voyages. Sereptie, unlike most *nga*, had to discover the way and interpret the signs for himself.

With the imagination of a visionary poet, he relates the magical and often perilous encounters with gods, spirits, and nature during his otherworld journey. Ultimately, after Sereptie has discovered all the origins and ways of disease, even his barely helpful spirit guide deserts him. He is left in the most terrifying of realms, confronted with the thing he most fears. Yet, by shamanizing, he finds his own way back to the middle world, where he awakens from his trance.[1]

When I was a young man I used to dream of all sorts of insignificant things just like any other man. But once, I saw myself going down a road until I reached a tree. With an axe in my hand, I went round the tree and wanted to fell it. Then I heard a voice saying: "(Fell it) later!" and I woke up.

Next day the neighbours said to me: "Go and fell a tree for the *kuojka*** sledge!" I set out, found a suitable tree and started to

---

*kuojka—holy family relics such as stones, anthropomorph and zoomorphic figures made of wood or metal. They were transported in special sledges.

cut it down. When the tree fell, a man sprang out of its roots with a loud shout. I was petrified with fear (from this unexpected event). The man asked: "Where are you going?" "What could I do —I am going to my tent." "Why, of course, since you have a tent, you must go there. Well, my friend, I am a man, who came out of the roots of the tree. The root is thick, it looks thin in your eyes only. Therefore I tell you that you must come down through the root if you wish to see me."—"What sort of a tree is that?" I asked. "I never could find it out." The man answered: "From times of old, it is of this tree that the *kuojka* sledges have been made and the shamans have been growing from. Rocked in the cradle, they become shamans—well that's what this tree is for."—"All right, I shall go with you."

Whilst preparing to descend, the man turned to me and said: "Just take a look at me and find out who I am?" His clothes at the sides reminded me of the wild reindeer's hide during moulting time. I did not ask him why he was wearing such clothes. Then again he said: "Don't be afraid of me, but find out why there are such patterns on my *parka* (winter garment), both black and white patches?" I replied: "On the left side you have the white spots because you dress in the attire of the (spirit of the) first snow; the black spots on the right side resemble the spots of the earth appearing in spring from under the snow—because you put on the attire (of the spirit) of the melting snow." My companion turned his back and, taking my hand, said: "Now let us go to our hosts!" I was afraid and thought that I was lost.

As I looked round, I noticed a hole in the earth. My companion asked: "What hole is this? If your destiny is to make a drum of this tree, find it out!" I replied: "It is through this hole that the shaman receives the spirit of his voice." The hole became larger and larger. We descended through it and arrived at a river with two streams flowing in opposite directions. "Well, find out this one too!" said my companion, "one stream goes from the centre to the north, the other to the south—the sunny side. If you are destined to fall into a trance, find it out!" I replied: "The northern stream originates from the water for bathing the dead, and the southern from that for the infants."—"Yes, indeed, you have guessed right," said he.

Then we set out on the shore of the northern stream. My

companion always led me by the hand. We saw nine tents before us, the nearest one being tied round with a rope. A tree stood on each side of its entrance—one on the northern, the other on the southern side. "What do you think these trees grew for?" asked the man. I replied again: "One of the trees is bright as if the sun were shining on it. Because the parents bring up their children loving and fostering them, this must be the (protecting) spirit of the children." Here my companion (as if to confirm my words) clapped his hands and smacked his knees with the palm of one hand. "The dark tree is the tree of the moon, the tree of birth, enabling the women to fix the date of the birth according to the moon." The man again clapped his hands and slapped his knees. Then he asked: "What is the meaning of the bars that hang horizontally above the fireplace of the tent?"* Suddenly I found one of the bars in my hand and struck my companion with it. "These bars are the borderline between two daybreaks, the backbone of the firmament. The northern bar is the beginning of the polar light, the southern one—the beginning of the cycle of dawns." When I said this, my companion praised me. I got frightened. "And what is the tent tied round with a rope?" asked my companion. And I said: "When men go mad and become shamans, they are tied with this rope." (I was quite unconscious and was tied up too.)

Then it seemed to me that we were in the street. We entered the first tent where we found seven naked men and women who were singing all the time while tearing their bodies with their teeth. I became very frightened. "Now I shall explain this to you, myself, because you will not guess it anyway," said my companion: "Originally, seven earths were created and it is through the spirits of these seven earths that (men) lose their minds. Some just start singing, others losing their minds, go away and die; others again become shamans. Our earth has seven promontories with a madman living on each of them. When you become a shaman, you will find them yourself."—"Where can I find them—you have led me to the wrong place"—thought I. "If I do not lead you to see (the spirits), how could you make magic for the insane? If you find the spirit of madness, you will begin to shamanize, initiating (new) shamans. You must be shown all the ways of diseases."

*The bars that serve to hang the tea pot or the kettle over the fire.

We came out of the first tent and went to the second that was placed on the northern promontory. The whole tent was covered with hoar frost and tied round in the middle with a black rope. Around the smoke hole, the tent was covered with something red. "Down there (to the south) is Asondu—they are Tungus," said my companion. "This is their tent. The black rope will serve you to cure stomach diseases, while the red stuff will help you heal madness that comes from headaches. The middle rope will serve you to cure epidemics. You will find out the meaning of this rope later on. When you will enchant, Tungus spirits will come to you and I, myself, do not understand them. When you enchant a Dolgan or a Tungus, come here and you will learn it." The frost-covered tent had two smoke holes, one of copper and the other of iron. We entered the second tent, but found nobody there. "Let us go back," said my companion.

We came out of the tent through another door and went into another tent which seemed to be covered with fishing nets. Inside, the fire was scarcely flickering. We found a disfigured old woman there in worn boots and otherwise naked, except for her upper clothes; she warmed herself by the fire. There was a dim light in the tent and shadows were flickering everywhere. The old woman asked: "Do you know me?"—"Find the answer yourself!" said my companion to me. I replied: "When a child is born, there is the afterbirth too, you are its spirit, are you not?" My companion and the old woman slapped their knees in astonishment. "You are a good guesser!" Then they asked again: "Why is the fire dark?" And I answered: "When a child is born, a new fire is kindled. You too, you are sitting here like a housewife who lights a new fire." Again they slapped their knees in astonishment. "In the southern part of the tent, the fire is very weak. Human beings are purified after birth by being fumigated with fire. This is the origin of the purifying fire." "That's right," said both of them. The tent had two kinds of *ńuk*s*—some were frost-covered, some were white. I guessed the meaning of these *ńuk*s too. "We wrap up the dead in *ńuk*s made of wild reindeer hide. Here, these rimy *ńuk*s are the *nil'ti*s** of the said *ńuk*s. The white *ńuk*s are the *nil'ti*s of our

---

ńuk—tent, cover of conical hut.
**nil'ti*—one of the life substances ("soul"? A.P.).

leather garment." Both confirmed the correctness of my words.

We went over to the fourth tent that stood in the middle of the water, behind three freezing waters. One part of it was covered with seven reindeer hides, instead of a *ńuk,* while the other was spread over with rippling water. I said: "Doesn't the shaman make his clothing out of seven reindeer hides? And since the other part of the tent is covered with waves, it must belong to the spirit of the water—that is why it is standing in the middle of the water." "You will shamanize, you go downwards," they said. We entered the tent where we found an old woman sitting among heaps of children's clothes and killed dogs. On each side of the tent there were two white salmons. "Do you recognize me?" asked the old woman. "Find it out," said my companion. And I replied: "This is the earth where we shall have to come in lean years. Here, she (the old woman) will show us where to find game and fish." "Find it out!"—they repeated. "Seven hides—these I shall find when I shamanize, I shall find and recognize them. Every man, when he becomes a shaman, makes himself a seat. I shall shamanize for seven days, sitting on these seven hides. Two fishes: one of them means that we blow on the fire and breath goes out of us. The breath has a soul. What is it when the fish (opening its mouth) is panting? When we light the fire, it flares up on its back. Seeing the fire on the back of one fish, the other blows it out. Therefore, in imitation of this fish, a wooden fish was made. When a child is born, men act in a similar fashion. One of the fishes is full of roe —the roe floats above. The child is to be rubbed with the roe. When a child is born, we smear it with grease. This is what it means. Then throwing the grease into the fire we feed the house *kuojka* and also smear its face with grease. When people become hungry, it is this that gives enough to eat. It is this (the fish) you have to ask." The southern side was closed with hides. Looking closer, I found that they looked like seven apertures instead of hides. From outside, they looked like hides, from inside, like apertures—through which one could look out. "Why should I find this one out?" "We shamans have seven resting places, henceforth you will find them. The seven apertures mean that when a man sinks under the water but has still some air left and you happen to be there, then you come and save him."

We came out of the tent—the northern side was covered all

over with ice. "You will find this out yourself," said my companion. "Don't come here, this is the way of another shaman." When I submerged, I arrived at these places, and it seemed as if I were swimming in the water. We went to another tent. On each side there stood an iron trunk. A one-horned reindeer doe was tied to the trunk on the right side, while a stag, with bruised antlers, was tied to the left trunk. One tine was broken, the other twisted. I tried to guess what the two animals were tied with and found that they were tied with the rays of the sun. "Well, that's strange"— I thought—"how is that these (ropes) do not break?" Although they were twisted, some of the threads were broken and hanging straight, like sticks. "Do you know this rein-hind?" they asked me. I answered: "No, I do not." "When you will be a shaman (surely you think that this is a real trunk—this is the spirit of everything humans do) and (during the ceremony) the men will beat your drum with the drumstick,* this trunk will split up. The rein-hind is the origin of the *kuojka* (made of stone or wood)." "And what is this rope for?" "It serves to brand the reindeer's fawn that is presented to the moon." "Why is the reindeer one-horned?" "Every man who becomes a shaman, makes divinations about the reindeer whose hide will serve him as a dress. When you become a shaman, (don't) ask them (the wild reindeer for the clothes) and don't make yourself a suit of the simple wild reindeer's hide. Provide yourself with clothes, but, first, ask for permission from the mother of the wild reindeer, she will give you instructions about the wild reindeer whose hide is to be used for your clothes. One of the wild reindeer is a stag, he is the master spirit of the wild reindeer stags. It is this spirit whom you will have to ask to know which tree you are to make your drum of, or else your life will not be long."

Walking round the tent, I saw that all the *ńuk*s were bright with decorations and fringes. We make fringes for ourselves, similar to the antlers of the reindeer. For we take hair from every animal to sew it on to the fringes of the attire similar to the cover of this tent. My companion said: "Then, when you come here, ask questions, and if you are given hair of an animal, make yourself

---

*The Nganasans, when appealing to the shaman during the ceremony, hit the drum with a stick.

fringes of it." Then I looked up to the smoke-hole and saw nine human figures made of iron. I don't remember any more, nor how I reached them, but I began to hit them with a stick, saying: "When shamanizing in the clean tent,* I shall ascend by them." "You will be a great shaman indeed, you find out everything," said (my companion) clapping his hands. "If this is so, I shall surely be a shaman. But I don't want to be a shaman," said I to myself. "No, you will be a shaman, since you have seen all these things"—they said.

We entered the tent and found there seven moon-figures made of copper, similar to those that are on the shamans' clothes. "Behold, they are yours," said (my companion) and began to give me the figures. I did not take them. "No, take them," said he and brought forth seven suns which he showed me. "What is this?" I thought, "probably I shall have to enchant for seven days." Then he gave me three times seven figures of the sun and said: "Find it out!"—"I don't know." My companion said: "You, being a new shaman, stand up (i.e. recover) and cure thrice seven men from their illness." When I shamanize, I walk round all these tents.

I came out of this tent and reached another. I think it was mine. To me, it seemed a strange one, not my own. People were sitting around the fire, men on one side and women on the other. I went in, not as a man but as a skeleton; I don't know who gnawed me off, I don't know how it happened. As I took a close look at them, they did not look like real human beings but like skeletons which had been dressed. At the bottom of the tent, there was a seven-bladed anvil. I saw a woman who looked as if she were made of fire. I saw a man holding (a pair of) pliers. The woman had seven apertures on her body. From these, the man pulled out iron pieces as from the fire, placed them on the anvil and struck them with the hammer. When the iron cooled down, the man replaced it in the aperture of the woman's body as if it were fire. Although there was fire in the fireplace, the man did not make use of it. I looked round. Near the fireplace there was a woman, stirring up the fire with animal hides, while the sparks were flying on every side. The man took a piece of iron, placed it on the anvil and

*The feast of the clean tent, a spring festivity celebrated together with the 7 or 9 day ceremony of the shaman.

hit it with the hammer which consisted in reality of seven small hammers on a single helve. At every blow on the iron, sparks rose into the air and flew out through the smoke hole. My companion asked me: "What do you think, what tent have we entered?" "I don't know," said I. "However, it must be here that the pendants of the shaman's clothes are forged and it is probably these people I have to ask (for pendants), for my clothes. The man (= shaman) descends from many places, this is surely one of them." "This is not all of them, anyway," they said. I tossed my head back and began to look at the smoke hole. "What are those seven figures in the upper part of the tent?" I asked. "They are the spirits of your future saw-toothed pendants," he said. "Do you give me these pieces of iron?" "No, the time has not yet come for it," they said. I began to feel uneasy. "Then why do you make me guess?" "Who are these two beings, the man and the woman; are they humans?" "So that is the origin of the shamans," I said. "Indeed." This is my fate—to lose my mind. "Whenever you become a shaman, ask them for permission to make yourself clothes and a drum. Ask them also to give you reindeer for your clothes; if you come to this tent they will provide you with the necessary things. The sparks are birds, catch them, imitate them, we have birds, geese made from them, on the back of the dress." When I entered as a skeleton and they forged, it meant that they forged me. The master of the earth, the spirit of the shamans, has become my origin. When a shin-bone or something else is hit and the sparks fly, there will be a shaman in your generation.

Then we came out of this tent and I began to look round. In front, there was a great river with sandy shores, and a hill with two tents on it. I began to guess what kind of a hill this was. It seemed as if the tent were standing on an iceberg, behind them were black spots of earth appearing from under the melting snow. The nearer tent was covered all over with white *ńuk*s, whereas the more remote one had *ńuk*s with checkerboard pattern.

When we went closer, we saw that tents were standing on both shores of the river. The checkered tent stood on the black spots of earth (on account of the melting snow), while the white tent was behind the river. It seemed as if I had come back to the river I had encountered at the beginning of the journey. One stream of the river continued southwards, the other northwards.

"Find it out," said my companion. "How long will you make me guess things? Anyway, when I become a shaman, the origin of my shamanship will be here. Whenever I submerge, I shall descend this water." "You will implore the place of confluence of these streams. When you submerge you will return swimming in the southern flow. Your throat, similar to the stream, will begin to talk, to conjure up this spirit. At the checkered tent, the upper parts of the smoke hole, the *ńuk*s are made of poor, small-haired hides. What does it mean?" I said: "The diseases devour everybody, yet they spare the half of mankind so that it may reproduce itself. Behold, these (the black squares of the checkerboard) cover the surviving men with the blackness of diseases." "Now that we have arrived here, I will leave you alone," said my companion. "If you return, you will be a man, if not—you will die. Henceforward I cannot lead you anymore. I have led you to all the origins and ways of diseases. Shamanizing, you will find your way, by yourself."

Standing near the tent, I looked at the river and saw a woman passing by. She was quite red, her face and hair included, and her dress was checkered. Some of the squares were red, the others blue. "Here," said my companion, "I have brought you here. It was only the way of the big disease that I have not showed you yet. That's why I have brought you here. You will shamanize with the big disease, take care not to curse but to implore when you shamanize. Can you guess who this woman is?" I: "Her body is quite red and her dress is strange. The shaman gets up and sits down when shamanizing. Why, he sits on different litters, obviously, the woman carries these litters of mine with her. The red disease (measles) sometimes occurs, she seems to be its mother. There were checkered *ńuk*s on the tent. This means that the tent was covered with the clothes of the woman. She took off the *ńuk*s and put them on." I looked at the tent—it was quite red. "If in case of such disease (measles) I shall come here and appeal to her I shall surely heal (the sick)," said I. "Yes," said my companion, "I have told you already that I shall leave you. Well, my friend, you must not even look at this tent, whoever may be there. You must not go there. I have brought you to this tent, where your forefather, the famous shaman died of pox. I leave you here to make friends and not to die of this plague."

I became terribly frightened. The woman said: "You have come from far away. Yet, I am obliged to send you back." And she breathed on me three times. As she was breathing I began to recognize the place. Yet she did not let me go immediately, but said: "My friend, there is a tent there, but you must not cross the river, and, from now on, you should only come up to me. If you want to obtain advice from that tent (from its female occupant), I shall give you advice. By now, she will have surely come to know that you are here. I shall notify her. When she opens her mouth and blows, the fog sets in. It is from this fog that men get sick."

Meanwhile, my companion stood sideways and listened. Then the fog came. "Find it out!" said the woman. I began to get angry, but still said: "Half of the fog is the breath of men; when I am a shaman, I shall be able to rescue the *nil'ti* of the dead from this fog." "Yes, indeed," said the woman. "Here is a reef* with a red tent on it. If the sick [person] is cured, the woman will come from the opposite direction. If the *nil'ti* falls beyond the reef, beyond the limit of the fog—that is the limit of life—he cannot be saved." Then I said to myself: "I am sure that I have reached the place whence every man descends" and, turning towards the woman, I said aloud: "You are surely the mistress of the earth who has created all life." "Yes, that is so," said she. "Well, my friend, we had three children, the second lives in the red tent, the eldest is beyond the river. You return from these places. If you want to enter their tents, you shall die. They are half *barusi*s, half *nguo*s.** Take care to look in the direction in which you have to return."

Then I made a few steps forward and, looking round, saw seven stone peaks. On one of them, there were seven willows, on the other seven thin trees, and so on—seven plants were growing on each peak. "What's that?" thought I. Everywhere on the plants, there were nests of all kinds of birds. On the highest peak, in the middle, a bumble-bee was hatching her young. Her wings were of iron. She looked as if she were hatching while lying in the fire. The woman pointed at these nests and said: "You are surely tired, come here, lie down, and find out what that is!" "This is the bumble-bee, who creates (plant) for the tinder, so that none of the men

*A rock rising above the water surface in the river.
**barusi—malevolent spirits, nguo—benevolent divinities and spirits.

should be in want of it. These seven peaks are the origin of every plant: the future shamans go around them. In these nests there are spirits—the master spirits of all the running and flying birds and game." "What can you see on the shore?" the woman asked. "I can see two stone peaks." "Find it out!" I replied: "When we reached at one of the peaks—this is the mistress of water, we can ask her for fish. The other peak is black. When a child is born, it is placed on a layer made of punk wood. Half of the peak is covered with such punk wood, the other half, with moss. When he gets here, the shaman can cure the child, in case of disease. The spirit of this lives here."

Then I left them and saw nothing but the earth. It seemed as if I were going along a river. One shore was pebbly, the other covered with coloured stones—yellow ochre and black earth (graphite). A woman began to talk: "The coloured stones are iron, copper and different metals. When you become a shaman, you make yourself pendants of them, therefore you go to them." Going on along the shore I saw two peaks; one of them was covered with bright-coloured vegetation, the other was black earth all over. Between them, there appeared to be an islet with some very nice red plants in blossom on it. They resembled the flowers of the cloudberry. "What is this," I thought. There was nobody near me, but I found it out myself. When a man dies, his face becomes blue and changes: then the shaman has nothing more to do. As I noticed the red grass grew upwards, the black downwards. Suddenly I heard a cry: "Take a stone from here!" The stones were reddish. Since I was marked out to survive, I snatched up a red stone. What I thought to be flowers were stones. Someone said to me: "When you have a clean tent made, have a fire lit with flint. When you get to your own tent, speak about this with the men, not sitting like this, but shamanizing, because you are a shaman singing with the throat of nine diseases."

Suddenly I recovered my senses: I must have been lying for a considerable time, near the root of the tree. So I felled that tree and made a *kuojka* sledge of it. This was our ancestral *kuojka*. Whenever I go shamanizing, I always hear the terrible songs on the peaks. Before coming to myself, I heard a voice saying: "If you become a shaman, you will live a long time." This was twenty years ago and I was not married. When I am shamanizing, I see a road to the north. When I am looking for a sick man, the road is narrow like a thread. I do not know who is leading me, in front I see the sun and the moon. On (the lower) part of the narrow road there are conical ramshackle tents; on this (road) you go for the breath of the man. The other part of the road (leading upwards) is quite entangled—I do not understand why. The man who is to recover has a breath like a white thread, while he who dies has one like a black thread. Going along the road, you look sideways and you proceed. Then you find the man's *nil'ti* and take it.

Half of my spirits comes from the men of the forest (the Tungus).

It was new moon, a bright weather in March when we three set off. I had been blindfolded with the hide of the wild reindeer and sent afoot to find a tree for the drum. The companions followed me on reindeer. The tree suitable for the drum, makes sounds like a drum. I ran forward, with my eyes covered, listening. The spirits do not give immediately the opportunity to find the tree, they mislead us. There are as many as three sounding trees instead of one—the third has to be chopped down.

Now, you are going to one of these trees—it is also coming towards you. "Am I to take this tree?" I asked myself and began to sneak up to it as if it were a wild reindeer. But if you try to take it, somebody pushes you away so that you leap aside. "Don't do it, or you shall die!" This is the tree where the spirits of your family live—the tree that protects your family against death and diseases. Realizing your mistake, you walk on before being pushed away.

Then you hear another tree sounding (like a drum) and coming towards you and you prepare to catch it. But you must not do so. This is the tree where the breath of your entire flock and the breath of the flocks of your home folk get, "mixed." If you touch this tree, you die.

Finally, I see a third tree, it stands and does not move. I begin to steal up to it. The tree says: "Come, come, I am for you!" Then I fell it. My companions did the work with the axe, not I. They must by no means be relatives. If, for all that, the tree is a false one and not the real one, you implore in vain when bending the hoop—that would break anyway, and then somebody belonging to the shaman's kin would die. But if you suspect this, do make a drum of this hoop, even if it will be a bad one, but previously perform a ceremony, so that nobody should die.

When, for a man's illness, I make ceremonies to the evil spirits, the latter would say: "Here, I have surrendered to you, what is he going to give me?" I ask: "What you require for him I shall settle." "The ill man has to kill a certain wild reindeer," says the disease. The man indeed kills such a wild reindeer, gives me its hide and I make a new dress of it for myself. It may happen that the spirit does not speak sincerely and says: "He should kill a wolf, a fox or some other game." But in reality, the ill man kills a reindeer.

Kyzlasov

SIBERIA/SAGAY

The famous *Kam* (shaman) Kyzlasov from the Sagay village of Kyzlan was very old when he gave this account of the fierce experiences that plagued him during his initiatory illness many years before. He granted the Hungarian ethnologist Vilmos Diószegi the rare privilege of this knowledge in spite of the usual reluctance among Siberian shamans to disclose the details of their initiatory trials.

Kyzlasov lived a distance from his village, behind the slope of a hill, in an isolated and impoverished yurta constructed of logs and surrounded by birch trees. The old man was apparently eager to communicate about the general nature of his profession as a *Kam*. When Diószegi inquired about how he had become a shaman, Kyzlasov fell into a deep silence, but his wife eagerly began to supply details: "Sickness seized him when he was twenty-three years old, and he became a shaman at the age of thirty. That was how he became a shaman. After the sickness, after the torture. He had been ill for seven years. While he was ailing he had dreams; he was beaten up several times, sometimes he was taken to strange places. He had been around quite a lot in his dreams, and he had seen many things."[2]

With a glance, Kyzlasov stopped her from going further. As Diószegi inquired about various other aspects of the shaman's illness and some of the psychosymbolic events, such as dismemberment, that occur in an initiatory crisis, the silence in the yurta grew oppressive. As Diószegi said, "The stillness was beginning to thump on my eardrums."[3] Finally, Kyzlasov, so alert and full of life, let his story pour forth, and the bond between the old, white-maned Sagay shaman and the Hungarian ethnographer was complete.[4]

My name is Yegor Mikhaylovich Kyzlasov. I live at the mouth of the river Yes, in the village of Kyzlan. I belong to the *Tag Harga* clan. *Pürigesh* has been my first ancestor. *Shtuk* was his son. *Shtuk* was a shaman. *Hizinah* was the son of Shtuk. He left two sons. The firstborn was not a shaman, but his younger brother, *Hizilas* became one. Hizilas left an only son: *Torah.* The son of Torah was *Payatay,* he had a son called *Ochi,* Ochi's son was *Mamay.* Mamay fathered me and I became a shaman.

It was not the talent I inherited, but the shaman spirits of my clan. . . .

* * *

I had been sick and I had been dreaming. In my dreams I had been taken to the ancestor and cut into pieces on a black table. They chopped me up and then threw me into the kettle and I was boiled. There were some men there: two black and two fair ones. Their chieftain was there too. He issued the orders concerning me. I saw all this. While the pieces of my body were boiled, they found a bone around the ribs, which had a hole in the middle. This was the excess-bone. This brought about my becoming a shaman. Because, only those men can become shamans in whose body such a bone can be found. One looks across the hole of this bone and begins to see all, to know all and, that is when one becomes a shaman . . . When I came to from this state, I woke up. This meant that my soul had returned. Then the shamans declared, "You are the sort of man who may become a shaman. You should become a shaman, you must begin to shamanize!"

* * *

When the shaman goes to the chief-shaman, that is, to the family-ancestor, he has to cross the *ham saraschan harazi* mountain along the way. On the top of that mountain there is a pine-tree, its trunk resembles a six-sided log. The shamans carve their symbols into it, between the edges. Whoever places his marking, his *tamga,* upon it, then becomes a real shaman. It happens sometimes that a certain tamga "falls down," it disappears from the tree. Then its owner dies. After resting at the foot of this tree, the journey is continued. Then the shaman arrives to a crossing where an invisible shaman is sitting. He guards the crossroads. This is the place where all paths begin: the path of all the animals offered to the spirits, the road of the spirit rabies, the path of the spirits of all other sicknesses, this is where all the wild animals of the forest enter upon their trails. When this crossroad is reached by one who became a shaman, through the spirit of sickness, he must pray to the invisible shaman and offer him wheat-brandy. The right path is shown him only after the offering has taken place. Then he may continue the journey along the appointed path. In the course of the journey the shaman arrives at a narrow plank-bridge across a very fast river and he must cross it. After having crossed the river he is not very far away from the ancestral shaman but there is still one more obstacle he must conquer. There are two cliffs there. Sometimes they close, and then again they withdraw from each other. They keep moving day and night. After they clash they then start to move away from each other again, this is when the shaman may slip across between them. But he, who is lazy and does not run, perishes there. In such cases the shaman becomes ill and dies. But if he succeeds, he is already treading upon the grounds of the ancestral shaman, covered with black rocks. So, this is where the ancestor lives. The shaman cannot see him, he merely senses his presence.

* * *

When I was asleep during my sickness . . . , my brother came to visit me . . . and told me: I crossed the mountains already! He told me also: You are ill because of the mountain! . . . Soon, however you would be healthy again! But I did not get any better for a long time to come. I wandered about in the mountains in my dreams. Then I went further and further, and my brother stayed behind. I even left the mountains behind me. I arrived in another land. There were some people there too. They were all writing something. Their tables were built of black earth and there were drums hung on the sides. There were some tables on the opposite side too, there were drums hanging on the sides of these too, but with their bottoms up. Here all the tables were also upside down. The shamans' garments were also turned inside out. I have heard before: these are the drums of those shamans who do not live long. He that [chooses] from these would die soon. At least the people said so . . . So I picked up a white drum and a garment from the other side. That is how I became a shaman.

* * *

As soon as I was better, I prepared all my equipment and became a shaman and I went to present myself to the chief shaman, accompanied by nine black-haired and seven straw-blonde men and three children. No shaman accompanied me. I ladled some gruel into a trough, put some boiled potatoes on top, and I went to the chief shaman, the ancestor. When I got there, he measured my drum, its circumference, its length and its height. He counted the pendants hanging from it. When he was ready, he gave me the men. (The shamans call their spirits *men.*) They are my friends. Sometimes they come upon me unexpectedly, then they disappear again. They are rather unstable. It is to them, I owe my well-being, it is through them, that when I hold the pulse of a sick person, it becomes clear to me, what is wrong with him. Then I began to shamanize.

Lizard's Son
AUSTRALIA/WIRADJURI

The son of Yibai-dthulin* was a Wiradjuri of the Murri subclass and the kangaroo totem. According to A. W. Howitt, this account was revealed to him only after Lizard's Son learned that Howitt himself had been initiated and was to be trusted with the unusual details of the sacred journey the apprentice shaman makes in the course of his initiatory experiences.

Lizard's Son was introduced into his apprenticeship by his father when he was a very small child. On reaching the age of ten, he underwent further initiation experiences, the details of which he gives in the account that follows. This phase of his apprenticeship includes journeys to the underworld and sky realm; encounters with the dead, animal allies, and spirit beings; a passage through "clashing gates"; and many other elements common to shamanism in all parts of the world.

*Howitt does not give us his name. *Dthulin* means "lizard." I have, therefore, given the son of Yibai-dthulin the name *Lizard's Son.*

The *Mulla-mullung* (shaman) of the Australian Wiradjuri obtains his power from supernatural sources that he encounters on his journeys to the otherworld. He is always capable of seeing the living and the dead in their incorporeal state, either as wraiths or as a spirit of one who is deceased. He can leave his body at will, traveling or being transported to distant environs, natural or supernatural. His power can be used for benign or malign purposes. Inevitably, the *Mulla-mullung* comes to his knowledge in dream and trance states; yet, his knowledge and power seem to be subject to easy dissolution, as was the case with Lizard's Son.[5]

My father is *Yibai-dthulin.* When I was a small boy he took me into the bush to train me to be a *Mulla-mullung.* He placed two large quartz crystals [*Wallungs*] against my breast, and they vanished into me. I do not know how they went, but I felt them going through me like warmth. This was to make me clever and able to bring things up. He also gave me some things like quartz crystals in water. They looked like ice and the water tasted sweet. After that I used to see things that my mother could not see. When out with her I would say, "What is out there like men walking?" She used to say, "Child, there is nothing." These were the *Jir* (ghosts) which I began to see.

When I was about ten years old, I was taken to the *Burbung* and saw what the old men could bring out of themselves; and when my tooth was out the old men chased me with the *Wallungs* in their mouths, shouting *"Ngai, Ngai,"* and moving their hands towards me. I went into the bush for a time, and while there my father came out to me. He said, "Come here to me"; and he then showed me a piece of quartz crystal in his hand, and when I looked at it he went down into the ground and I saw him come up all covered with red dust. It made me very frightened. He then said, "Come to me," and I went to him, and he said, "Try and bring up a *Wallung.*" I did try, and brought one up. He then said, "Come up with me to this place." I saw him standing by a hole in the ground, leading to a grave. I went inside and saw a dead man, who rubbed me all over to make me clever, and who gave me some *Wallung.* When we came out, my father pointed to a *Gunr* (tiger-snake) saying "That is your *Budjan* [totem]; it is mine also." There was a string tied to the tail of the snake, and extending to us. It was one of those strings which the Doctors bring up out of themselves, rolled up together.

He took hold of it, saying, "Let us follow him." The tiger-snake went through several tree trunks, and let us through. Then we came to a great Currajong tree, and went through it, and after that to a tree with a great swelling round its roots. It is in such places that *Daramulun* lives. Here the *Gunr* went down into the ground, and we followed him, and came up inside the tree, which was hollow. There I saw a lot of little *Daramuluns,* the sons of *Baiame.* After we came out again the snake took us into a great hole in the ground in which were a number of snakes, which rubbed themselves against me, but did not hurt me, being my *Budjan.* They did this to make me a clever man, and to make me a *Mulla-mullung.* My father then said to me, "We will go up to *Baiame's* camp." He got astride of a *Mauir* (thread) and put me on another, and we held by each other's arms. At the end of the thread was *Wombu,* the bird of *Baiame.* We went through the clouds, and on the other side was the sky. We went through the place where the Doctors go through, and it kept opening and shutting very quickly. My father said that, if it touched a Doctor when he was going through, it would hurt his spirit, and when he returned home he would sicken and die. On the other side we saw *Baiame* sitting in his camp. He was a very great old man with a long beard. He sat with his legs under him and from his shoulders extended two great quartz crystals to the sky above him. There were also numbers of the boys of *Baiame* and of his people, who are birds and beasts.

After this time, and while I was in the bush, I began to bring things up, but I became very ill and cannot do anything since.

Old K̈"xau
AFRICA/!KUNG

This extraordinary account by an old !Kung Bushman was recorded by Megan Biesele when she was a Harvard doctoral candidate in anthropology. Although I have edited and emended the text so that it reads as a narrative, the presence of Ms. Biesele and the relationship between

her and the energetic old curer can be strongly felt by the reader. She describes this interview as "a communication which came of its own accord, in a sustained burst of enthusiasm lasting several hours."[6] The ancient, blind K"xau was led to Biesele's home by his friend N//au. Old K"xau told the anthropologist, "Turn on your machine. I have something to say."[7]

Humorous and intense by turns, Old K"xau describes his voyage into the abysmal waters of the underworld, his ascent to God's camp on sky threads, and his own initiation into the mysteries of the medicine dance's power. K"xau weaves together his otherworld journeys, the curer's trance journey into the body of one afflicted, and his own initiation. As Biesele explains, "In a sense, all three of these themes—the curing journey into the body, the journey to the sky, and the reception of power *(n/um)* for the first time—are one in that they are all initiations, leaps of faith requiring that one dare the loss of soul."[8]

A word must be said about *n/um,* or healing medicine. Biesele describes it as not being a physical substance. "It is energy, a kind of supernatural potency whose activation paves the way for curing. Associated with it are other special powers, like clairvoyance, out-of-body travel, x-ray vision, and prophecy."[9] *N/um,* residing in the belly, is activated through strenuous trance dancing and the heat of the fire. It ascends or "boils up" the spinal column and into the head, at which time it can be used to pull out the sickness afflicting others.

Over half the men in !Kung society are curers, and many women are also able to assume this role. But only a few attain the fluency, imagination, and power of Old K"xau.[10]

Just yesterday, friend, the giraffe came and took me again. Kauha [God] came and took me and said, "Why is it that people are singing, yet you're not dancing?" When he spoke, he took me with him and we left this place. We traveled until we came to a wide body of water. It was a river. He took me to the river. The two halves of the river lay to either side of us, one to the left and one to the right.

Kauha made the waters climb, and I lay my body in the direction they were flowing. . . . My feet were behind, and my head was in front. That's how I lay. Then I entered the stream and began to move forward. I entered it and my body began to do like this [K"xau waves his hands dreamily to show how his body traveled forward, undulating in the water]. I traveled like this. My sides were pressed by pieces of metal. Metal things fastened my sides. And in this way I traveled forward, my friend. That's how I was stretched out in the water. And the spirits were singing.

The spirits were having a dance. I began to dance it, too, hopping around like this. I joined the dance and danced with them, but Kauha said to me, "Don't come here and start to dance like that: now you just lie down and watch. This is how you should dance," he said, as he showed me how to dance. So the two of us danced that way. We danced and danced. We went to my protector and Kauha said to him, "Here is your son." To me he said: "This man will carry you and put *n/um* into you." The man took hold of my feet. He made me sit up straight. But I was under water! I was gasping for breath! I called out, "Don't kill me! Why are you killing me?" My protector answered, "If you cry out like that, I'm going to make you drink. Today I'm certainly going to make you drink water. . . ." The two of us struggled until we were tired. We danced and argued and I fought the water for a long, long, time. We did it until the cocks began to crow.

[K"xau softly sings a medicine song.]

That's how my protector sang. He told me that was how I should sing. So, my friend, I sang that song and sang it and sang it until I had sung into the daybreak. Then, my friend, my protector spoke to me, saying that I would be able to cure. He said that I would stand up and trance. He told me that I would trance. And the trancing he was talking about, my friend—I was already doing it. Then he said he would give me something to drink. My friend, my little drink was about this size. . . . He made me drink it and said that I would dance the dance I had learned. And so, my friend, I have just stuck with that dance and grown up with it.

Then my protector told me that I would enter the earth. That I would travel far through the earth and then emerge at another place. When we emerged, we began to climb the thread—it was the thread of the sky! Yes, my friend. Now up there in the sky, the people up there, the spirits, the dead people up there, they sing for me so I can dance.. . .

When people feel bad, my friend, I don't dance. But if a person dies, . . . I carry him on my back and lay him down. I lay him out so that we are lying together. He lies with his feet this way. And his head lies across my shoulders. I lay him across my body and carry him on my back. I carry him and then lay him down again. . . . That's what I do, my friend. I dance him, dance him, dance him, dance him so that God will give his spirit to me. Then I return from God and put his spirit back into his body. My friend, I put it back, put it back, put it back, put it back, put it back and that's how he comes out alive. Sometimes I cure a person, and he dies, and God says, "This person is going to die today. I will take him and go away with him!" . . . He won't return . . . ! Not when he speaks like that. Now we who have been with this sick person, staying with him, when God tries to leave with him, we stinge [are stingy with] him! We do not want to let him go. Then God stabs him right here! [In the shoulder.] He stabs him with a piece of metal. God stabs him! [In the neck.] Then I who have been inside him crawl along his body and come out here. [He points to his midriff.]

* * *

For I am a big dancer. Yes, I am a big dancer. I teach other people to dance. When people sing, I go into a trance. I trance and put n/um into people, and I carry on my back those who want to learn n/um. Then I go! I go right up and give them to God!

My friend, when you go to visit God, you sit this way [in an attitude of respect, with arms folded across the knees]. People sit this way when they go to God, the great, great God, the master. Friend, this is how people sit. You sit this way, and the flies cluster all over your sides. "What do you want?" God asks. And the metal piece that sits there begins to wiggle back and forth. It shimmies, my friend. It shimmies like this. God's piece of metal. Friend, it shimmies like this. And mambas. Pythons. All sorts of things. Bees. Locusts. Everything. . . . When you go there, they bite you. Yes, they bite you [gestures to his legs]. . . . Yes, they bite your legs and bite your body. When you go there, you sit like this. The mamba bites you. It lies near you. Yes, the mamba lies there. That which Tswanas call the *Noga,* the mamba, it lies there and watches you. . . . My friend, it is a foul thing. It kills you and you die.

God's penis lies this way [K"xau's hands demonstrate its enormous size as it sticks out in front of him]. . . . Lo-o-ong! A bunch of people stand in a line before him and carry it on their shoulders. They take it and lay it out straight. . . . My friend, they take it upon their shoulders. One person stands here. Another person stands here. Another stands here. All of them lift it up and rest it on their shoulders. . . . And another person up front here. . . . His penis lies there! . . . A strange thing, this. The people have gotten together and are carrying it over their shoulders. They walk around with it. It has horns. They carry it to a chair and lay it down on the chair so that it doesn't lie on the sand. Friend, they set up a chair, and they bring it around and bring it so it lies on the opened chair. Friend, the thing sits there—a foul thing! A strange, terrible thing! Ak, ak, ak, a bad thing. God's wife [K"xau dangles wiggling fingers]. . . . They're this long, my friend, dreadful things, really [K"xau indicates that her labia are as long as his arms]. My friend, she's a terrible thing, pure and simple. Now, this woman is stirring porridge! She stirs maize porridge. She stirs sorghum porridge. Then she comes to scratch and claw you so you'll go away. My friend, people begin to eat. They eat, and she comes and sits down and watches them. And she wiggles, that's what she does. . . . While they eat, people watch out like this [K"xau demonstrates, turning his head from right to left and back]. They eat and keep watch. They look from side to side, because other people try to steal their food. People gather while they're eating and snatch away their food. . . . The spirits, my friend. That's what they do while you are trying to eat.

When you go there, women are singing, they are singing for a dance. [K"xau sings a line or two.] That's how they sing. You hear it, and you think about it, and you begin to dance, "huh, huh, huh!"

. . . They dance the giraffe dance. [K"xau sings.] What you do there, where God is, is to dance like this. . . . And the women sing like this [K"xau sings]. They sing and they sing. Then comes the ‡dwamananani.

Yes. He is a spirit. His one leg is missing. He has to sit like this [K"xau indicates how a person would sit if he had only a right leg]. This is how he stands. His other side is just empty—it has no leg. The other leg stands alone. So he just hops about when he dances. He hops and dances "huh-ahuh, huh-ahuh!"

Then there's another one whose legs are all soft. He comes and stands like this; he goes about propping himself up. His head looks like this. . . . He has horns. . . . Like this. And his ears stick out. His face, my friend, is this wide. . . . His face is big! It reaches all the way to here [K"xau's hands show how his face goes all the way to the back of his head]. And the hair hangs off his body down to here. [The spirit has long hair on his chest.] He's a terrible thing, my friend. A foul thing! A thing to make you run away. People have to cure themselves of it, because it's so bad. People fear it. . . .

When God sits on his chair, he watches all around. And when people come from somewhere else and see him, they tremble with fear. They tremble themselves to death over him! He's a terrible thing! Friend, that's what people say. When you come to him, he takes out his thing and you have to greet it. You ask, "how are you?" "I'm fine!" it says. You watch and he takes out a spear. He keeps a spear there. . . . It's just there in his house. Friend, that house is a bad place! People say there are leopards there. People say there are zebras. They say locusts. They say lions. They say jackals. . . . They're in his house, right in his very house. . . . And pythons, they say, come and go in that house. . . . Elands are there. Giraffes are there. Gemsboks are there. Kudu are there. . . . These things don't kill each other. They are God's possessions.

A horse is there, and God rides him! God's horse! Yes, friend, he rides that horse. He sits up on a saddle and rides. He has a gun, the kind of gun that goes "!Khwi!." He rides his horse and goes places. His boots—they come all the way to his knees. . . . Big ones! And they are made of metal. . . . God wears metal boots. And they're as high as his knees. Donkeys are there too. Friend, everything is there.

When you go there, friend, you make yourself small like this. Friend, when you go there, you don't go standing up straight. You make yourself small so that you are a mamba. When you go there, where God is, you are a mamba. That's how you go to him. Because if you do that, he'll let you live. If you go to him like a regular person, you'll die. . . . You won't come back. When you've gone back there, you have died and you aren't going to come back. But if you're a snake, friend, you'll stay alive. If you're a mamba, you'll stay alive. . . .

And when you arrive at God's place, you make yourself small. You have become small. You come in small to God's place. You do what you have to do there. Then you return to where everyone is, and you hide your face. You hide your face so you won't see anything. You come and come and come and finally you enter your body again. All the people, the zhũ/twãsi [!Kung] who have stayed behind waiting for you—they fear you. Friend, they are afraid of you. You enter, enter, enter the earth, and then you return to enter . . . the skin of your body. . . . And you say "he-e-e-e!" [K"xau makes the trembling moan of those who have "died" in trance and returned.] That is the sound of your return to your body. Then you begin to sing. [He sings.] The n/um k"xausi are there around! They take powder and blow it—Phew! Phew!— in your face. They take hold of your head and blow about the sides of your face. This is how you manage to be alive again! Friend, if they don't do that to you, you die! . . . You just die and are dead. Friend, this is what it does, this medicine [n/um] that I do, this n/um here that I dance.

Friend, when a person dies, I come into his body this way. . . . I enter at his buttocks. I enter his foot, my friend, and travel up his leg, travel up his leg, travel up his leg and go into his buttocks. I've got him. When I've got him, I lay his leg out straight. Here—yes!—here his legs are lying straight out, and then I start to cradle his soul in my arms. Friend, when I cradle him, I do like this [K"xau demonstrates his own trembling]. . . . I'm going "Ko-Ko-Ko" [the sound of trembling]. I tremble and tremble, and then I separate his legs. By then he is already alive! That's what I do. As you are my friend, I tell you that's what my n/um is like, this n/um that I do.

When another person dies, I will enter his body. I will enter here! [Points to his head.] . . . His fontanelle is where I enter! That's where I come in and begin to work my way down. When I get down inside his body, he is already alive! He's already alive. Friend, that's what I do. . . . I'm searching for him there. . . . I'm looking for his soul, that's what I'm doing.

Friend, this n/um here—when I was small like this, . . . I was nursing and Kauha came quietly, God came and gave me n/um. He dipped water and gave it to me to drink. . . . It was the water of his urine. . . . The waters from that long thing of his. . . . The waters of his long lower belly. That's what he gives you to drink. . . . Bitter stuff! When you drink it [he demonstrates trembling]. You tremble! You urinate, and then you vomit. "Wah, wah!" [K"xau demonstrates retching.] You vomit, of course, because it's urine. Such a thing—the waters of such a long thing, the waters that spill off the end of it. . . . Terrible thing. If you drink it, you'll die. Friend, that, by gum, is what he made me drink.

Friend, this *n/um* here—in all these many people there is no one who surpasses me. Friend, this is what it's like, this big medicine that I dance. When a giraffe is killed, I *tshwa* it [this is to eat ritually; trancers *tshwa* certain food so that they will not interfere with the *n/um* they are developing in themselves]. If an eland is killed, a male eland, I *tshwa* it. Or a male kudu—if one is killed, I *tshwa* it. When a female kudu has died, I *tshwa* it. Friend, that's what I do. Strong *n/um*. I *tshwa* lots of things like *n/n* berries [*grewia*]. I *tshwa* *n/n*. I *tshwa* *!gwa* [*grewia*]. I *tshwa* mongongo nuts. If I don't *tshwa* them, I'll die.

* * *

My friend, that's the way of this *n/um*. When people sing, I dance. I enter the earth. I go in at a place like a place where people drink water. I travel in a long way, very far. When I emerge, I am already climbing. I'm climbing threads, the threads that lie over there in the South. . . . I take them and climb them. I climb one and leave it, then I go climb another one. I come to another one and climb, then I come to another one. Then I leave it and climb on another. Then I follow the thread of the wells, the one I am going to go enter! The thread of the wells of metal. When you get to the wells, you duck beneath the pieces of metal. [K"xau weaves his fingers together and puts them over the back of his head.] And you pass beneath them. . . . It hurts. When you lift up a little, the metal pieces grab your neck. You lie down so that they don't grab you. When it grabs you, you have entered the well. Friend, when you've entered the well, you just return. And then you come out. That's what this *n/um* does. This medicine [*n/um*] is something else. . . .

Friend, that's how it is with this *n/um* that I do! Its possessions! They're many! Gemsboks, leopards, lions, things like that. When people sing, his possessions come, the great, great God's possessions! Friend, now that you have come to me here, God's animals will come to us. You will come and watch how people sing. The women will sing and you will watch. My friend, that's what we'll do.

Friend, if a person asks me to put n/um in him, I'll refuse. My medicine is a bad thing. . . . It would drive people crazy. Friend, it would drive a person so crazy that he'd be going like this [K"xau shows him running around in a circle]. Friend, he'd go round and round until I just stood him still. I'd come to him and enter his body. . . . And I'd lie inside him. [K"xau shows how he would go into the person's head and down into his stomach.] When he shivers, it is because I have entered his insides and am lying there. . . . My head comes to lodge here in his crotch. My feet are up around his head. My ass is here in his chest, so I am lying this way. And he sits there going "dhu-dhu-dhu-dhu" [the sound of trancing and of the heart thumping]. That's what he does.

He trances and trances. When he is finished, I come to his crotch and pop out! When I come to his crotch and jump out, he gets up! He's already alive, and sits up! That's what I do. That's my n/um.

A person who wants me to give him n/um is a person who speaks badly. It's too strong. But if I do put n/um in a person, I carry him on my back. We two will lie right at the fire's mouth. The fire is here and we are lying next to it. Friend, we lie here, and then the two of us go; I make him eat locusts up there in the sky. In God's house, in the house of great, great God. I turn his head and hold him that way, and I carry him to the house. His arms and legs are sprawled across my body. God asks me [gruffly], "Whose child is this?" I say, "My child." "No," he says, "that's someone else's child." But I refuse. I say, "No, it's my child. And I have brought it here to you for you to see." That's what I say.

Then God shoots him. That's what he does. . . . Arrows about this long [K"xau makes the motion of removing arrows from an invisible quiver on his back. They are about five inches long]. They smell. . . . They enter his diaphragm and pierce right through to his backbone. When God has shot him, the arrow lodges there near his backbone . . . and moves along it . . . inside his body. My friend, that's what it does. . . .

My friend, this medicine [n/um] here—I'm telling you! That's what it does. Friend, it's bad n/um!

3 The Quest for Vision

This Sioux Chief is adorned with a feathered headdress that appears like a radiance around his head, indeed like the rays of the sun. The figure is a detail from a painted buffalo skin. *(From: Musée de l'Homme.)*

Igjugarjuk
ESKIMO/CARIBOU

The Caribou Eskimos lived on the barren grounds in the Arctic wastes west of the northern reaches of Hudson Bay. The culture of these nomadic people, according to Rasmussen, was of an inland origin and the most primitive that he encountered during his entire expedition. Although the Caribou were coastal dwellers, the absence of implements and the simplicity of their ceremonies indicated that they had not been acculurated into the coastal peoples' older lifeway.[1]

Igjugarjuk, a Caribou shaman of great skill, described to Rasmussen how he became a wizard. The *angakoq* spoke so slowly and carefully that Rasmussen was able to write down his statement word for word. Although the Arctic explorer found it difficult to believe that any human being, even a shaman, could survive thirty to forty degrees of cold, sitting in a tiny snow hut, eating no food, and drinking but two sips of water over a thirty-day period, he never questioned Igjugarjuk about his vision quest. As Rasmussen said, "I was afraid of making him cautious by doubting or asking him questions, and, after all, what I wanted to know, here, as elsewhere, was these people's own beliefs. And there is not the slightest doubt that they themselves believed that the holy work itself, which consisted in being able to see into the riddles of life, imparted to novices and practitioners some special power that enabled them to go through what ordinary mortals would not be able to survive."[2]

Igjugarjuk chose to suffer and die by the two things that are most dangerous to human beings: starvation and cold. During the pitch of his crisis, when he had collapsed from exhaustion, a helping spirit came to him. She was a beautiful woman, like the helping spirit of the Siberian Gol'd shaman (see pp. 120–123), who endowed him with special powers. This female spirit is called *Pinga.* She is believed to dwell somewhere in space, manifesting only when she is needed.

When the neophyte *angakoq* was taken back to his people after his retreat in the harsh winter solitudes, he was so emaciated that he resembled a skeleton. After a year of sexual abstinence, special diet, and other prohibitions, he finally became a shaman.

Besides being a healer and seer, Igjugarjuk was a master initiator. He initiated Kinalik by shooting her through the heart and Aggjartoq by submerging him in an icy lake for five days.[3] However, according to Igjugarjuk, a man or woman cannot become an *angakoq* because he or she wishes to. Rather a "certain mysterious power" in the universe conveys this potential during a revelatory dream. This power is known as *Sila*. It is a force that is at the same time the universe, the weather, and a mixture of common sense, intelligence, and wisdom. It is, furthermore, a power that can be evoked and applied.[4]

When I was to be a shaman, I chose suffering through the two things that are most dangerous to us humans, suffering through hunger and suffering through cold. First I hungered five days and was then allowed to drink a mouthful of warm water; the old ones say that only if the water is warm will Pinga and Hila notice the novice and help him. Thereafter I went hungry another fifteen days, and again was given a mouthful of warm water. After that I hungered for ten days, and then could begin to eat, though it only had to be aklɛrnäŋicut, that is to say the sort of food on which there is never any taboo, preferably fleshy meat, and never intestines, head, heart or other entrails, nor meat that had been touched by wolf or wolverine while it lay in a cache. I was to keep to this diet for five moons, and then the next five moons might eat everything; but after that I was again forced to eat the meat diet that is prescribed for all those who must do penance in order to become clean. The old ones attached great importance to the food that the would-be shamans might eat; thus a novice who wished to possess the ability to kill had never to eat the salmon that we call hiuʳlχit. If they eat hiuʳlχit, they will, instead of killing others, kill themselves.

My instructor was my wife's father. Perqánâq. When I was to be exhibited to Pinga and Hila, he dragged me on a little sledge that was no bigger than I could just sit on it; he dragged me far over on the other side of Hikoligjuaq. It was a very long day's journey inland to a place we call Kíngârjuit: the high hills, which are at Tikerarjuaq (by the southeast shore of Hikoligjuaq). It was in winter time and took place at night with the new moon; one could just see the very first streak of the moon; it had just appeared in the sky. I was not fetched again until the next moon was of the same size. Perqánâq built a small snow hut at the place where I was to be, this snow hut being no bigger than that I could just get under cover and sit down. I was given no sleeping skin to protect me against the cold, only a little piece of caribou skin to sit upon. There I was shut in: uk·uᴀrtɔrpɔq kiziän·e haᵘnago: The entrance was closed with a block, but no soft snow was thrown over the hut to make it warm. When I had sat there five days, Perqánâq came with water, tepid, wrapped in caribou skin, a watertight caribou-skin bag. Not until fifteen days afterwards did he come again and hand me the same, just giving himself time to hand it to me, and then he was gone again, for even the old shaman must not interrupt my solitude. The snow hut in which I sat was built far from the trails of men, and when Perqánâq had found the spot where he thought it ought to be built, he stopped the little sledge at a distance, and there I had to remain seated until the snow hut was ready. Not even I, who was after all the one to have to stay there, might set my footprints in the vicinity of the hut, and old Perqànâq had to carry me from the sledge over to the hut so that I could crawl in. As soon as I had become alone, Perqánâq enjoined me to think of one single thing all the time I was to be there, to want only one single thing, and that was to draw Pinga's attention to the fact that there I sat and wished to be a shaman, piŋ·äp qaⁱjumaniᴀrmaŋa: Pinga should own me. My novitiate took place in the middle of the coldest winter, and I, who never got anything to warm me, and must not move, was very cold, and it was so tiring having to sit without daring to lie down, that sometimes it was as if I died a little. Only towards the end of the thirty days did a helping spirit come to me, a lovely and beautiful helping spirit, whom I had never thought of; it was a white woman; she came to me whilst I had collapsed, exhausted, and was sleeping. But still I saw her lifelike, hovering over me, and from that day I could not close my eyes or dream without seeing her. There is this remarkable thing about my helping spirit, that I have never seen her while awake, but only in dreams. She came to me from Pinga and was a sign that Pinga had now noticed me and would give me powers that would make me a shaman.

When a new moon was lighted and had the same size as the

one that had shone for us when we left the village, Perqánâq came again with his little sledge and stopped a long way from the snow hut. But by this time I was not very much alive any more and had not the strength to rise, in fact I could not stand on my feet. Perqánâq pulled me out of the hut and carried me down to the sledge and dragged me home in the same manner as he had dragged me to Kíngârjuit. I was now so completely emaciated that the veins on my hands and body and feet had quite disappeared: taqaˑruɓluᴀrluŋa. For a long time I might only eat very little in order to again get my intestines extended, and later came the diet that was to help to cleanse my body.

For a whole year I was not to lie with my wife, who, however, had to make my food. For a whole year I had to have my own little cooking pot and my own meat dish; no one else was allowed to eat of what had been cooked for me.

Later, when I had quite become myself again, I understood that I had become the shaman of my village, and it did happen that my neighbours or people from a long distance away called me to heal a sick person, or to "inspect a course" if they were going to travel. When this happened, the people of my village were called together and I told them what I had been asked to do. Then I left tent or snow house and went out into solitude: ahiᴀrmut, away from the dwellings of man, but those who remained behind had to sing continuously: quiahuŋnialukhiŋˑᴀrʟutik, just to keep themselves happy and lively. If anything difficult had to be found out, my solitude had to extend over three days and two nights, or three nights and two days. In all that time I had to wander about without rest, and only sit down once in a while on a stone or a snow drift. When I had been out long and had become tired, I could almost doze and dream what I had come out to find and about which I had been thinking all the time. Every morning, however, I could come home and report on what I had so far found, but as soon as I had spoken I had to return again, out into the open, out to places where I could be quite alone. In the time when one is out seeking, one may eat a little, but not much. If a shaman "out of the secrets of solitude" finds out that the sick person will die, he can return home and stay there without first having allowed the usual time to pass. It is only in cases of a possible cure that he must remain out the whole time. On the first night after returning from such a spirit wandering in solitude, the shaman must not lie with his wife, nor must he undress when going to sleep, nor lie down at full length, but must sleep in a sitting position.

These days of "seeking for knowledge" are very tiring, for one must walk all the time, no matter what the weather is like and only rest in short snatches. I am usually quite done up, tired, not only in body but also in head, when I have found what I sought.

We shamans in the interior have no special spirit language, and believe that the real angatkut do not need it. On my travels I have sometimes been present at a seance among the saltwater-dwellers, for instance among the coast people at Utkuhigjalik (Back River, or Great Fish River). These angatkut never seemed trustworthy to me. It always appeared to me that these salt-water angatkut attached more weight to tricks that would astonish the audience, when they jumped about the floor and lisped all sorts of absurdities and lies in their so-called spirit language; to me all this seemed only amusing and as something that would impress the ignorant. A real shaman does not jump about the floor and do tricks, nor does he seek by the aid of darkness, by putting out the lamps, to make the minds of his neighbours uneasy. For myself, I do not think I know much, but I do not think that wisdom or knowledge about things that are hidden can be sought in that manner. True wisdom is only to be found far away from people, out in the great solitude, and it is not found in play but only through suffering. Solitude and suffering open the human mind, and therefore a shaman must seek his wisdom there.

But during my visits to the salt-water shamans, both down about Iglugârjuk and Utkuhigjalik, I have never openly expressed my contempt for their manner of summoning their helping spirits. A stranger ought always to be cautious, for—one may never know—they may of course be skilful in magic and, like our shamans, be able to kill through words and thoughts. This that I am telling you now, I dare to confide to you, because you are a stranger from a far away country, but I would never speak about it to my own kinsmen, except those whom I should teach to become shamans. While I was at Utkuhigjalik, people there had heard from my wife that I was a shaman, and therefore they once asked me to cure a sick man, a man who was so wasted that he could no longer swallow food. I summoned all the people of the village together and asked them to hold a song-feast, as is our custom, because we believe that all evil will shun a place where people are happy. And when the song-feast began, I went out alone into the night. They laughed at me, and my wife was later on able to tell me how they mocked me, because I would not do tricks to entertain everybody. But I kept away in lonely places, far from the village, for five days, thinking uninterruptedly of the sick man and wishing him health. He got better, and since then nobody at that village has mocked me.

Lame Deer
NORTH AMERICA/SIOUX

John Fire Lame Deer, a full-blooded Lakota born on the Rosebud Reservation in South Dakota, did many things during his long life. He painted signs and picked spuds. He was a soldier, a tribal policeman, and a prisoner. He sang, was a radio clown and a bootlegger, and herded sheep. Behind this extraordinary range of professions and misfortunes was the fruit of a great vision he attained during the traditional vision quest he undertook as a young man, the vision that brought him to his true vocation, that of healer–shaman–medicine man. Lame Deer once said, "The find-out, it has last me my whole life. In a way I was always hopping back and forth across the boundary line of the mind."[5] Lame Deer is now dead. But his humor and wise heart seem to have brought him a long and incredibly rich and courageous life. His face, a rugged reflection of the Badlands, and his eyes, shining like those of an eagle, have been memorialized by his close friend, photographer Richard Erdoes.

Lame Deer told Erdoes one day: I believe that being a medicine man, more than anything else, is a state of mind, a way of looking at and understanding this earth, a sense of what it is all about. Am I a *wičasa wakan?* I guess so. What else can or would I be? Seeing me in my patched-up, faded shirt, with my down-at-the-heel cowboy boots, the hearing aid whistling in my ear, looking at the flimsy shack with its bad-smelling outhouse which I call my home—it all doesn't add up to a white man's idea of a holy man. You've seen me drunk and broke. You've heard me curse or tell a sexy joke. You know I'm not better or

wiser than other men. But I've been to the hilltop, got my vision and
power; the rest is just the trimmings.⁶˒ ⁷

I was all alone on the hilltop. I sat there in the vision pit, a
hole dug into the hill, my arms hugging my knees as I watched old
man Chest, the medicine man who had brought me there, disappear far down in the valley. He was just a moving black dot among
the pines, and soon he was gone altogether.

Now I was all by myself, left on the hilltop for four days and
nights without food or water until he came back for me. . . .

Indian children are never alone. They are always surrounded
by grandparents, uncles, cousins, relatives of all kinds, who fondle
the kids, sing to them, tell them stories. If the parents go some-
place, the kids go along.

But here I was, crouched in my vision pit, left alone by myself
for the first time in my life. I was sixteen then, still had my boy's
name and, let me tell you, I was scared. I was shivering and not
only from the cold. The nearest human being was many miles
away, and four days and nights is a long, long time. Of course,
when it was all over, I would no longer be a boy, but a man. I
would have had my vision. I would be given a man's name.

Sioux men are not afraid to endure hunger, thirst, and loneliness, and I was only ninety-six hours away from being a man. The
thought was comforting. Comforting, too, was the warmth of the
star blanket which old man Chest had wrapped around me to
cover my nakedness. My grandmother had made it especially for
this, my first *hanblechia,* my first vision-seeking. It was a beautifully designed quilt, white with a large morning star made of many
pieces of brightly colored cloth. That star was so big it covered
most of the blanket. If Wakan Tanka, the Great Spirit, would give
me the vision and the power, I would become a medicine man and
perform many ceremonies wrapped in that quilt. I am an old man
now and many times a grandfather, but I still have that star blanket my grandmother made for me. I treasure it; some day I shall
be buried in it.

The medicine man had also left a peace pipe with me, together
with a bag of *kinnickinnick*—our kind of tobacco made of red willow
bark. This pipe was even more of a friend to me than my star
blanket. . . .

For us Indians there is just the pipe, the earth we sit on and the open sky. The spirit is everywhere. Sometimes it shows itself through an animal, a bird or some trees and hills. Sometimes it speaks from the Badlands, a stone, or even from the water. That smoke from the peace pipe, it goes straight up to the spirit world. But this is a two-way thing. Power flows down to us through that smoke, through the pipe stem. You feel that power as you hold your pipe; it moves from the pipe right into your body. It makes your hair stand up. That pipe is not just a thing; it is alive. Smoking this pipe would make me feel good and help me to get rid of my fears.

As I ran my fingers along its bowl of smooth red pipestone, red like the blood of my people, I no longer felt scared. That pipe had belonged to my father and to his father before him. It would someday pass to my son and, through him, to my grandchildren. As long as we had the pipe there would be a Sioux nation. As I fingered the pipe, touched it, felt its smoothness that came from long use, I sensed that my forefathers who had once smoked this pipe were with me on the hill, right in the vision pit. I was no longer alone.

Besides the pipe the medicine man had also given me a gourd. In it were forty small squares of flesh which my grandmother had cut from her arm with a razor blade. I had seen her do it. Blood had been streaming down from her shoulder to her elbow as she carefully put down each piece of skin on a handkerchief, anxious not to lose a single one. It would have made those anthropologists mad. Imagine, performing such an ancient ceremony with a razor blade instead of a flint knife! To me it did not matter. Someone dear to me had undergone pain, given me something of herself, part of her body, to help me pray and make me stronghearted. How could I be afraid with so many people—living and dead—helping me?

One thing still worried me. I wanted to become a medicine man, a *yuwipi*, a healer carrying on the ancient ways of the Sioux nation. But you cannot learn to be a medicine man like a white man going to medical school. An old holy man can teach you about herbs and the right ways to perform a ceremony where everything must be in its proper place, where every move, every word has its own, special meaning. These things you can learn—like spelling, like training a horse. But by themselves these things mean nothing. Without the vision and the power this learning will do no good. It would not make me a medicine man.

What if I failed, if I had no vision? Or if I dreamed of the Thunder Beings, or lightning struck the hill? That would make me at once into a *heyoka*, a contrariwise, an upside-down man, a clown. "You'll know it, if you get the power," my Uncle Chest had told me. "If you are not given it, you won't lie about it, you won't pretend. That would kill you, or kill somebody close to you, somebody you love."

Night was coming on. I was still lightheaded and dizzy from my first sweat bath in which I had purified myself before going up the hill. I had never been in a sweat lodge before. I had sat in the little beehive-shaped hut made of bent willow branches and covered with blankets to keep the heat in. Old Chest and three other medicine men had been in the lodge with me. I had my back against the wall, edging as far away as I could from the red-hot stones glowing in the center. As Chest poured water over the rocks, hissing white steam enveloped me and filled my lungs. I thought the heat would kill me, burn the eyelids off my face! But right in the middle of all this swirling steam I heard Chest singing. So it couldn't be all that bad. I did not cry out "All my relatives!" —which would have made him open the flap of the sweat lodge to let in some cool air—and I was proud of this. I heard him praying for me: "Oh, holy rocks, we receive your white breath, the steam. It is the breath of life. Let this young boy inhale it. Make him strong."

The sweat bath had prepared me for my vision-seeking. Even now, an hour later, my skin still tingled. But it seemed to have made my brains empty. Maybe that was good, plenty of room for new insights.

Darkness had fallen upon the hill. I knew that *hanhepi-wi* had risen, the night sun, which is what we call the moon. Huddled in my narrow cave, I did not see it. Blackness was wrapped around me like a velvet cloth. It seemed to cut me off from the outside world, even from my own body. It made me listen to the voices within me. I thought of my forefathers who had crouched on this hill before me, because the medicine men in my family had chosen this spot for a place of meditation and vision-seeking ever since the day they had crossed the Missouri to hunt for buffalo in the White River country some two hundred years ago. I thought that I could sense their presence right through the earth I was leaning against. I could feel them entering my body, feel them stirring in my mind and heart.

Sounds came to me through the darkness: the cries of the wind, the whisper of the trees, the voices of nature, animal sounds, the hooting of an owl. Suddenly I felt an overwhelming presence. Down there with me in my cramped hole was a big bird. The pit was only as wide as myself, and I was a skinny boy, but that huge bird was flying around me as if he had the whole sky to himself. I could hear his cries, sometimes near and sometimes far, far away. I felt feathers or a wing touching my back and head. This feeling was so overwhelming that it was just too much for me. I trembled and my bones turned to ice. I grasped the rattle with the forty pieces of my grandmother's flesh. It also had many little stones in it, tiny fossils picked up from an ant heap. Ants collect them. Nobody knows why. These little stones are supposed to have a power in them. I shook the rattle and it made a soothing sound, like rain falling on rock. It was talking to me, but it did not calm my fears. I took the sacred pipe in my other hand and began to sing and pray: "Tunkashila, grandfather spirit, help me." But this did not help. I don't know what got into me, but I was no longer myself. I started to cry. Crying, even my voice was different. I sounded like an older man, I couldn't even recognize this strange voice. I used long-ago words in my prayer, words no longer used nowadays. I tried to wipe away my tears, but they wouldn't stop. In the end I just pulled that quilt over me, rolled myself up in it. Still I felt the bird wings touching me.

Slowly I perceived that a voice was trying to tell me something. It was a bird cry, but I tell you, I began to understand some of it. That happens sometimes. I know a lady who had a butterfly sitting on her shoulder. That butterfly told her things. This made her become a great medicine woman.

I heard a human voice too, strange and high-pitched, a voice which could not come from an ordinary, living being. All at once I was way up there with the birds. The hill with the vision pit was way above everything. I could look down even on the stars, and the moon was close to my left side. It seemed as though the earth and the stars were moving below me. A voice said, "You are sacrificing yourself here to be a medicine man. In time you will be one. You will teach other medicine men. We are the fowl people, the winged ones, the eagles and the owls. We are a nation and you shall be our brother. You will never kill or harm any one of us. You are going to understand us whenever you come to seek a vision here on this hill. You will learn about herbs and roots, and you will heal people. You will ask them for nothing in return. A man's life is short. Make yours a worthy one."

I felt that these voices were good, and slowly my fear left me. I had lost all sense of time. I did not know whether it was day or night. I was asleep, yet wide awake. Then I saw a shape before me. It rose from the darkness and the swirling fog which penetrated my earth hole. I saw that this was my great-grandfather, Tahca Ushte, Lame Deer, old man chief of the Minneconjou. I could see the blood dripping from my great-grandfather's chest where a white soldier had shot him. I understood that my great-grandfather wished me to take his name. This made me glad beyond words.

We Sioux believe that there is something within us that controls us, something like a second person almost. We call it *nagi*, what other people might call soul, spirit or essence. One can't see it, feel it or taste it, but that time on the hill—and that once only —I knew it was there inside of me. Then I felt the power surge through me like a flood. I cannot describe it, but it filled all of me. Now I knew for sure that I would become a *wicasa wakan*, a medicine man. Again I wept, this time with happiness.

I didn't know how long I had been up there on that hill—one minute or a lifetime. I felt a hand on my shoulder gently shaking me. It was old man Chest, who had come for me. He told me that I had been in the vision pit four days and four nights and that it was time to come down. He would give me something to eat and water to drink and then I was to tell him everything that had happened to me during my *hanblechia*. He would interpret my visions for me. He told me that the vision pit had changed me in a way that I would not be able to understand at that time. He told me also that I was no longer a boy, that I was a man now. I was Lame Deer.

Leonard Crow Dog
NORTH AMERICA/SIOUX

Leonard Crow Dog comes from a family of medicine men. His fore-
bears were as famous in their own times as Crow Dog is today. He was
born in 1942 on the Rosebud Reservation, in a countryside of pine-
studded rolling hills, grassy plains, and rivers. The holy men of his
tribe realized early that the young boy was endowed with powers, and
they never permitted him to attend the white man's school because
that would have interfered with his long, arduous training as a medicine man.

The first Crow Dog, Leonard's great-grandfather, a close friend of
Chief Crazy Horse, was a leader in the Ghost Dance movement that
led to the massacre at Wounded Knee in 1890. Leonard himself was the
medicine man at the 1973 siege of Wounded Knee, and in the spring
of 1974, he initiated a revival of the Ghost Dance. Native Americans
from all over the United States and from Canada and Mexico gathered
to participate in this powerful messianic event. From November 1975
to March 1977, Leonard was imprisoned for his political activities at
Wounded Knee.

Crow Dog is not only a political figure and a traditional Sioux
medicine man; he is also a Sun Dancer who has pierced himself many
times, a singer of the sacred chants of his people, a Road Man of the
Native American Church, and an activist philosopher who desires to
unify all Indian nations by creating a pan-Indian faith. He is an ac-
knowledged medicine man in more than eighty tribes in North America and has practiced his medicine from coast to coast and from Canada
to Mexico. His metaphysical views, according to his close friend Richard Erdoes, have continued to evolve and deepen in the twenty-five
years that have passed since he became a practicing medicine man at
the age of twelve.[8]

They know me as Leonard Crow Dog, but Leonard is just a
white man's name that we must have. The important name, which
was given to me when I was a small boy, my Indian name, is
Defends His Medicine. Few people know it. I am trying to wrap
my life around this name. I have not always defended my medicine well, but I am trying.

Before I could be instructed in the way of a medicine man, I had to purify myself, I had to go up on the hill to *hanbleceya,* to cry for a dream, to ask for a vision that would show me the way. This is a hard thing to do, especially for a young boy. It took all the courage I had. Before I could go on my vision quest, I had to cleanse myself in the *oinikaga* tipi, the *inipi,* the sweat lodge. My uncle, Good Lance, and my father prepared everything for me. Good Lance would direct the ceremony; my father would be the helper. The *inipi* is probably our oldest ceremony because it is built around the simplest, basic, life-giving things: the fire that comes from the sun, warmth without which there can be no life; *iñyañ wakan,* or *tunka,* the rock that was there when the earth began, that will still be there at the end of time; the earth, the mother womb; the water that all creatures need; our green brother, the sage; and encircled by all these, man, basic man, naked as he was born, feeling the weight, the spirit of endless generations before him, feeling himself part of the earth, nature's child, not her master.

It is also the simplest of all ceremonies. All you need is a patch of earth some six feet across, six saplings that will bend, rocks, wood for a fire, a few blankets, a pail of fresh, cold water from the nearest brook. A person alone, with nobody to help, nobody to comfort him, could find solace, a great uplift by performing this ceremony. He would need no money, no collar-wearing preacher to help him; he could make a sweathouse in half an hour. Many have done this, I am sure, when they felt the need.

Now I was going to purify myself for the first time, my first sweat bath, which was put up specially for *me!* I felt very solemn, overawed, stiff, awkward. My father and my uncle, as well as the few other relatives, put me at my ease by cracking jokes and making funny little remarks. Life is holiness and everyday humdrum, sadness and laughter, the mind and the belly all mixed together. The Great Spirit doesn't want us to sort them out neatly. He lets the white people do it, who have one way of behaving on Sunday in church and another for the rest of the week. We were doing something sacred, but this didn't mean we shouldn't laugh while we gathered wood for the fire. "This *inipi* for my son is an important one," said my father. "Let only the sacred wood, cottonwood, *can-wakan,* be used." This was done. Good Lance placed four sticks on the ground first, a square, and then placed another four across these while he prayed to the West, the North, the East, and the South. In a sacred manner, he built up a cone-shaped pile of wood for the fire.

The little pile of gray rocks was already there waiting, rocks from many previous sweat baths, good, tried rocks that would not crack and explode in the fire. They were the kind called *sintkala wakshu,* bird rocks. They sometimes are covered with designs, thin and faint as spiderwebs, that quickly fade in the sunlight. Scientifically, if you want to know, they are limestone. Beside the heap of rocks was a huge bleached buffalo skull with a lightning symbol painted on it. Its eye sockets were filled with two balls of sage and grass. Good Lance tied a short string of tobacco offerings to one of the horns. He was, as I said before, determined that all the rituals at which he was present should be done in the right, ancient way. He had made sure that no Bull-Durham was used in one of his ceremonies, only *čanshasha,* our old red willow bark tobacco. He made a face when he saw the shiny new metal pail with its equally shiny new dipper. He took out of his old, battered suitcase an ancient ladle made of buffalo horn. "We'll use this instead," he said, "as for the pail, we really should use a buffalo's stomach paunch for a water receptacle, but you cannot get one nowadays, so this thing here"—and he kicked the offending pail lightly— "will have to do." Good Lance was very different in this way from the other medicine men, who had long given up being fussy over details, over what they said were just unimportant externalities. "And don't go into the *oinikaga* tipi with your underwear on, jockstraps, fancy shorts with little flowers printed on them," Good Lance told us. "The Spirit doesn't like this. You go in naked."

My father and my uncle then made a sweat lodge for me. They took twelve willow saplings and stuck them upright in the ground so that they formed a circle, six on one side and six on the other. They bent these sticks toward each other so that they became a dome, about waist high, binding them together with strips of red trade cloth. Six bundles of tobacco offerings were tied to this framework. "These are the cones of the *oinikaga* tipi; now we must put flesh and skin on them," said Good Lance. He then covered the frame with blankets and quilts, spreading a big, faded tarp over the whole. Now the lodge was finished, looking very much like a canvas-covered igloo, as an anthropologist once described it. I, too, was allowed to help, gathering sage and covering the floor of the little hut with it. Besides my father, Good Lance, and myself, there were four more relatives who were to purify themselves with me. I wondered how they would all fit; the lodge looked so small.

They then dug the fire pit, a round hole in the exact center of the little hut. "That's the universe, the whole universe contained within this tiny *oinikaga tipi*," my father told me. "The whole world is in there with us to listen when we pray." From the earth scooped out of the fire pit, they made a straight ridge leading out of the lodge to a distance of about nine feet, and what was left of it they made into a little mound. "This represents *Unči*, Our Grandmother the Earth. Remember it," I was told. "And the little ridge leading to it, that is *čanku-wakan*, the Sacred Road of Life. Walk it straight." The pit in the hut, the little mound, the stack of wood were all in one line. Close to one entrance, on the right side, two small forked sticks with a third twig placed horizontally across them formed a rack against which our sacred pipe, handed on from father to son, was placed.

Now all was ready. The fire in which the stones were heated was already blazing brightly. We stripped and entered the lodge. Good Lance was the leader, so he entered first, sitting on the right side with his pail of water. I went in next to last. The last one in was my father, who was the helper. Small as I was, I had to crawl inside on my hands and knees. "That will remind you," said someone, "of your brothers the buffalo, the elk, the antelope, who walk on four legs. Pray for them today." The entrance of the *initipi* faced *wiyohpe*, the West. I could see the setting sun through the entrance; the heated air around the fire seemed to make his rays dance. I was surprised how easily we all fitted inside.

"Don't sit sloppy, like a *washichu*," said my cousin next to me. "Sit on your knees like an Indian."

Good Lance took a twist of sweet grass and lit it with a match. He also lit a little bundle of sage. I'll never forget how sweet it smelled that first time. After so many years, it still affects me the same way, whenever I take a sweat bath. "This will make your body sacred," said Good Lance, smoking me up, waving the smoldering sweet grass over and around me. He encouraged me to inhale the fragrance, to put my palms close to the burning end of the herbs, to rub them together, to rub the sweet smell all over me.

Someone crushed another herb, *wahpe-washtemna,* Indian perfume, between his hands and rubbed his body with it. Good Lance then asked for silence. "This is the moment. I want you to be quiet. Stop chattering. When I place the rocks, remember *wakichagapi,* remember your dead relatives and friends; pray for them in your minds." He then called for the first six rocks.

One of my older cousins was the fire keeper. He did everything that was needed on the outside. On a forked stick, he brought the first six rocks and passed them inside one by one in total silence. As each stone appeared, Good Lance grabbed the large forked stick and guided it into the fire pit. My cousin would have liked to use a shovel for this because that would have been easier, but Good Lance did not allow it. He placed one rock first in the center of the pit, then four rocks around it, then one more rock on top of the middle one. These represented the earth, the four directions of the universe, and the sky. The helper outside closed the flap, and we sat in darkness. The rocks glowed a dull red, like iron heated in a forge. They gave off a thousand tiny sparks and made a noise like a disturbed ant heap. And were they hot! I edged away from them as far as I could, pressing my back against the wall of the sweat lodge, being very conscious of all that went on: of the heat, the feel of sage under my backside, the red-hot glow in the center.

"If things get too hot for you," whispered my father to me, "say *mitakuye oyasin,* all my relatives, and we'll open the flap and let some coolness in. But don't do it unless you have to."

With his buffalo horn ladle, Good Lance poured ice-cold water over the red-glowing stones. There was a tremendous hiss as we were instantly enveloped in a cloud of searing white steam. It was so hot, it came like a shock wave upon me. It was as if I had stuck my head inside our old kitchen range when its bottom was covered with live coals. I dared not breathe; I thought that if I did I would burn my lungs into charcoal. But I did not cry out. I just stuck my head between my knees. Good Lance prayed. He used ancient words, some of which I did not understand. He prayed for the dear dead ones, for our soldiers on duty overseas in Korea, Okinawa, Germany. He prayed for the earth, the animals, the plants. He prayed to Tunkashila, the Grandfather Spirit: "Let this young boy here have a good dream, a good vision. Let him walk the medicine road; let him be worthy."

After every sentence, we all said, *"Hau, ohan, Tunkashila onshimala ye."* We all tried to catch this hot steam in our palms, rub it on us.

"This steam is the holy breath of the universe. Hokshila, boy, you are in your mother's womb again. You are going to be reborn." They all sang two songs, very ancient songs, going way back to the days when we Sioux roamed the prairie, when we planted corn near the Great Lakes. I suddenly felt wise with the wisdom of generations. The men, my relatives, sang loud and vigorously, while I could barely breathe. I wondered how they could do it.

Good Lance called out, *"Ho, mitakuye oyasin,"* and my cousin outside opened the flap, let the steam escape, let light and wonderful coolness enter. My father lit the sacred pipe, raised its stem in prayer, took four puffs, and passed it to me. I drew up the smoke as strongly as I could, hoping the pipe would not go out on me because that would have been a bad sign. My father made sure that it did not by gently stirring up the tobacco in the pipe bowl with a small poker of sage wood. This poker, I knew, had once pierced the breast of a Sun Dancer. I took my four puffs and passed the pipe on.

"This *chanunpa,* this sacred pipe," said my father, "let it be your guide. It is the soul of our people. Its red stone is the blood and flesh of the Lakota. Its stem is our backbone; the feather tied to the stem has within it the wisdom of *Wanblee,* the eagle. The smoke rising from it is Tunkashila's breath. With the pipe, you cannot lie. If ever you say anything untrue while smoking it, lightning will strike you." The tobacco tasted and smelled good. Its fragrance filled the sweat lodge. I felt wonderfully happy, proud to smoke with the grown-ups. I felt as one with them. I passed the pipe on.

When Good Lance had taken his turn with it, he called for more stones, not any particular number. He didn't warn us to be especially quiet. It had been the first six that were the important ones. Again, hot rocks were brought in and the flap closed. The heat, the steam, the tobacco had made me giddy and light-headed. It had emptied my mind so that the spirits could enter it. I felt weak, but I also felt power streaming through my veins, a new, strange power. As I stared into the glowing stones, I thought I saw a small bird in them. I recognized it as an eagle. I had hardly done so when it turned into a pipe. It all happened in a flash, in a twinkling of an eye, but it was very real to me.

"The red, the heat, the flame, the fire, *peta-owihankeshni*, the fire without end. Your grandfather lit it for your father who is lighting it for you now," someone said in the dark. "Hokshila, boy, tend this fire; pass it on to the next generation, to the son you will have sometime, so that he can pass it on to his children." Again, the water was poured. Again, we were wrapped in the hot, whirling steam. This time it felt good. I liked feeling it heating up my lungs, spreading its hotness throughout my body.

The power must have entered the other ones, too. The songs rose to a new pitch, a new strength, a new intensity, as I never had heard songs before. The little hut was shaken as if in the grip of a giant hand. It was trembling as a leaf trembles in the wind. Beneath us the earth seemed to move.

"Grandfather is here," said Good Lance. "The spirits are here; the eagle's wisdom is here."

We all believed it, knew it. The pipe was passed to the right, and we smoked again. Four times in all the stones were brought; four times the water was poured; four times we prayed and sang; four times we smoked.

After the last time, Good Lance told me, "Hokshila, you have been purified; you are no longer a child; you are ready now and made strong to go up there and cry for a dream. *Hechetu.*"

Then all of us in turn said, *"Mitakuye oyasin,* all my relatives!" That meant all two-legged ones, all four-legged ones, even those with eight legs or no legs at all. It meant those with wings and those with fins, those with roots and leaves, everything alive, all our relatives. My father then took the pipe apart and carefully cleaned the bowl. My first *inikagapi* was over.

But the sweat bath had only been the beginning, just the first part of *hanbleceya*. After rubbing my glistening body with sage to dry myself, I dressed. I felt good, tingling, as if that had been my first day on earth. I saw my sisters standing together a little way off toward the river. Delphine was making a flesh offering to help me fast. She was standing there quietly, holding a peace pipe, a small, L-shaped, red pipe, the stem pointing up into the clouds.

Some of her cousins were cutting little pieces of flesh from her arms, lifting the tiny squares of skin with a needle, slicing them off with a razor blade. A thin rivulet of blood was flowing down my sister's arm from the shoulder to the elbow. She just stood there, silent, not moving at all, looking straight ahead. Our cousins picked up each little piece of flesh and put it on a square of red trade cloth.

After she had given twenty pieces, the red cloth containing them was made into a small bundle and tied to the pipe, which my sister handed to me, saying, "If you get scared or discouraged, just grab hold of this."

Think that by your suffering you can help someone you love. If you have a relative who is sick and you want him to get well, if you have nothing else, why, you have your flesh to give, and you sacrifice it for him. My sister's offerings were so many silent prayers for me, and the thought of this made me almost cry.

Good Lance also gave me a medicine bundle with a stone in it and some tobacco ties.

My father gave me an eagle-bone whistle. "When things get rough," he advised, "you blow on it." There was nothing more to be done but go up that hill.

My father and an uncle of mine, Joe Yellow Wolf, took me up. The Crow Dogs' fasting place, their holy spot, is on Grass Mountain, a steep hill with a good view of our house, the river, the valley, a whole chain of hills on the other side. Part of that hill is a wide plateau where stray cattle sometimes roam. The plateau narrows toward the end and becomes heavily wooded. The grass and herbs come halfway up your legs. There, among the pine trees, is our vision pit, an L-shaped hole dug into the ground, first straight down and then a short horizontal passage deep under the roots of the trees. You sit at the end of that passage and do your fasting.

A grown-up man fasts anywhere from one to four days. A medicine man who needs a big vision always fasts four days. I know one healer, Pete Catches, who has fasted even longer. His wife went on a long fast, too. In my case, it was decided I should stay up there alone without food or water for two days and two nights. I was only a boy, so four days would be too much. On the other hand, I wanted to be a medicine man, so it should be more than just one day.

"Hokshila, son, do you think you can stand it that long?"

I said, "Yes" with my heart in my mouth.

They put prayer flags—red, black, yellow, and white—at four points around the fasting hole. They put a string of 105 tobacco bundles in a square around it. They put the buffalo skull right at the entrance. Then it was time for me to strip and go down into the hole. My father and uncle crawled in with me, though there was really no room for them. They wrapped me in a star quilt and tied me up in it with a deer hide thong. That was symbolic of the fact that it was hoped I would one day be a *yuwipi wichasha*, a kind of medicine man who conducts his ceremonies wrapped and tied up in a blanket like a mummy. Well, they patted me on the back, mumbled some encouragements, and left me there, my heart pounding, a very scared little bundle.

The first hours were the hardest. It was pitch dark and deathly still. I sat there without moving. My arms and legs went asleep. I could neither hear nor see nor feel. I became almost disembodied, a thing with a heart and wild thoughts but no flesh or bones. Would I ever be able to see and hear again? I kept my fingers clamped around the little pipe, fingered the bundle with my sister's flesh in it. I found that it did give me a little courage. I don't know how long I sat there. All sense of time had left me long ago. I didn't know whether it was day or night, had not even a way to find out. I prayed and prayed, tears streaming down my cheeks. I wanted water but kept praying. Toward evening of the second day—and this time is only a wild guess—I saw wheels before my eyes forming up into one fiery hoop and then separating again into bright, many-colored circles, dancing before my eyes and again contracting into one big circle, a circle with a mouth and two eyes.

Suddenly, I heard a voice. It seemed to come from within the bundle that was me, a voice from the dark. It was hard to tell exactly where it came from. It was not a human voice; it sounded like a bird speaking like a man. My hackles rose; the tiny hairs on my back stood up. My flesh crawled; I had goose pimples. I tried to understand the voice, grasping the sacred pipe hard enough to break it. "Remember the hoop," said the voice that was not like a human's. "This night we will teach you." And I heard many feet walking around in my small vision pit. And suddenly I was out of my hole, in another world, standing in front of a sweat bath on a prairie covered with wild flowers, covered with herds of elk and buffalo.

I saw a man coming toward me; he seemed to have no feet; he just floated toward me out of a mist. He held two *wagmuha,* two rattles, in his hand. He said, "Boy, whatever you tell your people, do not exaggerate; always do what your vision tells you. Never pretend." The man was wearing an old-fashioned buckskin outfit decorated with quillwork. I stretched my hands out to touch him, when suddenly I was back inside my star quilt. My hand was on the medicine bundle with the stones and the tobacco ties. I still have it. I shall always keep it. I still heard the voice: "Remember the hoop; remember the pipe; be its spokesman." I was no longer afraid. Whoever was talking meant me no harm.

Suddenly, before me stretched a coal-black cloud with lightning coming out of it. The cloud spread and spread; it grew wings; it became an eagle. The eagle talked to me: "I give you a power, not to use for yourself, but for your people. It does not belong to you. It belongs to the *ikche wichasha,* the common folks." I saw a rider on a gray horse coming toward me, he held in his one hand a hoop made of sage. He held it high. Like the man I had seen before, this horse had no legs. It, too, just came floating up to me. And again everything dissolved into blackness, with just me cowering naked in my blanket. And again out of the mist came a strange creature floating up, covered with hair, pale, formless. He wanted to take my medicine away from me, but I wrestled with him, defended it. He did not get my medicine. He, too, disappeared.

Suddenly somebody shook me by the shoulder. "Wake up, boy." I bit my lip not to cry out, but it was only my father and my uncle coming for me. The two days and nights were over.

Back at the house I told them what I had seen. *"Takoja,* grandson," said Good Lance, "you had a fine dream; it will take you a long way. Hokshila, you will be a medicine man, a *yuwipi.* But before that you will be a hoop dancer for four years, until you grow up. I will do something for you now." Up to this time, I had trouble with my speech. I was tongue-tied; I couldn't talk; I stammered. Whenever I met a stranger, I couldn't get a word out.

Nobody could understand me. Good Lance put his hands on my head and mouth. He fanned me with an eagle wing. He prayed, "Tunkashila, make this boy talk." And when I woke up the next morning, I could speak better; and in a short while, I was talking a streak. After the prayer, Good Lance said, "I will give you something good for a gift: a hoop and a horse. Now sleep."

I went to bed but couldn't sleep. I just drifted in and out of half wakefulness. I still had visions, could not stop them, didn't try to. I saw gourds dancing before my eyes, stars, and many, many colors, all the colors of the rainbow, wheeling and wheeling in never-ending circles. I reached underneath my pillow. I had put my medicine bundle there, the one with the stone and tobacco ties. I clenched my fist firmly around it. Thus I finally fell asleep contented. I had defended my medicine well, even if only in a dream.

Brooke Medicine Eagle
NORTH AMERICA/NEZ PERCÉ AND SIOUX

I found some dry, bleached bones today,
and gathered them to put into a bag
for casting to ask the future,
when modern means have failed me.

Brooke Medicine Eagle—her sacred name is Daughter of the Rainbow of the Morning Star Clan Whose Helpers Are the Sun and Moon and Whose Medicine Is the Eagle—is the great-great-grandniece of Grandfather Joseph, the Nez Percé Indian leader and holy man. Brought up on the Crow Reservation in Montana, where Native American traditions were fading, she found her path by returning to the ancient sacred ways of her people. Medicine Eagle was in her twenties when she undertook ritual training with the Northern Cheyenne medicine woman Stands Near the Fire (Josie Limpie), who is also called The Woman Who Knows Everything. Stands Near the Fire, one of the highest traditional religious leaders among her people, is The Keeper of the Sacred Buffalo Hat.

The description of Medicine Eagle's vision on Bear Butte is that of a woman whose concerns and work are focused on global issues in-

volving peoples of all races and traditions. She believes that the dreams and visions of Black Elk and other seers are now coming true. "His place [Black Elk's] was to wait. Our generation must now go back to our origins to know that beauty about which he spoke and reap the harvest without guilt. Guilt does not allow us receive the source of his great vision."

Raised in economically impoverished circumstances, she was awarded a full scholarship to the University of Denver, where she earned a bachelor's degree in psychology and mathematics and a master's degree in counseling psychology. She then worked in various universities, saved money, gave up on Western education, and cast her fate to the winds.

Medicine Eagle is a poet and chanter of sacred songs, a dancer of traditional forms, and a healer.[9]

The vision quest that I have done was with my teacher who is a Northern Cheyenne woman. She is eighty-five years old and is known as The Keeper of the Sacred Buffalo Hat. Her people call her The Woman Who Knows Everything. She and a younger medicine woman took me to a place called Bear Butte, South Dakota; it's plains country that goes up into the Black Hills. That's the traditional fasting, vision-questing place of the Sioux and Cheyenne and has been for centuries and centuries. What is usually done among the Cheyenne is that you fast and cleanse yourself bodily, emotionally, and psychically. Then you go atop a mountain for four days and nights with just a breechcloth on and a buffalo robe, and you stay there without food or water, praying for vision. This is the kind of quest that I did.

The younger medicine woman took me up the butte. She prepared and blessed a bed of sagebrush on a very rocky hill halfway up the mountain. This was to be my bed. After we smoked a pipe and offered prayers, she left me. So I spent the time there fasting and praying for vision.

It was just getting to be dark. Up on the mountain, I can look down over the country: There's a lake down below me; in the far-off distance are the Black Hills, and I can see the lights of Rapid City. I'm hoping it won't rain because I really don't want to be rained on up here. A few little clouds are flitting across the sky, but it is relatively warm, the late fall. I'm just lying here very peacefully. And beside me there comes a woman, older than me, but not really an old woman. She's dressed very simply, buckskin. And I'm surprised that she doesn't have beading on her dress. She has raven black hair in long braids. And she stands beside me and begins to talk to me. As she talks to me, her words come, but not in my ears; I don't really hear her say anything. It's as though she's feeding something in at my navel, and it comes through me, and I can interpret part of it in words but not all of it, like she's giving me something through my stomach and letting it come up. So the words that I put to it have to be my own, and I have discovered more and more of what she told me as time has gone on.

Just then the little clouds that were over the moon move off, and as they move away, the moonlight shining on her dress creates a flurry of rainbows, and I can see that her dress is beaded with crystal beads, hundreds of tiny crystal beads; the slightest movement she makes sends little flurries of soft rainbows all over. About this time, something else starts to happen. Down off the high part of the mountain, it starts to become light, and I hear soft drumbeats begin, very soft. There's a kind of dance that the women do that is very soft. And down off that mountain in a slow, soft, and gentle step come the old women, spirits of that land, that mountain, old gray-haired women, Indian women, dancing down. They either *are* light or carry light. They wind down the mountain and then circle around the hill I am on. And as they dance around in a circle, very quickly, into that circle comes another circle, this of young women, of my age and time, young women that I know, and they, too, are dancing. Those two circles are dancing and moving, and then they begin to weave in and out of each other, sway in and out of each other. And then inside of that circle comes another circle of seven old grandmothers, white-haired women, women who are significant to me, powerful old women.

In the Indian tradition, there is an amazing amount of humor. And the humor comes when all this very solemn, very slow, and very beautiful ceremony is taking place. Running off the mountain, with her hair flying, is this friend of mine. She's always late. She is a very high person, but she is very unstable. Into the circle comes Dianne, flying, with her hair streaming, late as always. And on her hand she is carrying a dove. The Rainbow Woman looks down on me and says, "Her name is Moon Dove," and she smiles. Dianne then lets the dove fly.

The circles around me disappear, and I am again alone with the Rainbow Woman.

She said to me that the earth is in trouble, that the land is in trouble, and that here on this land, this Turtle Island, this North American land, what needs to happen is a balancing. She said that the thrusting, aggressive, analytic, intellectual, building, making-it-happen energy has very much overbalanced the feminine, receptive, allowing, surrendering energy. She said that what needs to happen is an uplifting and a balancing. And because we are out of balance, we need to put more emphasis on surrendering, being receptive, allowing, nurturing. She was speaking to me as a woman, and I was to carry this message to women specifically. But not only do women need to become strong in this way; we all need to do this, men and women alike.

Women are born into that kind of space. It's more natural for us to be receptive and nurturing. That's what being a woman in this body is about. But even the women in our society don't do that very well. None of us has ever been taught how to do that. We know how to *do* something; we know how to *make* something, how to *do*, how to *try*. But we need to allow, to be receptive, to surrender, to serve. These are things we don't know very well. So she told me that women especially need to find that place, to find the strength of their place, and that also the whole society, men and women, need that balance to bring ourselves into balance.

Another thing she said to me was that we on this North American continent are all children of the rainbow, all of us; we are mixed-bloods. And especially me she was speaking to, saying that she felt that I would be a carrier of the message between the two cultures, across the rainbow bridge, from the old culture to the new, from the Indian culture to the dominant culture, and back again. And in a sense, all of us in this generation can be that. We can help bridge that gap, build that bridge into the new age of balance.

Those are the kind of things that she talked about, about cleansing ourselves so that we can allow love and light and surrender to come through us. And when she finished talking, she stood quietly for a moment. Her feet stayed where they were, but she shot out across the sky in a rainbow arc that covered the heavens, her head at the top of that arc. And then the lights that formed that rainbow began to die out, almost like fireworks in the sky, died out from her feet and died out and died out. And she was gone.

When I woke up the next morning, on the other side of the sky was the completion of the rainbow that had started the night before. And for days and days after that, rainbows kept appearing in my life.

There are very few women who are on the path of the shaman, and yet, this is my way. I was raised on the Crow Reservation in Montana. My blood is Sioux and Nez Percé. The Indian tradition was very much hidden when I was growing up on the reservation. However, I am getting back, more and more, to the tribal way. This happened as I began to have visions; I was drawn back to the old ways by my visions. I did not choose it outwardly. It just came about.

One of the things that I feel about the quest for vision: The traditional Indians, when they prayed, their prayers were always "Not only for myself do I ask this, but that the people may live, the people may live." Any of us can dream, but when you seek a vision, you do this not only for yourself but that the people may live, that life might be better for all of us, not only for me but for all people.

I feel my purpose is to help in any way I can to heal the earth. I feel that we are in a time when the earth is in dire need of healing. We see it everywhere, the droughts, earthquakes, storms, pollution. Yes, the earth itself is in need of healing. And I feel that any way that I can help, that is my mission: to make it whole, to pay attention to that wholeness, not only in ourselves but also in relation to the earth.

The Indian people are the people of the heart. When the white man came to this land, what he was to bring was the intellect, that analytic, intellectual way of being. And the Indian people were to develop the heart, the feelings. And those two were to come together to build the new age, in balance, not one or the other.

It has been only a couple of hundred years now, and I think we're beginning to see the force of this land, that receptive force, come back again, and that balance is beginning to happen. And I feel that what we are is that land. We are those children Rainbow

Woman talked about. We are the ones who are going to have to do it. We are that blend.

In the philosophy of the true Indian people, Indian is an attitude, a state of mind; Indian is a state of being, the place of the heart. To allow the heart to be the distributor of energy on this planet; to allow your heart, your feelings, your emotions to distribute your energy; to pull that energy from the earth, from the sky; to pull it down and distribute it from your heart, the very center of your being—that is our purpose.

Several different traditions talk about four or five different worlds and say that the Creator made all these worlds with one simple law: that we shall be in harmony and in balance with all things, including the sun. And time and again people have destroyed that harmony; we have destroyed that harmony. And we have done it again needlessly. Unless we bring about that balance again, this is our last chance.

We need to achieve a clarity and lack of resistance before we seek vision—a surrendering, a relinquishing. If you are unwilling to be in your experience now, then vision will not open for you. You need to get on that circle where there is no resistance, no up, no down, where there are no square corners to stumble on. Then, someday, you become that circle.

4 Seeing in a Sacred Way

A Samoyed shaman beats his drum on his journey to the underworld. Riding a bear to the land of the dead, currents of energy seem to flow from his spine; on his back are wings, and his head is adorned with the antlers of the sacred deer, indicating knowledge of death and rebirth. *(After Prokofieva.)*

Black Elk

The Oglala Sioux Hehaka Sapa, known to most as Black Elk, was born "in the Moon of the Popping Trees (December) on the Little Powder River in Winter When the Four Crows Were Killed (1862)." He knew the days when his people had the freedom of the plains and still hunted the bison. He fought in the terrible battles at Little Bighorn and Wounded Knee and lived to see the time when the spiritual hoop of Indian life was broken and the Sacred Tree was dead.

In May 1931, John Neihardt, with the help of Black Elk's son, Ben, began to record the narrative of this holy man's life. At the conclusion of his immensely moving story of this life of great suffering and great vision, the nearly blind *wičaṣa wakan,* desiring to return to the origin of his great vision, enjoined his listeners to go with him to the summit of Harney Peak, the place where the spirits had communed with him many years ago. And so, after several days, they made the ascent up this sacred mountain. At its summit, Black Elk, like a fragile fire, offered his prayers to the Great Spirit:

> . . . To the center of the world you have taken me [Great Spirit] and showed me the goodness and the beauty and the strangeness of the greening earth, the only mother—and there the spirit shapes of things, as they should be, you have shown to me and I have seen. At the center of this sacred hoop you have said that I should make the tree to bloom.
>
> With tears running, O Great Spirit, Great Spirit, my Grandfather—with running tears I must say now that the tree has never bloomed. A pitiful old man, you see me here, and I have fallen away and have done nothing. Here at the center of the world, where you took me when I was young and taught me; here, old I stand, and the tree is withered, Grandfather, my Grandfather!
>
> Again, and maybe the last time on this earth, I recall the

great vision you sent me. It may be that some little root of the sacred tree still lives. Nourish it then, that it may leaf and bloom and fill with singing birds. Hear me, not for myself, but for my people; I am old. Hear me that they may once more go back into the sacred hoop and find the good red road, the shielding tree![1]

Blind, his body broken with age, Black Elk lived on with his sacred vision welling up from the depths of his soul until his death in August 1950.[2, 3]

It was the summer when I was nine years old, and our people were moving slowly toward the Rocky Mountains. We camped one evening in a valley beside a little creek just before it ran into the Greasy Grass, and there was a man by the name of Man Hip who liked me and asked me to eat with him in his tepee.

While I was eating, a voice came and said: "It is time; now they are calling you." The voice was so loud and clear that I believed it, and I thought I would just go where it wanted me to go. So I got right up and started. As I came out of the tepee, both my thighs began to hurt me, and suddenly it was like waking from a dream, and there wasn't any voice. So I went back into the tepee, but I didn't want to eat. Man Hip looked at me in a strange way and asked me what was wrong. I told him that my legs were hurting me.

The next day the camp moved on to where the different bands of our people were coming together, and I rode in a pony drag, for I was very sick. Both my legs and both my arms were swollen badly, and my face was all puffed up.

When we had camped again, I was lying in our tepee and my mother and father were sitting beside me. I could see out through the opening, and there two men were coming from the clouds, headfirst like arrows slanting down, and I knew they were the same that I had seen before. Each now carried a long spear, and from the points of these a jagged lightning flashed. They came clear down to the ground this time and stood a little way off and looked at me and said: "Hurry! Come! Your Grandfathers are calling you!"

Then they turned and left the ground like arrows slanting upward from the bow. When I got up to follow, my legs did not hurt me any more and I was very light. I went outside the tepee, and yonder where the men with flaming spears were going, a little cloud was coming very fast. It came and stooped and took me and turned back to where it came from, flying fast.

*   *   *

Now suddenly there was nothing but a world of cloud, and we three were there alone in the middle of a great white plain with snowy hills and mountains staring at us; and it was very still; but there were whispers.

Then the two men spoke together and they said: "Behold him, the being with four legs!"

I looked and saw a bay horse standing there, and he began to speak: "Behold me!" he said. "My life-history you shall see." Then he wheeled about to where the sun goes down, and said: "Behold them! Their history you shall know."

I looked, and there were twelve black horses all abreast with necklaces of bison hoofs, and they were beautiful, but I was frightened because their manes were lightning and there was thunder in their nostrils.

Then the bay horse wheeled to where the great white giant lives (the north) and said: "Behold!" And there were twelve white horses all abreast. Their manes were flowing like a blizzard wind and from their noses came a roaring, and all about them white geese soared and circled.

Then the bay wheeled round to where the sun shines continually (the east) and bade me look; and there twelve sorrel horses, with necklaces of elk's teeth, stood abreast with eyes that glimmered like the daybreak star and manes of morning light.

Then the bay wheeled once again to look upon the place where you are always facing (the south), and yonder stood twelve buckskins all abreast with horns upon their heads and manes that lived and grew like trees and grasses.

And when I had seen all these, the bay horse said: "Your Grandfathers are having a council. These shall take you; so have courage."

Then all the horses went into formation, four abreast—the blacks, the whites, the sorrels, and the buckskins—and stood behind the bay, who turned now to the west and neighed; and yonder suddenly the sky was terrible with a storm of plunging horses in all colors that shook the world with thunder, neighing back.

Now turning to the north the bay horse whinnied, and yonder all the sky roared with a mighty wind of running horses in all colors, neighing back.

And when he whinnied to the east, there too the sky was filled with glowing clouds of manes and tails of horses in all colors singing back. Then to the south he called, and it was crowded with many-colored, happy horses, nickering.

Then the bay horse spoke to me again and said: "See now your horses all come dancing!" I looked, and there were horses, horses everywhere—a whole skyful of horses dancing round me.

"Make haste!" the bay horse said; and we walked together side by side, while the blacks, the whites, the sorrels, and the buckskins followed, marching four by four.

I looked about me once again, and suddenly the dancing horses without number changed into animals of every kind and into all the fowls that are, and these fled back to the four quarters of the world from which the horses came, and vanished.

Then as we walked, there was a heaped up cloud ahead that changed into a tepee, and a rainbow was the open door of it; and through the door I saw six old men sitting in a row.

The two men with the spears now stood beside me, one on either hand, and the horses took their places in their quarters, looking inward, four by four. And the oldest of the Grandfathers spoke with a kind voice and said: "Come right in and do not fear." And as he spoke, all the horses of the four quarters neighed to cheer me. So I went in and stood before the six, and they looked older than men can ever be—old like hills, the stars.

The oldest spoke again: "Your Grandfathers all over the world are having a council, and they have called you here to teach you." His voice was very kind, but I shook all over with fear now, for I knew that these were not old men, but the Powers of the World. And the first was the Power of the West; the second, of the North; the third, of the East; the fourth, of the South; the fifth, of the Sky; the sixth, of the Earth. I knew this, and was afraid, until the first Grandfather spoke again: "Behold them yonder where the sun goes down, the thunder beings! You shall see, and have from them my power; and they shall take you to the high and lonely center of the earth that you may see; even to the place where the sun continually shines, they shall take you there to understand."

And as he spoke of understanding, I looked up and saw the rainbow leap with flames of many colors over me.

Now there was a wooden cup in his hand and it was full of water and in the water was the sky.

"Take this," he said. "It is the power to make live, and it is yours."

Now he had a bow in his hands. "Take this," he said. "It is the power to destroy, and it is yours."

Then he pointed to himself and said: "Look close at him who is your spirit now, for you are his body and his name is Eagle Wing Stretches."

And saying this, he got up very tall and started running toward where the sun goes down; and suddenly he was a black horse that stopped and turned and looked at me, and the horse was very poor and sick; his ribs stood out.

Then the second Grandfather, he of the North, arose with a herb of power in his hand, and said: "Take this and hurry." I took and held it toward the black horse yonder. He fattened and was happy and came prancing to his place again and was the first Grandfather sitting there.

The second Grandfather, he of the North, spoke again: "Take courage, younger brother," he said; "on earth a nation you shall make live, for yours shall be the power of the white giant's wing, the cleansing wind." Then he got up very tall and started running toward the north; and when he turned toward me, it was a white goose wheeling. I looked about me now, and the horses in the west were thunders and the horses of the north were geese. And the second Grandfather sang two songs that were like this:

> *They are appearing,*
> *They are appearing,*
> *The thunder nation is appearing.*

> *They are appearing,*
> *They are appearing,*
> *The white geese nation is appearing.*

And now it was the third Grandfather who spoke, he of where the sun shines continually. "Take courage, younger brother," he said, "for across the earth they shall take you!" Then he pointed to where the daybreak star was shining, and beneath the star two men were flying. "From them you shall have power," he said, "from them who have awakened all the beings of the earth with roots, and legs and wings." And as he said this, he held in his hand a peace pipe which had a spotted eagle outstretched upon the stem; and this eagle seemed alive, for it was poised there, fluttering, and its eyes were looking at me. "With this pipe," the Grandfather said, "you shall walk upon the earth, and whatever sickens there you shall make well." Then he pointed to a man who was bright red all over, the color of good and of plenty, and as he pointed, the red man lay down and rolled and changed into a bison that got up and galloped toward the sorrel horses of the east, and they too turned to bison, fat and many.

And now the fourth Grandfather spoke, he of the place where you are always facing (the south), whence comes the power to grow. "Younger brother," he said, "with the powers of the four quarters you shall walk, a relative. Behold, the living center of a nation I shall give you, and with it many you shall save." And I saw that he was holding in his hand a bright red stick that was alive, and as I looked it sprouted at the top and sent forth branches, and on the branches many leaves came out and murmured and in the leaves the birds began to sing. And then for just a little while I thought I saw beneath it in the shade the circled villages of people and every living thing with roots or legs or wings, and all were happy. "It shall stand in the center of the nation's circle," said the Grandfather, "a cane to walk with and a people's heart; and by your powers you shall make it blossom."

Then he rose very tall and started running toward the south, and was an elk; and as he stood among the buckskins yonder, they too were elks.

Now the fifth Grandfather spoke, the oldest of them all, the Spirit of the Sky. "My boy," he said, "I have sent for you and you have come. My power you shall see!" He stretched his arms and turned into a spotted eagle hovering. "Behold," he said, "all the wings of the air shall come to you, and they and the winds and the stars shall be like relatives. You shall go across the earth with my power." Then the eagle soared above my head and fluttered there; and suddenly the sky was full of friendly wings all coming toward me.

Now I knew the sixth Grandfather was about to speak, he who was the Spirit of the Earth, and I saw that he was very old, but more as men are old. His hair was long and white, his face was all in wrinkles and his eyes were deep and dim. I stared at him, for it seemed I knew him somehow; and as I stared, he slowly changed, for he was growing backwards into youth, and when he had become a boy, I knew that he was myself with all the years that would be mine at last. When he was old again, he said: "My boy, have courage, for my power shall be yours, and you shall need it, for your nation on the earth will have great troubles. Come."

He rose and tottered out through the rainbow door, and as I followed I was riding on the bay horse who had talked to me at first and led me to that place.

* * *

I looked below me where the earth was silent in a sick green light, and saw the hills look up afraid and the grasses on the hills and all the animals; and everywhere about me were the cries of frightened birds and sounds of fleeing wings. I was the chief of all the heavens riding there, and when I looked behind me, all the twelve black horses reared and plunged and thundered and their manes and tails were whirling hail and their nostrils snorted lightning. And when I looked below again, I saw the slant hail falling and the long, sharp rain, and where we passed, the trees bowed low and all the hills were dim.

Now the earth was bright again as we rode. I could see the hills and valleys and the creeks and rivers passing under. We came above a place where three streams made a big one—a source of mighty waters—and something terrible was there. Flames were rising from the waters and in the flames a blue man lived. The dust was floating all about him in the air, the grass was short and withered, the trees were wilting, two-legged and four-legged beings lay there thin and panting, and wings too weak to fly.

Then the black horse riders shouted "Hoka hey!" and charged down upon the blue man, but were driven back. And the white troop shouted, charging, and was beaten; then the red troop and the yellow.

And when each had failed, they all cried together: "Eagle Wing Stretches, hurry!" And all the world was filled with voices of all kinds that cheered me, so I charged. I had the cup of water in one hand and in the other was the bow that turned into a spear as the bay and I swooped down, and spear's head was sharp lightning. It stabbed the blue man's heart, and as it struck I could hear the thunder rolling and many voices that cried "Un-hee!," meaning I had killed. The flames died. The trees and grasses were not withered any more and murmured happily together, and every living being cried in gladness with whatever voice it had. Then the four troops of horsemen charged down and struck the dead body of the blue man, counting coup*; and suddenly it was only a harmless turtle.

Joe Green
NORTH AMERICA/PAVIOTSO

Joe Green, a Paviotso Indian from Pyramid Lake, Nevada, was a highly intelligent and conscientious individual. For a short time, he was a practicing shaman, but he lost his power by not following the dream instructions given to him by his spirit animal, Otter.

The Paviotso world is described as being infused with inanimate beings, the spirits of creatures of nature; spirits that live in sacred caves of certain mountains; spirits of wind, thunder, and clouds; water babies that live in lakes or water holes; water serpents; and spirits of deceased individuals. The shaman is in contact with this unseen world, from which he or she derives the power to heal the sick and locate disembodied souls who are lost. All curing, then, depends on the manipulation of power *(puha),* which is a sign of the shaman's rapport with nature.

Joe Green, whose father was also a shaman, acquired his power from the otter, the animal spirit of his father. As is usual for the Paviotso shaman-doctor, this came about in the course of a series of dream experiences. His acquisition of power commenced with a vivid

*To "count coup" is to strike the body of an enemy.

auditory dream of a sacred song "coming just a few feet above the ground."[4] In later dreams, the spirit of the Otter appeared to the neophyte and told him how to prepare his primary object of power, an otter skin adorned with eagle feathers. It was the mishandling of the otter skin that caused Joe Green to sicken and lose his power.[5]

There are two nights. The second one comes behind the night that everybody sees. This second night is under the darkness. It tells the shaman where the pain is and what caused the sickness. When the second night comes it makes the shaman feel that he is a doctor. The power is in him to doctor. Only shamans can see this second night. The people can only see the darkness. They cannot see the night under it.

I was getting to be a doctor. My father was a doctor, and I got to be one just the same as he. In my dream, I heard a song. It was coming from the north. It was coming just a few feet above the ground. I heard that song. I heard it just one night. The song came all night. That was all I heard the first night.

In dreams after that I saw a horse coming from the east. When I first heard him, he was on the other side of the mountain. Then I saw him come over the ridge. He came toward me and when he got close, he made a big circle around me. Then he went back. That horse had nothing to do with my power.

My father used to doctor. He had power from the otter. I had the same power. After I dreamed about the horse, the otter came to me in my dreams. He told me to get his skin and to cut it into a strip about four inches wide down the length of the back from the head to the top of the tail and including the eyes and ears. Then he told me to get two eagle tail-feathers and put them in two holes in the skin at the neck and to tie them inside with buckskin. The feathers lay flat on the fur side of the skin. The otter told me to keep the skin and the eagle-feathers. He told me to use the skin and feathers when sickness is bad and hard to cure. He said, "When there is very bad sickness and no doctor can cure it, take the skin out of your sack and put it in front of you. Then you are going to try to cure." I was ready to doctor then. When I doctored, the otter gave me my songs.

* * *

Indians were put here on this earth with trees, plants, animals, and water, and the shaman gets his power from them. One shaman might get his power from the hawk that lives in the mountains. Another may get his power from the eagle, the otter, or the bear. A long time ago, all the animals were Indians (they could talk). I think that is why the animals help the people to be shamans.

* * *

When a shaman gets his power from the otter it means that the spirit is from many otters. The chief otter spirit tells the man to be a good doctor. It is this main otter that cannot be seen by the common people. He is the one that makes a man a shaman. He lives in a certain place in the water. Only the shaman can see him there. He knows where the otter is. He dreams about the otter and after a while he learns where the otter lives.

* * *

After I got my power, I tried doctoring a few times. Then one night the otter came to me again in a dream. He told me that I should get another tail-feather of the eagle. He said, "Take a round piece of abalone shell about the size of a quarter and fasten it to the feather." It was then that I spoiled my power. I had been thinking for some time that the otter-skin was too long. It was about four feet from the head to the tip of the tail. So I cut the head off. After I had done this I got sick. The last time I dreamed about the otter was when I was sick. I felt dizzy. I did not feel very good. I saw the otter jump into the upper end of Pyramid Lake. Then I saw him running on the desert. That was the last time I saw the otter. I had to call in a powerful shaman [Tom Mitchell] to cure me. He came and doctored me. He said to me, "I found out that you cut off the otter's head. That is what made you sick. When you did that the otter went away. You will never see him again. You cut the head off and now you are just like the otter. He does not know anything, and you are the same way." I never dreamed again of the otter when I got well. If I had not cut that piece from the skin I would now be a doctor.

Rosie Plummer
NORTH AMERICA/PAVIOTSO

For the Paviotso, the unsolicited dream was the field of experience that
was central to the acquisition of shamanic power. The shaman knew
that he or she must carefully and faithfully follow the instructions
communicated in the dream by the spirit beings who bestowed power
on the healer. Not to do so meant sickness or death.

Rosie Plummer inherited her vocation as shaman from her father,
who in turn had been heir to his power from his shaman brother. All
three in this family had as their spirit animal rattlesnake. Like many
Paviotso shamans, Rosie Plummer did not receive her power until her
later years. In her fifties, she had a series of three or four dreams in
which her father appeared and instructed her to become a *puhágəm*
(shaman-doctor). After this, she began to have experiences of power
during her dreams. Later, the rattlesnake spirit appeared in her
dreams, and she recognized it as her spirit guide.

The Paviotso—hunters, fishers, and gatherers—once roamed the
semiarid areas of western Nevada and Honey Lake valley, California.
Although their traditional way of life began to disappear with the
dwindling of their numbers and the strictures of reservation life, their
sacred life, especially the practice of shamanism, persisted.

Rosie Plummer lived with her daughter, Daisey Lopez, at Schurz
on the Walker River Reservation in western Nevada.[6]

When my uncle was dying, he told my father to take his
power. He wanted my father to have the power to doctor. He told
my father to dream about the power and get instructions for
doctoring that way. The next day my uncle died. Soon after that
my father began to have dreams. My uncle would appear in these
dreams. He came every night in dreams. Each time he came a
different way. My father did not like the dreams. He was afraid
that his brother was trying to get him away [so he would die]. My
uncle, before he died, had given my father a little piece of lead
with a hole in the center. The hole was filled with eagle down. My
father buried the lead and the eagle down. Then his brother's
ghost did not bother him again. That lead and the feathers represented my uncle's power. After that my father became a powerful
shaman. His power told him to catch rattlesnakes. They did not

bite him. He was told to put sage-brush in his nostrils so the snakes would not hurt him.

Rattlesnake was my uncle's power; then my father had rattlesnake for his power. Now the snake gives me power. Rattlesnake came to my father in dreams. That is how he learned to treat snake-bites. Rattlesnake told him to catch rattlesnakes and take two fangs from each. He was to do this until he had ten fangs. Then he was told to take ten stone beads that were colored like rattlesnake eyes. He strung the beads and the fangs together. He used this string of beads to treat rattlesnake bites. He could also cure people who were sick.

Sometimes my father caught rattlesnakes and put them around his waist. He used to ride home carrying rattlesnakes that way. One time he put a rattlesnake on me. He told me not to move. The snake crawled all over me, but it did not bite. He had rattlesnakes with him all the time.

My father died about twenty years ago. Nearly fifteen years later, when I was about fifty, my father began to come to me in dreams. He brought his power to me. He told me to doctor. I dreamed about him three or four times before I believed that I would doctor. After a while the power started to come to me when I dreamed. Then I stopped dreaming about my father. The rattlesnake told me what to do. The snake helps me doctor now. It comes to me when I dream. Several times it has told me to catch snakes, but I have not done it. This has not yet made me sick.

* * *

Some shamans get their power from the water-babies. They are the only people who can talk to them. They tell the rest of the people not to make fun of water-babies. These shamans can take the water-babies out of the lake.

The water-babies came to life by their own power. They formed themselves. Some water-babies live in water-holes, and these holes never dry up. People call these water-babies the "breath of the water-holes." There is a cool breeze all the time in the mountains where they live. They have the power to cause wind to blow, even a very strong wind. The wind is their breath.

There are also women in the lakes where the water-babies live. These women are like the water-babies. They have the same power. Big serpents live in the lake, too. Like the water-babies, these serpents have strong power. They give power to some shamans.

Autdaruta
GREENLAND/ESKIMO

Arctic explorer Knud Rasmussen first learned of Autdaruta, the Greenland Eskimo shaman and renowned storyteller, from a missionary paper written years earlier. In a diary kept by a priest, Autdaruta, whose baptismal name was Christian, had had a strange effect on his religious instructor: "Sometimes I am seized by an incomprehensible disquiet when I have to instruct Christian. I have a feeling that it is Satan incarnate whom I have before me . . . Today as I was about to start out to my teaching of the heathens, I was again seized with this terror of facing Christian, and I was obliged to let them wait while I went down to the seashore to fortify myself in solitude by prayer to Almighty God."[7]

These few lines whetted Rasmussen's desire to know the man. Autdaruta had been not only a magician, a shaman, but also a ruthless murderer in his youth. Later, appalled by his own deeds, he was filled with a terrible and haunting remorse.

After living with Christian for some time, Rasmussen seemed to have won his confidence, but he himself commented that Christian remained an enigma to him: "His eyes always make me doubtful. I only remember . . . [having] seen that timorous, despairing look in the eyes of a stricken reindeer . . . Sometimes a twitch would shoot across his face that would give him an extraordinary resemblance to a tired and tamed wild beast."[8]

Although Christian was reluctant to speak of his infamous murders, he showed no reluctance in sharing with Rasmussen the astonishing experiences he had had during his training as a shaman. He told of his encounter with his helping spirits, his apprenticeship to a master shaman who gained power by allowing himself to be devoured repeatedly by a bear, and his encounters with the fire people.[9]

When my father died, I often went out for long rambles among the hills, because I felt that I had been left alone. It was at the season when stonecrop springs up, and I gathered it, to preserve in blubber for the winter.

One day, up among the rocks, I heard someone begin to sing; I looked, but could see no one.

"Now why should I have heard this song?" I thought to myself, and went home.

The next morning, towards daybreak, I went up again to the hills, and then I heard the same thing again; it was some one beginning to sing. "Now why is this happening to me?" thought I. Just then I saw two men coming towards me. They were inland-dwellers.

"We are sorry for you, because you were an orphan; so we have come to help you," they said, and so they became my first helping-spirits. Then I began to be a magician, but did not speak to any one about it. The year afterwards we moved south; that was in the season when the small birds come, and we settled down in company with an old and much venerated magician. He could not stand upright, and could only walk by propping up his thighs with his arms. He could not carry his kayak up and down himself, and so it came about that I used to help him.

One day he came and said to me—

"Travel east with me, and I will teach you something; you may need help yet, my poor, fatherless boy."

So we travelled together, and he told me on the way that he was going to make a great magician of me. We went ashore up a fjord, close to a cave, and the old man took off his clothes and crept inside. And he told me to watch carefully what happened next. I lay hidden a little way off and waited. It was not long before I saw a great bear come swimming along, crawl ashore, and approach the magician. It flung itself upon him, crunched him up, limb for limb, and ate him.

Then it vomited him out again and swam away.

When I went up to the cave, the old man lay groaning. He was very much exhausted, but was able to row home himself. On the way back he told me that every time he allowed himself to be devoured alive by the bear he acquired greater power over his helping-spirits.

Some time afterwards, he took me on a journey again, and this time it was so that I myself might be eaten by the bear; this was necessary if I wished to attain to any good. We rowed off and came to the cave; the old man told me to take my clothes off, and I do not deny that I was somewhat uncomfortable at the thought of being devoured alive.

I had not been lying there long before I heard the bear coming. It attacked me and crunched me up, limb by limb, joint by joint, but strangely enough it did not hurt at all; it was only when it bit me in the heart that it did hurt frightfully.

From that day forth I felt that I ruled my helping-spirits. After that I acquired many fresh helping-spirits and no danger could any longer threaten me, as I was always protected.

Once I had been out seal-hunting far out at sea in my kayak, towing a large bearded seal home to land; not suspecting danger, I paddled slowly forward. The sea was quite calm. All at once I found myself surrounded by many kayaks and saw a umiaq come rowing towards me.

"We will have both the man and the bearded seal in the umiaq!" they exclaimed, and immediately they lay up alongside my kayak and began to unloose the towing-line my seal was fastened to.

I had shipped my oars, and was only waiting for what might happen next, as it was impossible for me to defend myself against so many.

Then all at once a great commotion arose among the strange kayaks; they belonged to the fire people, who live in a country which is said to lie between the sea and the land.

The fire people began to flee, and when I tried to discover what was happening, I saw that they were pursued by a kayak of remarkable appearance. The prow of it was like a great mouth, which kept opening and shutting all the time; and if those in its path did not move away quickly, they were simply cut in two. I think that the umiaq and the kayaks all sank to the bottom of the sea, for they were gone at once. This is the peculiarity of the fire people; they can appear suddenly, but they can disappear again just as suddenly.

Then afterwards the man with the dragon in his prow came back to me and told me that he himself belonged to the fire people, but had helped me because he knew that I was a great magician. After that he became my helping-spirit.

Later on, I had a great many helping-spirits among the fire people, and they were often of great assistance to me, especially when I was overtaken by a storm or by foul weather. When I made up my mind to journey to the West coast to be baptized, they appeared to me and urged me not to do so. But I did what I willed, all the same. Since then they have not shown themselves to me, because I betrayed them by my baptism.

Sanimuinak

ESKIMO/ANGMAGSALIK

Gustav Holm visited the Angmagsalik Eskimos of Greenland between 1884 and 1885. There he encountered Sanimuinak, whose training to become an *angakoq* (shaman) although arduous and vision provoking, was not without humor. His spirit-helpers included a sea monster with claws like shears and two little men. One had long black arms and wore a white frock; the other had a pointed head and cried like a baby. Sanimuinak was also attended by a man-eating bear.

Only the Angmagsalik *angakoq* can see his spirit-helpers, and only he can communicate with them. Before attaining access to the world of spirits, the neophyte shaman is apprenticed to a master shaman, an elder who can teach the apprentice "how . . . [he is] to seek for that which may put . . . [him] in communication with the spirit world." The apprenticeship can last up to ten years. The first three or four years are spent attempting to contact and collect spirit-helpers *(tartoks).* There is quite an astonishing variety of these entities. *Tarajuatsiaktes* can gain control of the gods of the elements at the behest of their shaman-masters; abduct the soul of a sleeping, sick, or injured person; or recover the lost soul of the one who is ill. *Inersuaks* are spirits of the water's depths who assist the *angakoq* in getting marine animals close to the shore. *Timerseks* steal souls. *Amortortoks,* who act as oracles during shamanic performances, have long black arms and are dangerous to approach; those who touch them blacken and die. *Ungatortoks,* like the *Amortortoks,* walk with a heavy tread and cry like a baby.[10]

Among the Angmagsalik, all shamans are inevitably devoured by a *angakok* bear. Although much larger than an ordinary bear, this shaman-creature is so thin that all its ribs are quite visible. At the end of the apprentice's probation, the *angakoq* bear makes a thorough meal of him, swallowing him whole and later regurgitating him bone by bone. The dismembered shaman is then reassembled and clothed with new flesh.[11]

During the lengthy apprenticeship, the future *angakoq* has to observe certain prohibitions. For example, he must adhere to a strict diet, above all being careful not to eat the entrails of animals. Working in iron is also forbidden to him. Yet, most important of all, the neophyte should reveal to no one the fact that he is pursuing the vocation of shaman.[12]

When I was quite a small boy, I once made a sledge, for which I was beaten by my mother with the upright of the sledge. I then made up my mind to become an angakok.

We were living in those days at *Umivik,* having previously had our home at *Norsit.* I then went out to Norsit to a certain cleft in the mountain which faces the sun-rise, laid a large stone over the cleft, and another on top of it. I now began to rub the upper stone round against the lower "the way of the sun," and continued till I was almost lame in the arms. I now heard a voice from the depths of the cleft calling to me; but I understood not the words, grew numb with fear, and the bowels jumped up into my throat. When the voice died away, my bowels dropped down again from my throat, but I had no strength left to bear me up on my way home. Henceforth I ate no more entrails, hearts, nor livers of seals, nor did I work in iron.

The next day I went out again to the cleft, and ground the stones against each other, as on the previous day. Once more I heard the voice from the depths of the cleft; my bowels and heart flew up to my throat, and I was seized with the most horrible pains. The following day all went in the same manner as before, but . . . I now heard the voice say: "Shall I come up?" I was numb with terror, but said: "Yea, come up!" The stones lifted and a "sea-monster armed with claws like shears," came up and looked towards the sun-rise. It was much larger than those which are to be found in the sea.* Presently the monster vanished, and I travelled back home. This was my first spirit *(tartok).* The winter waned

---

*Sanimuinak showed that those which are in the sea are of the size of a large hand (a crab?).

to its close, and when it was spring again, I went back to the same spot and rubbed the stones; and when I grew tired and had no strength in me to rub them any longer, the stones went on of themselves moving round "the way of the sun." There came a little man up from the ground; he looked towards the sun-rise. He was half as long as a man, was clad in a white frock, and had black arms. His hair was curly, and in his hand he carried a wooden implement, with which he caught salmon. I lost consciousness, and when I came to myself again, the man had gone. He was my second spirit.

The following year I repaired to a place where a brook was flowing from a little lake. A little man with a pointed head, which was quite bald, came up from the stream. He cried like a little child: *"Unga! unga!"* He was my third spirit.

Next year I went inland to *Tasiusak.* Here I cast a stone out into the water, which was thereby thrown into great commotion, like a storm at sea. As the billows dashed together, their crests flattened out on top, and as they opened, a huge bear was disclosed.

He had a very great, black snout, and, swimming ashore, he rested his chin upon the land; and, when he then laid one of his paws upon the beach, the land gave way under his weight. He went up on land and circled round me, bit me in the loins, and then ate me. At first it hurt, but afterwards feeling passed from me; but as long as my heart had not been eaten, I retained consciousness. But, when it bit me in the heart, I lost consciousness, and was dead.

When I came to myself again, the bear was away, and I lay wearied out and stark naked at the same place by the lake. I went down to the sea, and, having walked a little, I heard someone coming running after me. It was my breeches and boots that came running, and, when they had got past me, they fell down on the ground, and I drew them on. Again I heard something running. It was my frock, and when it had got past me, it fell down, and that too I put on. Peering down the river, I saw two little folks, as big as a hand. One of them had an *amaut* on in which there was a little child. Both the bear and the three little folks became my spirits.

Once when I was standing by the shore at *Umivik,* I saw three kaiakers coming in, dragging a narwhal. When they came in to shore, the kaiaks flew up in the air like three black guillemots, and the narwhal sank like an *ovak* (cod).

At *Pikiutdlek* I got me two spirits, one of which was called *Kuitek* and shrieked: *"Unga! Unga,"* like a new-born babe. The other was called *Amortortok* and shrieked: *"Amo! Amo!"* They were both *Tarajuatiaks* (*tarajuadat* = shades). Amortortok is from the south, and speaks the same tongue as the *Kavdlunaks*. At *Tasiusak* too I met a spirit with a pointed head and without hair.*

Once I have seen *Tornarsuk*. He was sitting bent over with his back towards me, holding his privy parts with both hands. I leapt up on his back, and then lost consciousness. When I came to myself again, I was lying on a large stone.

Aua
ESKIMO/IGLULIK

Arctic explorer Knud Rasmussen[13] gives a vivid description of the meeting with Aua, the Iglulik *angakoq:*

> The 27th of January was fine, but cold; it was bright starlight towards the close of the journey, but we had had a long and tiring day, and wished for nothing better than to find shelter without having to build it ourselves.
>
> Suddenly out of the darkness ahead shot a long sledge with the wildest team I have ever seen. Fifteen white dogs racing down at full speed, with six men on the sledge. They came down on us at such a pace that we felt the wind of them as they drew alongside. A little man with a large beard, completely covered with ice, leapt out and came towards me, holding out his hand white man's fashion. Then halting he pointed inland to some snow huts. His keen eyes were alight with vitality as he uttered the ringing greeting "Qujangnamik" (thanks to the coming guests).
>
> This was Aua, the angakoq.[14]

*In Hanserak's journal it is mentioned that *Sanimuinak*'s chief spirit is *Arrussak,* an *ataussak*(?) living in the sea, which is as big as a man. His second spirit is *Amok,* who dwells in a crumbling stone, and his third spirit *Ungortortok,* who barks like a fox, dwells in a dried-out lake, and is as big as a hand (a frog?).

Rasmussen soon found himself in a complex of wonderfully constructed snowhouses. The unquestioned master of the extended family that inhabited these bold, multiple structures was the genial Aua, a kind, hospitable, and humorous man of many skills and the spiritual leader of the group.

The poetic and philosophical abilities of Aua are comparable to those of the Hiuchol shaman Ramón Medina Silva. His ideas concerning the nature of death, the existence of reincarnation, the description of the soul, and the origin of the cosmos were recondite. His knowledge of mythology, cosmology, and eschatology was vast. His gift of poetic metaphor was particularly beautiful. Rasmussen wrote that Aua was always "clear in his line of thought, and with a remarkable power of expressing what he meant."[15]

Of death, he told Rasmussen:

> Mysterious as the manner in which death came into life, even so mysterious is death itself. . . .
>
> We know nothing about it for certain, save that those we live with suddenly pass away from us, some in a natural and understandable way because they have grown old and weary, others, however, in mysterious [ways], because we who lived with them could see no reason why they in particular should die, and because we knew that they would gladly live. But that is just what makes death the great power it is. Death alone determines how long we may remain in this life on earth, which we cling to, and it alone carries us into another life which we know only from the accounts of shamans long since dead. We know that men perish through age, or illness, or accident, or because another has taken their life. All this we understand. Something is broken. What we do not understand is the change which takes place in a body when death lays hold of it. It is the same body that went about among us and was living and warm and spoke as we do ourselves, but it has suddenly been robbed of a power, for lack of which it becomes cold and stiff and putrefies. Therefore we say that a man is ill when he has lost a part of his soul, or one of his souls; for there are some who believe that man has several souls. If then that part of a man's vital force be not restored to the body, he must die. Therefore we say that a man dies when the soul leaves him.[16]

* * *

> It would be . . . incomprehensible, . . . unreasonable, if, after a life short or long, of happy days or of suffering and misery, we were then to cease altogether from existence. What we have

heard about the soul shows us that the life of men and beasts does not end with death. When at the end of life we draw our last breath, that is not the end. We awake to consciousness again, we come to life again, and all this is effected through the medium of the soul. Therefore it is that we regard the soul as the greatest and most incomprehensible of all.[17]

Aua's knowledge of life and death and his vocation as an *angakoq* was foreseen by the shaman Ârdjuaq, who tended his mother before his birth and assisted her shortly after Aua was born. The pregnancy was precarious, and Aua was born with the umbilical cord twisted around his neck. Ârdjuaq announced that "He [Aua] is born to die, but he shall live."[18]

For many, many years, Aua and his family had to observe strict taboos in order to preserve his well-being. In spite of this, his efforts to become a shaman failed. Finally, Aua fell into a terrible state of melancholy, and it was this sorrow that led to his great joy and his understanding. Through his suffering, he attained the "shaman-light of brain and body."[19] It was this light that attracted his helping spirits to him.

I was yet but a tiny unborn infant in my mother's womb when anxious folk began to enquire sympathetically about me; all the children my mother had had before had lain crosswise and been stillborn. As soon as my mother now perceived that she was with child, the child that one day was to be me, she spoke thus to her house-fellows:

"Now I have again that within me which will turn out no real human being."

All were very sorry for her and a woman named Ârdjuaq, who was a shaman herself, called up her spirits that same evening to help my mother. And the very next morning it could be felt that I had grown, but it did me no good at the time, for Ârdjuaq had forgotten that she must do no work the day after a spirit-calling, and had mended a hole in a mitten. This breach of taboo at once had its effect upon me; my mother felt the birth-pangs coming on before the time, and I kicked and struggled as if trying to work my way out through her side. A new spirit-calling then took place, and as all precepts were duly observed this time, it helped both my mother and myself.

But then one day it happened that my father, who was going

out on a journey to hunt, was angry and impatient, and in order to calm him, my mother went to help him harness the dogs to the sledge. She forgot that in her condition, all work was taboo. And so, hardly had she picked up the traces and lifted one dog's paw before I began again kicking and struggling and trying to get out through her navel; and again we had to have a shaman to help us.

Old people now assured my mother that my great sensitiveness to any breach of taboo was a sign that I should live to become a great shaman; but at the same time, many dangers and misfortunes would pursue me before I was born.

My father had got a walrus with its unborn young one, and when he began cutting it out, without reflecting that my mother was with child, I again fell to struggling within the womb, and this time in earnest. But the moment I was born, all life left me, and I lay there dead as a stone. The cord was twisted round my neck and had strangled me. Ârdjuaq, who lived in another village, was at once sent for, and a special hut was built for my mother. When Ârdjuaq came and saw me with my eyes sticking right out of my head, she wiped my mother's blood from my body with the skin of a raven, and made a little jacket for me of the same skin.

"He is born to die, but he shall live," she said.

And so Ârdjuaq stayed with my mother, until I showed signs of life. Mother was put on very strict diet, and had to observe difficult rules of taboo. If she had eaten part of a walrus, for instance, then that walrus was taboo to all others; the same with seal and caribou. She had to have special pots, from which no one else was allowed to eat. No woman was allowed to visit her, but men might do so. My clothes were made after a particular fashion; the hair of the skins must never lie pointing upwards or down, but fall athwart the body. Thus I lived in the birth-hut, unconscious of all the care that was being taken with me.

For a whole year my mother and I had to live entirely alone, only visited now and again by my father. He was a great hunter, and always out after game, but in spite of this he was never allowed to sharpen his own knives; as soon as he did so, his hand began to swell and I fell ill. A year after my birth, we were allowed to have another person in the house with us; it was a woman, and she had to be very careful herself; whenever she went out she [had to] throw her hood over her head, wear boots without stockings, and hold the tail of her fur coat lifted high in one hand.

I was already a big boy when my mother was first allowed to go visiting; all were anxious to be kind, and she was invited to all the other families. But she stayed out too long; the spirits do not like women with little children to stay too long away from their house, and they took vengeance in this [way]: the skin of her head peeled [off], and I, who had no understanding of anything at that time, beat her about the body with my little fists as she went home, and made water down her back.

No one who is to become a skilful hunter or a good shaman must remain out too long when visiting strange houses; and the same holds good for a woman with a child in her amaut.

At last I was big enough to go out with the grown up men to the blowholes after seal. The day I harpooned my first seal, my father had to lie down on the ice with the upper part of his body naked, and the seal I had caught was dragged across his back while it was still alive. Only men were allowed to eat of my first catch, and nothing must be left. The skin and the head were set out on the ice, in order that I might be able later on to catch the same seal again. For three days and nights, none of the men who had eaten of it might go out hunting or do any kind of work.

The next animal I killed was a caribou. I was strictly forbidden to use a gun, and had to kill it with bow and arrows; this animal also only men were allowed to eat; no woman might touch it.

Some time passed, and I grew up and was strong enough to go out hunting walrus. The day I harpooned my first walrus my father shouted at the top of his voice the names of all the villages he knew, and cried: "Now there is food for all!"

The walrus was towed in to land, while it was still alive, and not until we reached the shore was it finally killed. My mother, who was to cut it up, had the harpoon line made fast to her body before the harpoon head was withdrawn. After having killed this walrus, I was allowed to eat all those delicacies which had formerly been forbidden, yes, even entrails, and women were now allowed to eat of my catch, as long as they were not with child or recently delivered. Only my own mother had still to observe great caution, and whenever she had any sewing to do, a special hut had to be built for her. I had been named after a little spirit, Aua, and it was said that it was in order to avoid offending this spirit that my mother had to be so particular about everything she did. It was my guardian spirit, and took great care that I should not do anything that was forbidden. I was never allowed, for instance, to remain in a snow hut where young women were undressing for the night; nor might any woman comb her hair while I was present.

Even after I had been married a long time, my catch was still subject to strict taboo. If there but lived women with infants near us, my own wife was only allowed to eat meat of my killing, and no other woman was allowed to satisfy her hunger with the meat of any animal of which my wife had eaten. Any walrus I killed was further subject to the rule that no woman might eat of its entrails, which are reckoned a great delicacy, and this prohibition was maintained until I had four children of my own. And it is really only since I have grown old that the obligations laid on me by Ârdjuaq in order that I might live have ceased to be needful.

Everything was thus made ready for me beforehand, even from the time when I was yet unborn; nevertheless, I endeavoured to become a shaman by the help of others; but in this I did not succeed. I visited many famous shamans, and gave them great gifts, which they at once gave away to others; for if they had kept the things for themselves, they or their children would have died. This they believed because my own life had been so threatened from birth. Then I sought solitude, and here I soon became very melancholy. I would sometimes fall to weeping, and feel unhappy without knowing why. Then, for no reason, all would suddenly be changed, and I felt a great, inexplicable joy, a joy so powerful that I could not restrain it, but had to break into song, a mighty song, with only room for the one word: joy, joy! And I had to use the full strength of my voice. And then in the midst of such a fit of mysterious and overwhelming delight I became a shaman, not knowing myself how it came about. But I was a shaman. I could see and hear in a totally different way. I had gained my quamanɛq, my enlightenment, the shaman-light of brain and body, and this in such a manner that it was not only I who could see through the darkness of life, but the same light also shone out from me, imperceptible to human beings, but visible to all the spirits of earth and sky and sea, and these now came to me and became my helping spirits.

My first helping spirit was my namesake, a little aua. When

it came to me, it was as if the passage and roof of the house were lifted up, and I felt such a power of vision, that I could see right through the house, in through the earth and up into the sky; it was the little aua that brought me all this inward light, hovering over me as long as I was singing. Then it placed itself in a corner of the passage, invisible to others, but always ready if I should call it.

An aua is a little spirit, a woman, that lives down by the sea shore. There are many of these shore spirits, who run about with a pointed skin hood on their heads; their breeches are queerly short, and made of bearskin; they wear long boots with a black pattern, and coats of sealskin. Their feet are twisted upward, and they seem to walk only on their heels. They hold their hands in such a fashion that the thumb is always bent in over the palm; their arms are held raised up on high with the hands together, and incessantly stroking the head. They are bright and cheerful when one calls them, and resemble most of all sweet little live dolls; they are no taller than the length of a man's arm.

My second helping spirit was a shark. One day when I was out in my kayak, it came swimming up to me, lay alongside quite silently and whispered my name. I was greatly astonished, for I had never seen a shark before; they are very rare in these waters. Afterwards it helped me with my hunting, and was always near me when I had need of it. These two, the shore spirit and the shark, were my principal helpers, and they could aid me in everything I wished. The song I generally sang when calling them was of few words, as follows:

> Joy, joy,
> Joy, joy!
> I see a little shore spirit,
> A little aua,
> I myself am also aua,
> The shore spirit's namesake,
> Joy, joy!

These words I would keep on repeating, until I burst into tears, overwhelmed by a great dread; then I would tremble all over, crying only: "Ah-a-a-a-a, joy, joy! Now I will go home, joy, joy!"

Once I lost a son, and felt that I could never again leave the spot where I had laid his body. I was like a mountain spirit, afraid of human kind. We stayed for a long time up inland, and my helping spirits forsook me, for they do not like live human beings to dwell upon any sorrow. But one day the song about joy came to me all of itself and quite unexpectedly. I felt once more a longing for my fellow-men, my helping spirits returned to me, and I was myself once more.

Gol'd Shaman
SIBERIA/GOL'D

We do not know the name of this shaman, although the interview with the Russian ethnologist Lev Iakovlevich Shternberg in the early 1900s seems to be complete in all other details. Shternberg collected this material from the first shaman that he encountered among the Gol'd, a Southern Tungus tribe, and it provides a fascinating example of the way in which shamans, at least those from Siberia, were selected for their sacred vocation.

Shternberg states that all Gol'd shamans were "prompted to sha-manistic service by a special spirit who offered them love and with whom they cohabit in sleep."[20] On the basis of his extensive fieldwork and scholarly research, he concluded that this situation applied to all Siberian shamans. The ancestor-guide simply functions as a match-maker, leading the souls of shamans into the celestial realms, where they are introduced then to "various ladies and daughters of the gods." A divine marriage ensues, creating a bond between the world of gods and spirits and the earthly realm.[21]

Among the Teleuts, for example, entire love stories unfold be-tween the neophyte shaman and his spirit-lover, who enchants him with sublime hospitality: "Hearing of your arrival a month ago, I prepared food in a golden dish, on the day before your coming I placed the food in a silver dish, oh my beloved, my dear shaman! We will sit at the table together, food there will be from a silver dish; we will sit at a silver table, we will eat from a golden dish. . . ."[22]

The Gol'd shaman of this narrative, though at first full of dread when approached by the *ayami,* soon finds himself wedded to her in body as well as spirit.[23]

My ancestors lived in the village of Urmil (15 versts from Chabarovsk). Their gens is said to have migrated there from the lower reaches of the Amur. Long, long ago, we were Ainu. The old folks say that some generations back there were three great shamans of my gens. No shamans were known amongst my nearest forefathers. My father and mother enjoyed perfect health. I am now forty years old. I am married, but have no children. Up to the age of twenty I was quite well. Then I fell ill, my whole body ailed me, I had bad headaches. Shamans tried to cure me, but it was all of no avail. When I began shamaning myself, I got better and better. It is now ten years that I have been a shaman, but at first I used to practice for myself only, and it is three years ago only that I took to curing other people. A shaman's practice is very, very fatiguing, it is much harder than felling trees, but there is nothing to be done about that.

Once I was asleep on my sick-bed, when a spirit approached me. It was a very beautiful woman. Her figure was very slight, she was no more than half an arshin (71 cm) tall. Her face and attire were quite as those of one of our Gold women. Her hair fell down to her shoulders in short black tresses. Other shamans say they have had the vision of a woman with one-half of her face black, and the other half red. She said: "I am the *ayami* of your ancestors, the shamans. I taught them shamaning. Now I am going to teach you. The old shamans have died off, and there is no one to heal people. You are to become a shaman."

Next she said: "I love you, I have no husband now, you will be my husband and I shall be a wife unto you. I shall give you assistant spirits. You are to heal with their aid, and I shall teach and help you myself. Food will come to us from the people."

I felt dismayed and tried to resist. Then she said: "If you will not obey me, so much the worse for you. I shall kill you."

She has been coming to me ever since, and I sleep with her as with my own wife, but we have no children. She lives quite by herself without any relatives in a hut, on a mountain, but she often changes her abode. Sometimes she comes under the aspect of an old woman, and sometimes under that of a wolf, so she is terrible to look at. Sometimes she comes as a winged tiger. I mount it and she takes me to show me different countries. I have seen mountains, where only old men and women live, and villages, where you see nothing but young people, men and women: they look like Go'lds and speak Go'ldish, sometimes those people are turned into tigers. Now my *ayami* does not come to me as frequently as before. Formerly, when teaching me, she used to come every night. She has given me three assistants—the *jarga* (the panther), the *doonto* (the bear) and the *amba* (the tiger). They come to me in my dreams, and appear whenever I summon them while shamaning. If one of them refuses to come, the *ayami* makes them obey, but, they say, there are some who do not obey even the *ayami*. When I am shamaning, the *ayami* and the assistant spirits are possessing me: whether big or small, they penetrate me, as smoke or vapour would. When the *ayami* is within me, it is she who speaks through my mouth, and she does everything herself. When I am eating the *sukdu* (the offerings) and drinking pig's blood (the blood of pigs is drunk by shamans alone, lay people are forbidden to touch it), it is not I who eat and drink, it is my *ayami* alone. I also care for the needs of my assistant spirits, but I only scatter meat and gruel for them, and they pick it up themselves. Have you ever seen a shaman at some solemn commemoration for the dead? How can a man drink so much vodka? The *ayami* drains it all! One has to feed the *ayami* and the assistant spirits (to bring offerings). If you do not feed them, they scold you and say: "We help thee to cure people and thou art stingy of feeding us." Then you have to slaughter a pig. The sick help to feed them. When they get well, they bring groats, vodka, and a pig. Then I go about the huts, shamaning everywhere, and then I kill a pig, pour the blood into a special vessel and have the meat cooked. In the evening I array myself in my vestments, summon the spirits, and put all the dishes before them; the blood I drink myself, the viands I scatter about and sprinkle vodka all about, and the spirits are quite satisfied.

There are three degrees of shamans: 1) the *siurku samán*, the shaman who only knows how to heal, 2) the *nyemanti samán*—who performs the commemoration office,* and 3) the greatest shaman —the *kassati samán*, who conveys the souls of the deceased to the other world. The *ayami* teaches them all. There have been shamans who have lived through all their life without becoming a *kassati-*

---

*A special ceremony performed over a deceased man's soul a day or two after his death.

shaman. As for me, the *ayami* only taught me to heal. I do not know, whether I am to be a great shaman: that is as the *ayami* wills it. The *ayami* taught me to make myself a shaman's garment and what to draw on it, but for the present she only allows me to wear an apron, and she also told me to make a drum; before that I used to borrow one when shamaning. She has not taught me to make a shaman pole; it is too early, one has to see what is to become of me. There is much work to be done. Then she told me to make images of my assistant spirits and to wear them on [my] neck. After they had been carved out, as the *ayami* had prescribed, I hung them on the wall and brought them offerings and gave them [food] to eat and burned incense for them; then I beat my drum, summoning the spirits to enter the images, and they obeyed my call.

* * *

There can be no shaman without an *ayami.* What assistant spirit will come to him without one? The *ayami* is the shaman's teacher, he is like a god of his. A man's *ayami* is always a woman, and a woman's—a man, because they are like husband and wife. Some shamans sleep also with all their assistant spirits, as with a woman. There was one great shaman woman who lived without a husband. She had many spirit-servants, and she slept with them all. They say there is one shaman whose *ayami* comes to him as a man. I have not seen such shamans myself. But the *ayamis* are also of great variety. Some of them deceive men. They come up to a man, exhort him to become a shaman, send him many spirits, sleep with him and then run away and do not reappear any more, and load him with a disease, besides. But those are not real *ayamis,* they are rather ambas (wicked spirits). Without *ayamis* there are no gods. The ambanso (the master tiger), the doonta (the master bear) and the jargá (the panther)—all of them have powerful *ayamis* who give them their power, but their *ayamis* are of a peculiar kind, not like those of the shaman. Those *ayamis* are more to be dreaded by man than the "gods" themselves. It is they, e.g., who are sent to steal souls.

Tankli
AUSTRALIA/KURNAI

**Tankli, a Kurnai of the Brataua clan, became a *Mulla-mullung* through
the power he obtained in three intricate initiatory dreams. On all three
occasions, the ancestral ghost of his father visited him to assist him in
acquiring the knowledge and power appropriate to a shaman. In the
last of these dreams, Tankli was taken on a journey to the otherworld
by means of a magical cord made of whale sinew. Like the Huichol
Indian making the first trip to Wirikúta, the Sacred Land of Peyote,
where the neophyte is blindfolded as he or she crosses the threshold
between the ordinary world and paradise, Tankli was blindfolded
when he traveled from one realm into another through a paradoxical
passage of clashing rocks.**

**Although Tankli became a shaman after his initiatory dreams, he
was unable to hold onto his power after he began to drink. One night,
he dreamed that his wife threw menstrual blood at him, and his magical quartz crystal disappeared from his medicine bag. He tried in vain
to regain his power, but his dreams never returned it to him.[24]**

When I was a big boy about getting whiskers I was at Alber-
ton camped with my people. Bunjil-gworan was there and other
men. I had some dreams about my father, and I dreamed three
times about the same thing. The first and second time he came
with his brother and a lot of older men, and dressed me up with
lyre-bird's feathers round my head. The second time they were all
rubbed over with *Naial* (red ochre), and had *Bridda-briddas** on. The
third time they tied a cord made of whale's sinews round my neck
and waist, and swung me by it and carried me through the air over
the sea at Corner Inlet, and set me down at *Yiruk.* It was at the front
of a big rock like the front of a house. I noticed that there was
something like an opening in the rock. My father tied something
over my eyes and led me inside. I knew this because I heard the
rocks make a sound as of knocking behind me. Then he uncovered
my eyes, and I found that I was in a place as bright as day, and
all the old men were round about. My father showed me a lot of

---

*A *Bridda-bridda* is a kind of kilt that the men wore in front and behind hanging
from the cord that was wound round the waist as a belt.

shining bright things, like glass, on the walls, and told me to take some. I took one and held it tight in my hand. When we went out again my father taught me how to make these things go into my legs, and how I could pull them out again. He also taught me how to throw them at people. After that, he and the older men carried me back to the camp, and put me on the top of a big tree. He said, "Shout out loud and tell them that you are come back." I did this, and I heard the people in the camp waking up, and the women beginning to beat their rugs for me to come down, because now I was a *Mulla-mullung.* Then I woke up and found that I was lying along the limb of a tree. The old men came out with fire-sticks, and when they reached the tree, I was down, and standing by it with the thing my father had given me in my hand. It was like glass, and we call it *Kiin.* I told the old men all about it, and they said that I was a doctor. From that time I could pull things out of people, and I could throw the *Kiin* like light in the evening at people, saying to it *Blappan* (go!). I have caught several in that way. After some years I took to drinking, and then I lost my *Kiin* and all my power, and have never been able to do anything since. I used to keep it in a bag made of the skin of a ring-tail opossum, in a hole of a tree. One night I dreamed that I was sleeping in the camp, and my wife threw some *Kruk* [menstrual blood] at me, and after that my *Kiin* went out of my bag, I do not know where. I have slept under the tree where I left it, thinking that my power might come back, but I have never found the *Kiin,* and I never dream any more about it.

5 Wondrous Medicine

Piltzintecuhtli, an aspect of Xochipilli, the Sun God and
Prince of Flowers, here receives instructions from
Quetzalcoatl on the origins and use of the sacred
hallucinogenic mushrooms. *This image of Xochipilli is found
in the central section (page 24) of the fifteenth-century
Mixtec Codex (the Vienna Codex).*

María Sabina
MESOAMERICA / MAZATEC

High above the Mazatec village of Huautla de Jiménez, next to Nindo Tocoxho, the Mountain of Adoration, is a humble daub and wattle hut of three tiny rooms. Its walls are crumbling, the uneven earthen floors seem to be eaten with age, and the interior of the dwelling is barren except for the simplest altar and a few pieces of rudimentary furniture. In the winter of 1977, I came to this place at the kind invitation of Alvaro Estrada to meet the holy woman and healer María Sabina, the shaman who introduced Gordon Wasson to the ancient cult of the wondrous mushroom in 1955.

María Sabina was born on March 17, 1894, and her years of suffering were engraved deeply in her strong brown face and in the bend of her tiny body. She was dressed in rags, like the poorest Mazatec, and was surrounded by ever curious villagers and children, who would most certainly steal anything we offered her. Her right forearm was covered with cruel wounds from the bites of a jealous relative who had attacked her a few days earlier. A terrible question rose in my mind: Why is it that visionaries and saints like María Sabina, Black Elk, and Ramón Medina Silva must always lead a life full of suffering. Even now, as an old woman too frail to take the psilocybine mushroom, her suffering continues. And so it must be, I learned, for behind the mask of pain, a light seemed to emanate from the eyes of this woman, a quality that imparts to those who are with her a sense of the divine awakened.

As the eminent ethnomycologist Wasson has described her, María Sabina is a woman "with out blemish, immaculate, one who has never dishonored her calling by using her powers for evil . . . [a woman of] rare moral and spiritual power, dedicated in her vocation, an artist in her mastery of the techniques of her vocation.'[1] For many decades, she has practiced her art with the hallucinogenic mushrooms, and many hundreds of sick and suffering people have come to her wretched hut to ingest the sacrament as she chants through the night in the darkness before her altar.[2]

I am María Sabina. She is the woman who waits; she is the woman that tries; she is the woman of victory; she is the woman of thought, the woman who creates; she is the woman who cures; she is the Sun Woman, the Moon Woman, the woman who interprets.

There is a world beyond ours, a world that is far away, nearby, and invisible. And there it is where God lives, where the dead live, the spirits and the saints, a world where everything has already happened and everything is known. That world talks. It has a language of its own. I report what it says.

The sacred mushroom takes me by the hand and brings me to the world where everything is known. It is they, the sacred mushrooms, that speak in a way that I can understand. I ask them, and they answer me. When I return from the trip that I have taken with them, I tell what they have told me and what they have shown me.

The father of my grandfather, Pedro Feliciano, my grandfather, Juan Feliciano, my father, Santo Feliciano—all shamans— they ate the *teo-nanácatl* and had great visions of the world where everything is known. With the exception of my father, I have never known these men. And also my father—I have known him for so short a time, I almost cannot remember him. He died when I was four years old. But I knew what he had done by his father and the father of his father. The mushroom was in my family as a parent, a protector, a friend.

My father had just died, and we were very poor. I used to go into the forests with my sister to pasture the beasts. We were hungry, but we knew that there were mushrooms and that the mushrooms were our friends and that from them only good could come. So we looked for them, and we ate them as they were—raw, just gathered.

Then I did not know how to distinguish the sacred mushrooms as *el derrumbe, San Isidro, pajaritos* or from those that were not. I ate them, without knowing what they were, just because I was

so hungry. But one day, I don't know how long a time had elapsed,
I began to have visions. My hands had ripped from the earth the
teo-nanácatl, and the *teo-nanácatl* had entered my mouth and my soul.
The goats were grazing on the mountain, and I was there sitting
on the grass as though drunk. My soul was coming out of my body
and was going toward the world that I did not know but of which
I had only heard talk. It was a world like this one, full of sierras,
of forests, of rivers. But there were also other things—beautiful
homes, temples, golden palaces. And there was my sister, who had
come with me, and the mushrooms, who were waiting for me—
mushrooms that were children and dwarfs dressed like clowns,
children with trumpets, children that sang and danced, children
tender like the flesh of the flowers. And the mushrooms talked,
and I talked to the mushrooms, crying, "What are we going to do?"
I said, "We are so poor. How are we going to live? What will
happen to us?" And the *teo-nanácatl* answered with the words of
hope and peace, saying that they would protect us, that when we
needed something, we should go to them and they would give it.
When I returned from my first trip, my sister returned, too, and
she had seen also the same things and heard the same words. From
then on, I wanted to get to know better those friends that I had
just met and to distinguish the sacred mushrooms from those that
were not; and so I made my grandmother, who knew many things
because she had learned them from her husband and from my
father, explain many things. And my grandmother told me everything with pleasure because she saw that I was destined to become
the priestess of the *teo-nanácatl.*

> *God is an immense clock*
> *That contains the universe.*

I was eight years old when a brother of my mother fell sick.
He was very sick, and the shamans of the sierra that had tried to
cure him with herbs could do nothing for him. Then I remembered
what the *teo-nanácatl* told me: that I should go and look for them
when I needed help. So I went to take the sacred mushrooms, and
I brought them to my uncle's hut. I ate them in front of my uncle,
who was dying. And immediately the *teo-nanácatl* took me to their
world, and I asked them what my uncle had and what I could do

to save him. They told me that an evil spirit had entered the blood of my uncle and that to cure him we should give him some herbs, not those that the *curanderos* gave him, but others. I asked where these herbs could be found, and they took me to a place on the mountain where tall trees grew and the waters of the brook ran, and they showed me the herb that I should pull from the earth and the road that I had to take to find them. When I returned from the trip in the world of the *teo-nanácatl,* I came out from the hut, and I took the direction shown by the mushrooms. I arrived in a place where tall trees grew and the waters of a brook ran; it was the same place that I had seen during the trip, and they were the same herbs. I took them, I brought them home, I boiled them in water, and I gave them to my uncle. A few days later, the brother of my mother was cured.

That was the first cure that the *teo-nanácatl* permitted me to do. After that, there were many others. Men, children, old ones, women. There was the cure of María Dolores, whose whole body had swollen—feet, hands, face, belly—so swollen that it looked as if it would burst. The woman could not walk anymore, nor move anymore. We took the *teo-nanácatl* together, and we left together for the world where everything is known. We met there, and there the *teo-nanácatl* made me say to María Dolores what she had to do to get better. When we came back from the trip, María Dolores began to deflate. The belly was cured; the face was cured; the legs and the feet were cured. María Dolores lived fifteen years longer. But I meanwhile had stopped taking *teo-nanácatl.*

A man, a merchant, Serapio Martínez, asked me to be his wife. Three children were born one after another, and I did not have time to dedicate to the *teo-nanácatl.* I had to take care of the children if I wished them to grow well. Then Serapio Martínez died, and I remained alone with three children, with all of my time taken to maintain them, to cut the coffee in the plantations, to sew *huipiles,* to keep up the small trade in pots and pans, blankets, and ponchos that had been Serapio Martínez's.

I remained alone thirteen years until another man, Marcial Calvo, asked me. And I went with him, and from him, I had nine children. Marcial was a shaman and a *curandero,* and he cured with herbs, but he was also a mean and violent man, always drunk, with liquor and tequila. He beat me and beat my children. He knew that

I, many years before, had used the *teo-nanácatl* and had entered the world where everything is known, but he did not want me to begin to take trips again. Perhaps he was envious of what the *teo-nanácatl* would say to me, of what I had learned or could learn. He laughed and beat me when I spoke of the *teo-nanácatl;* he used to get drunk and beat me. I suffered much with him. Anyhow, it was while I was with him that I began to take it again, after many years. I did it to cure two elderly sick people. Marcial had tried to cure them with his herbs but had not been able to. But I was able to with the mushrooms. But when Marcial came to know it, he beat me in front of the two old ones that I had saved until I bled. Then Marcial began to go with other women. He also went with a married woman until, one night, her husband and her children waited for him near a house. They killed him by blows of a stick. They split his head. I found him the following morning, lying on the path, dead.

The mushroom is similar to your soul. It takes you where the soul wants to go. And not all souls are the same. Marcial had taken the *teo-nanácatl,* had had visions, but the visions had served no purpose. Many people of the sierra have taken it and are taking it, but not everybody enters into the world where everything is known. Also Ana María, my sister, began taking them together with me, had the same visions, talked to the mushrooms, but the mushrooms did not reveal all their secrets. The secrets that they revealed to me are enclosed in a big Book that they showed me and that is found in a region very far away from their world, a great Book. They gave it to me when Ana María fell ill. Suddenly, she would fall on the ground, and her body used to become black and like stone. She used to fall on the ground, and she lay there like a black stone. The *curanderos* had tried to cure her with herbs and magic rites, burying eggs in some parts of the room where my sister lay. But Ana María was ill and seemed almost near death. So I decided to return again to the *teo-nanácatl.* I took many, many more than I had ever taken before: thirty plus thirty. I loved my sister and was ready to do anything, even to make a very long trip, just to save her. I was sitting in front of her with my body, but my soul was entering the world of the *teo-nanácatl* and was seeing the same landscape that it had seen many other times, then landscapes that it had never seen because the great number of mushrooms had taken me into the deepest of the depths of that world. I was going ahead until, at one point, a *duende,* a spirit, came toward me. He asked a strange question: "But what do you wish to become, you, María Sabina?"

I answered him, without knowing, that I wished to become a saint. Then the spirit smiled, and immediately he had in his hands something that he did not have before, and it was a big Book with many written pages.

"Here," he said. "I am giving you this Book so that you can do your work better and help people who need help and know the secrets of the world where everything is known."

I thumbed through the leaves of the Book, many written pages, and I thought that unfortunately I did not know how to read. I had never learned, and therefore that would not have been of any use to me. Suddenly, I realized I was reading and understood all that was written in the Book and that I became as though richer, wiser, and that in one moment I learned millions of things. I learned and learned.

I also learned that for curing Ana María I had to anoint her belly with herbs and destroy all that the *curanderos* had done for her, disinterring the eggs and throwing them away. Suddenly, when I had understood that, I saw there, in the world where I was, the room of my sister and the floor of beaten earth and the buried eggs that came out by themselves from the earth in the spots where they had been hidden. When I came to myself, I was there, sitting in front of my sister, but the floor was full of scattered eggs that had been broken. I had not moved from there; the eggs had come out by themselves. I looked for the herbs that the Book had indicated to me, and I did exactly what I had learned from the Book. And also Ana María got well.

I didn't need to see the Book again because I had learned everything that was inside it. But I again saw the spirit that gave it to me and other spirits and other landscapes; and I saw, close by, the sun and moon because the more you go inside the world of *teo-nanácatl,* the more things are seen. And you also see our past and our future, which are there together as a single thing already achieved, already happened. So I saw the entire life of my son Aurelio and his death and the face and the name of the man that was to kill him and the dagger with which he was going to kill him because everything had already been accomplished. The murder had already been committed, and it was useless for me to say to my son that he should look out because they would kill him, because there was nothing to say. They would kill him, and that was it. And I saw other deaths and other murders and people who were lost—no one knew where they were—and I alone could see. And I saw stolen horses and ancient buried cities, the existence of which was unknown, and they were going to be brought to light. Millions of things I saw and I knew. I knew and saw God: an immense clock that ticks, the spheres that go slowly around, and inside the stars, the earth, the entire universe, the day and the night, the cry and the smile, the happiness and the pain. He who knows to the end the secret of the *teo-nanácatl* can even see that infinite clockwork.

Ramón Medina Silva
MESOAMERICA/HUICHOL

> You have seen how it is when we walk for the peyote. How we go, not eating, not drinking, with much hunger, with much thirst. With much will. All of one heart, of one will. How one goes, being Huichol. That is our unity, our life. That is what we must defend. [3]

Some 9,000 people known to themselves as Wixárika and to us as Huichol live on tiny ranchos in the remotest areas of the Sierra Madre Occidental of Mexico. The archaic traditions of these people have remained intact in spite of Aztec and Spanish pressures. Their religious practice comes through a complex mythological system at the center of which is the Sun, Tayaupá, and our Grandfather Fire, Tatewarí, the First Shaman. The sacrament giving depth and vision to their rituals is *hikuri,* the hallucinogenic cactus peyote.

For most Huichol, the peyote vision is a very private and intensely personal experience, one that is not to be shared directly with others. The beauty of the visions and the profoundly spiritual condition that graces the experiencer represent individual awakenings into an all-encompassing cosmos that is already known to those who have found that unity. The shaman, however, may share visions with others. The *mara'akáme* knows well the deities who use the shaman as a vehicle for their messages, which emanate from the realms underlying the ordinary world of waking consciousness.[4]

Here, Ramón gives a simple and moving description of the peyote experience. The startling richness of these mystical events, however, is more evident in the mythologies, chants, and *nieríkas* (yarn paintings)—the aesthetic expressions of his visionary world.

Ramón was born in San Sebastian in the early 1930s. His family was extremely poor, even by Huichol standards. His grandfather was a renowned *mara'akáme,* and his mother was devoted to the sacred traditions of her people. When Ramón was five or six years old, his father deserted the family. At this time, Ramón began to have dreams in which Tayaupá, the Sun, would reassure him that one day all would be well with him, that he would know many, many things and would make objects of great beauty. When Ramón was eight years old, he was bitten by a poisonous serpent. His shaman-grandfather was summoned in an effort to save the young boy's life. After sucking out the poison and chanting through the night, the grandfather revealed to Ramón and his family that this terrible misfortune was a result of Ramón's father not keeping his promise to the deities to make a pilgrimage to Wirikúta, the Sacred Land of Peyote. The old *mara'akáme* told Ramón that if he survived, he would one day be a great shaman; Tatewarí, our Grandfather Fire, the First Shaman, had chosen him for this sacred vocation.

During the six months of his paralysis, Ramón reflected on his destiny. As he said years later, "It takes many years, much thought, to do such things. Much work, much sacrifice. Now I see that I grew up well."[5]

The first time one puts peyote into one's mouth, one feels it going down into the stomach. It feels very cold, like ice. And the inside of one's mouth becomes dry, very dry. And then it becomes wet, very wet. One has much saliva then. And then, a while later, one feels as if one were fainting. The body begins to feel weak. It begins to feel faint. And one begins to yawn, to feel very tired. And after a while one feels very light. The whole body begins to feel light, without sleep, without anything.

And then, when one takes enough of this, one looks upward and what does one see? One sees darkness. Only darkness. It is very dark, very black. And one feels drunk with the peyote. And when one looks up again it is total darkness except for a little bit of light, a tiny bit of light, brilliant yellow. It comes there, a brilliant yellow. And one looks into the fire. One sits there, looking into the fire which is Tatewarí. One sees the fire in colors, very many colors, five colors, different colors. The flames divide—it is all brilliant, very brilliant and very beautiful. The beauty is very great, very great. It is a beauty such as one never sees without the peyote. The flames come up, they shoot up, and each flame divides into those colors and each color is multicolored—blue, green, yellow, all those colors. The yellow appears on the tip of the flames as the flame shoots upward. And on the tips you can see little sparks in many colors coming out. And the smoke which rises from the fire, it also looks more and more yellow, more and more brilliant.

Then one sees the fire, very bright, one sees the offerings there, many arrows with feathers and they are full of color, shimmering, shimmering. That is what one sees.

But the *mara'akáme,* what does he see? He sees Tatewarí, if he is chief of those who go to hunt the peyote. And he sees the Sun. He sees the *mara'akáme* venerating the fire and he hears those prayers, like music. He hears praying and singing.

All this is necessary to understand, to comprehend, to have one's life. This we must do so that we can see what Tatewarí lets go from his heart for us. One goes understanding all that which Tatewarí has given one. That is when we understand all that, when we find our life over there. But many do not take good care. That is why they know nothing. That is why they do not understand anything. One must be attentive so that one understands that which is the Fire and the Sun. That is why one sits like that, to listen and see all of that, to understand.

Desana Shaman
SOUTH AMERICA/DESANA

The Tukano, one phratry (kin group) of which are the Desana, number around 7,000. They live in scattered dwellings along the rivers and small streams weaving through the vast equatorial rain forests of the northwest Amazon. In this little-explored region of the upper Amazon basin, the traditions of the various Tukano peoples have remained more or less intact.

The Desana *payé* (shaman) is the intellectual of his culture as well as a priest and healer. One of the shaman's main activities, however, is establishing contact with the Master of the Game Animals, who controls the success of hunting efforts and therefore the source of food. The *payé* is a mediator and moderator between the spirit elements that govern the field of life and the social network that is vulnerable to supernatural forces.[6]

The Desana *payé* must, of necessity, develop many qualities of mind. His knowledge of mythology and ritual play a central role in his ability to maintain balance in the community. A keen memory, a good singing voice, and physical stamina are all essential. They make it possible for the *payé* to conduct the lengthy séances, using various hallucinogenic substances, that bring him into contact with the nonordinary world that must then be translated to the people of the tribe. Most important, the *payé's* soul should shine with a strong inner light, a supernatural luminescence that makes what is obscure visible for others in order that they might survive.[7]

The anthropologist Gerardo Reichel-Dolmatoff has said: "To the Indians this 'other' dimension is just as real as that of ordinary everyday life, and for the individual to pass from one to the other is an experience shared by all. To accomplish this change, to see beyond the surface of things—through the hills and the waters and the sky—there exist means that can be handled and controlled; there is concentration, abstinence, and trance. Or sometimes this 'other' dimension will manifest itself quite suddenly and unexpectedly, allowing a brief and terrifying glimpse of dark powers. But more often the perception of this dimension will be produced quite consciously by chemical means, by powerful drugs under the influence of which the mind will wander into the hidden world of animals and forest spirits, of divine beings and mythical scenes. And in the preparation of these drugs the Indians of the Vaupés are specialists."[8, 9]

The yajé vessel is painted with yellow and white designs. The yellow color we call *boré* and the white color we call *ebohohó*. It is with these colors that the vessel is adorned.

There must be two men who blow tobacco smoke over the vessel. And while they are blowing they chant: "This is what we are going to see when we are drinking yajé!" They begin with the snake, a snake like a bead necklace. Singing of this snake they speak of its colors which are like those of a necklace with bright designs, blurred designs, and white designs. Then they sing of the white and the black boa constrictor. They imagine the two boa snakes as the central beams of the roof of the maloca, the white boa lying on the left and the black one to the right. The houseposts, too, they imagine as shining brightly, and they imagine the houseposts as entwined by snakes that are curled around them. And they sing: "We shall have bright visions, we shall have blurred visions." The *yonero* snakes come, too, and, grasping their shapes and colors, they push them into the maloca. Then come the *boréka* [fish] snakes and, grasping them—their shapes and their colors—they push them into the maloca. Then comes the *mahká* [boa constrictor] snake, and they push it into the maloca. There is a light-colored boa constrictor, with bright and blurred markings, and the image of this snake they push up onto the houseposts. "All this we are going to see," they sing. And again they blow smoke over the vessel. They smoke the same tobacco that is used during the gatherings. Then they sing of *buia* and they imagine the maloca to be painted the color of *carayurú* [red]. They also push the yellow and the yellowish colors into the maloca. Then they sing of the ornaments and feather headdresses, and they imagine them as fruits, and push them into the maloca. They put the red and the yellow colors in the center. "This we shall see," they sing, "when we are drinking yajé." They are not sitting quietly; they are preparing the images. "The conical design must be in the center," they sing. "The shrimp-shaped designs, the female design, must be heard; the *vahsú* [rubber tree] design must be heard. When we are under the influence of yajé, we shall hear these sounds; we shall feel as if we are drowning," they sing. They take the black deer-bone flute and the white deer-bone flute, and put their sounds into the maloca. The sound is: oré-oré-oré-rooo-rooo-rooo-erúuuu-erúuuu-erúuuu. All this they will hear later under the influence of yajé. Whatever music they play now, they will hear later. The red deer-bone flute sounds: pi-pari-pá-pira-pu. "This we shall hear," they say; "And the sound of the music shall overpower us and we shall fall silent." Then they shall hear the sound of the clay trumpet: mooo-mooo-virá-virá-virá-mooooo. All these sounds they are shaping while blowing tobacco smoke over the yajé vessel. And again the sound of the flutes: te-to-te-to-teto-te-rooo-te-rooo. "This we shall hear," they say. With their words, and blowing smoke over the yajé vessel, they create these sounds. And they take the vessel and lift it up high, and when they do this they know that their visions will be bright. When they do this, the people will not become nauseated. To sing well, they support it with macaw feathers. If we do not do this, one cannot sing well.

Manual Córdova-Rios
SOUTH AMERICA / AMAHUACA

In 1902, fifteen-year-old Manuel Córdova-Rios, a rubber cutter, was suddenly kidnapped from his camp on a small tributary of the Rio Jurua by a band of Amahuaca Indians. He was taken deep into the Amazon jungle, where his captors slowly and carefully introduced him to their way of life by means of intensive training sessions with the potent hallucinogenic vine *Banisteriopsis caapi.* During his six years with the Amahuaca, he learned through the visions evoked by the *nixi honi xuma* (banisteriopsis) the language and customs of his captors as well as the ways of the creatures of the tropical forest. It soon became apparent that the old chief, Xumu, had chosen Córdova-Rios to be his successor.

At the age of twenty-one, Córdova-Rios escaped from his tribe and returned to Iquitos, Peru, and his family. He had been experiencing a sense of deepening alienation from the people for whom he was now a chief and shaman. In a session with the visionary vine, he had also seen the death of his mother. (Telepathic and clairvoyant experiences were apparently not uncommon with the *nixi honi xuma.*) And so his escape led him back to his birthplace and his father, who had survived the death of both his mother and his sister.

Although Córdova-Rios left the Amahuaca, his extraordinary knowledge of healing practice and plants was not lost. At the age of ninety-five, he still sees twenty to thirty patients a day. In his account of his return to Western life, he stated: "All that I learned from . . . [Xumu]—the insight I developed of the inner workings of the mind and the human psyche, as well as the knowledge of the natural medicinal plants of the forest and how to use them—all this has remained a part of me in the years that have passed since I left the Huni Kui, years that have brought both joy and sorrow to me. My use of all that Xumu taught me, in a much wider world than he envisioned, has brought me to this point where men and women come in sickness and in pain. . . . My one frustration is knowing that I have not been able to impart my knowledge to someone who could continue to use it."[10, 11]

After the raid, since the enemy invading our territory had apparently withdrawn, life in the village settled down. Although the routine of daily life still seemed strange to me, it was a known pattern for the Indians. The tension was gone; the women went back to work in their little cleared and planted plots in the forest; the men again took up organized hunting. The chief kept a close watch over all these activities, giving the necessary directions to keep things moving according to his wishes and plans.

My own position had noticeably improved after I took part in the defense of the village against the invasion threat. And my ability to shoot the rifle without flinching from the awesome noise of thunder exploding when I pulled the trigger gave me a special status among the Indians, to whom the rifle was a strange and awesome thing.

I soon found that the chief's program for my training was far from finished. He prepared now a series of combined herbal purges, baths and diet that had subtle effects on my feelings and bodily functions. I cooperated without hesitation now, since the recent events made me sure that I was in a secure position within the tribe. Before my life among these Indians had begun I had heard the usual rumors of Indian medicine and witch-doctor activities. There had always been a certain fascination in this for me, so now I was determined to observe and learn all that I could.

After several days of preparation in which every detail was closely supervised by old Xumu, we began a series of incredible sessions with the extract of the vision vine, nixi honi xuma.

A small shelter was built especially for the two of us at a spot slightly removed from the village. It was just within the edge of the forest that surrounded our small settlement. There was only room to swing two hammocks with a small fire between. Outside there was also a small clear space in which to swing hammocks among the trees. Here we were well guarded from intrusion of any kind. Food was brought only on signal from the chief and always by the same old woman. Sounds from the village did not reach us.

The chief and I went to this secluded site alone one morning. On the way I remember wondering how old this man might be. Actually, his physical features did not give the usual signs of age. His skin was not unusually wrinkled and the flesh did not sag on his bones. Nevertheless, he gave the impression of being ancient, and it was evident that reverence and admiration dominated the feelings of the tribe toward their headman. He maintained a calm, distant aloofness from the people and their activities, yet gave the feeling of complete awareness of present, past and future events. And one felt that their awe of him was justified.

He led the way toward the forest at his usual slow, deliberate walk, which also gave the impression of great age. He seemed to choose each step with care. On the way he started a low chant, seemingly to himself:

> Spirits of the forest
> revealed to us by honi xuma
> bring us knowledge of the realm
> assist in the guidance of our people
> give us the stealth of the boa
> penetrating sight of the hawk and the owl
> acute hearing of the deer
> brute endurance of the tapir
> grace and strength of the jaguar
> knowledge and tranquillity of the moon
> kindred spirits, guide our way

It was a clear, still day of the early dry season. A few isolated cotton puffs of clouds drifted in an azure sky as we stepped from the village clearing into the mottled shade of the cool forest. Preparations had been made for our arrival, but no one was present. The old man sounded a birdcall that was answered from somewhere out of sight.

I looked around. A tiny, newly kindled fire glowed in the center of a small opening in the forest undergrowth. Beside it was a bunch of the leaves used for the fragrant ceremonial smoke. The small clearing revealed the massive buttresses to the columns that supported the leafy roof of the forest a hundred feet above our heads. These columns, draped in vines and hanging plants, were also visible in the diffuse filtered light that was occasionally broken by a brilliant shaft of direct sunlight. Details otherwise unnoticed would stand out momentarily in vivid clarity in these illuminating shafts of light from above.

At a motion from the chief, I sat down comfortably in a hammock swung low outside the shelter. Chanting, the old man deliberately put a bunch of leaves on the fire. Billowing clouds of fragrant smoke filled the still air.

> *O most powerful spirit*
> *of the bush with the fragrant leaves*
> *we are here again to seek wisdom*
> *give us tranquillity and guidance*
> *to understand the mysteries of the forest*
> *the knowledge of our ancestors*

We savored the fragrant tranquillity of the scene as the smoke drifted around us and up into the vaulted structure of the forest. Every immediate sound and movement seemed suspended by the magic smoke. Before the enchanted spell drifted away with the smoke, Xumu poured a single large gourd cupful of honi xuma from a pot and began another low chant:

> *Phantom revealing spirit of the vine*
> *we seek your guidance now*
> *to translate the past into the future*
> *to understand every detail of our milieu*
> *to improve our life*
> *reveal the secrets that we need*

He came over to me and said: "You drink alone this time. I will be present to guide you. All is well. Your preparations have been completed. Every reaction is favorable. Drink it all at once, without hurry and without fear, and prepare for visions. Pleasant and profound visions will come to you."

He took back the empty cup, calmly sat down opposite me in the other hammock and said, "The diets and purges have prepared you well. No unpleasant reactions will appear this time. With care, we can direct the flow of visions into desired channels. I will not leave your side. I have done this times without number. When prepared with care, it comes out well."

We both lay back in our hammocks. Imperceptibly a feeling of euphoria entered my consciousness. I heard a brief pulsating hum in one ear, which seemed to float off, up into the treetops. My eyes tried to follow it, and as my glance wandered in the treetops I became aware of undreamed beauty in the details of the textures of leaves, stems and branches. Every leaf, as my attention settled on it, seemed to glow with a greenish golden light. Unimaginable detail of structure showed. A nearby bird song—the irregular arpeggios of the *siete cantos* (seven songs)—floated down. Exquisite and shimmering, the song was almost visible. Time seemed suspended; there was only now and now was infinite. I could separate the individual notes of the bird song and savor each in its turn. As the notes of the song were repeated, I floated in a sensation that seemed somewhere between smelling an elusive intoxicating fragrance and tasting a delicate ambrosia. A breath of cool air drifting in from the forest created an ecstacy of sensations as it cooled my exposed skin. Sensations of a pleasant aroma again seemed involved.

The chief spoke in a low, pleasant tone, "Visions begin." He had completely captured my attention with two words of magic. I instantly felt a melting away of any barrier between us; we were as one. The mere glance of an eye had infinite meaning. The slightest change of expression conveyed full intent. We had complete rapport at all levels of understanding. I knew his thought as he knew mine. Did this telepathic facility come from some primitive recess of the mind used before ancestral man communicated in formal language?

Xumu said, "From the hunting camp we find there is much of the forest that you do not see and understand. We will change this. You must have complete knowledge of the forest to lead the men in vision ceremonies to improve their hunting. Thus they can eat well and be content." A few simple words and slight gestures transmitted the full intent of his message.*

---

*Córdova stopped his story and explained to me (Bruce Lamb) at this point: "You must realize, my friend, that the deeper we go into this, both written and

Aua (right) and Orulo.
*Photograph by Peter
Freuchen, 1922. Courtesy the
National Museum of Denmark.*

Kinalik, standing. *Photograph by Knud Rasmussen, 1922. Courtesy the National Museum of Denmark.*

Orpingalik (right). *Photograph by Knud Rasmussen, 1922. Courtesy the National Museum of Denmark.*

Igjugarjuk. *Photograph by Knud Rasmussen, 1922. Courtesy the National Museum of Denmark.*

Najagneq, 1924. *Courtesy the National Museum of Denmark.*

Fringe.
*Courtesy the
Smithsonian Institution.*

Plenty Coups.
Courtesy the Smithsonian Institution.

Geronimo.
Courtesy the Smithsonian Institution.

Yakut shaman.
Photograph courtesy American Museum of Natural History.

Leonard Crow Dog. *Copyright © Richard Erdoes.*

Lame Deer. *Copyright © Richard Erdoes.*

K'xau (left) with an Herero woman.
Photograph by Richard Katz.

Australian shaman (atop pole).
Photograph courtesy *American Museum of Natural History*.

Josie Limpie.
Copyright © *Richard Erdoes*.

Brooke Medicine Eagle.
Copyright © *Wernher Krutein*.

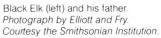
Ramón Medina Silva.
Photograph by Barbara Myerhoff.

Black Elk.
Photograph by Joseph Epes Brown.
Courtesy the Smithsonian Institution.

Black Elk (left) and his father.
Photograph by Elliott and Fry.
Courtesy the Smithsonian Institution.

Ramón Medina Silva (left) and Lupe.
Photograph by Barbara Myerhoff.

Manuel Córdova-Rios (standing). *Photograph by Bruce Lamb.*

María Sabina (right) and daughter Apolonia. *Photograph by Alan Richardson, © R. Gordon Wasson.*

Petaga Yuha Mani (Pete Catches). *Copyright © Richard Erdoes.*

Isaac Tens (second from right), over patient.
Photographs courtesy National Museums of Canada.

Prem Das.
Copyright © Diana Clark.

Warao shaman (right). Photograph courtesy Peter T. Furst

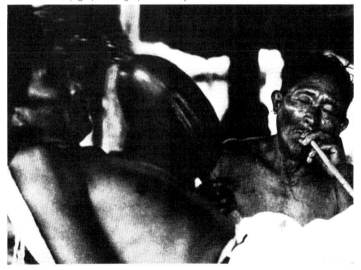

The chief said, "Let us start with the birds. You know the medium-sized tinamou, the partridge that gives the plaintive call at sunset because he does not like to sleep alone on the ground. Visualize one for me there on the ground between the trees in the alternating light and shadow."

There he was! I saw him in infinite detail with his rounded tailless rump, plumage olive gray, washed and barred with shades of cinnamon, chestnut and dusky brown, colors that blended imperceptibly with the light and shadows on the leafy forest floor. My visual perception seemed unlimited. Never had I perceived visual images in such detail before.

"Yes, Chief, I see him," was my response, mentally if not aloud.

"He will move around now. Watch closely."

A few shy, furtive movements and the bird was in another pattern of light and shadow where he was much more difficult to see. But I had followed him there and could pick out every detail still. The chief then brought a female, and the male went through his mating dance. I heard all of the songs, calls and other sounds. Their variety was beyond anything I had known. Finally a simple saucer-shaped nest appeared on the ground between the birds, with two pale-blue eggs in it. The male then sat on the nest, to my surprise. "Yes, he raises the children," said the chief.

We went from the various tinamous to the trumpeter, the curassows and other important game birds, all seen in the same infinite and minute detail.

Then the chief said, "Close your eyes now and let the visions flow before we go on to other things."

I do not know how much time had passed—time had lost its meaning for me. As I closed my eyes vague traceries of light and shade developed, gradually taking on a bluish green color as the patterns changed. They seemed like living, changing arabesques, moving in rhythm over a geometric background, with infinite variety of form. Sometimes they slightly resembled familiar pat-

---

spoken words of formal language become less and less adequate as a medium of expression. If I could arrange it we would have a session of visions ourselves and then you would then understand. But that would take time. Meanwhile we will continue with indifferent words and inflexible modes of expression."

terns of spider webs or butterfly wings. A moving current of air with a barely perceptible fragrance translated itself on this visual screen of my mind as a faint violet wash over the moving arabesques. A birdcall or buzz of cicada—a brilliant flash of color or a subtle rippling of waves, depending on its character.

All the senses seemed to be intensely acute and integrated into a single system. A stimulant to one was immediately translated to the others. The imagery gradually faded away, and the chief was aware of this.

He spoke, and I roused myself. It was late afternoon.

"We have night work to do," he said. "It will take another cup of honi xuma to make it effective. You will find this second cup even more illuminating. Listen for my instructions and have no fear."

He built up the smoldering fire so there was a dancing flame in the gathering dusk. Then he handed me another large cupful of the clear green liquid, which I drank without hesitation.

There was an almost immediate reaction. As the darkness deepened I became aware of an acute depth of visual perception far beyond anything known to me before. The mighty trees around us took on a deep spiritual quality of obedient benevolence that set the character of the whole scene. As the fire died back down to a glowing coal, the darkness settled over everything. At the same time my visual powers were so augmented that I could see things that in other circumstances would have been totally invisible to me. This explained how the Indians could travel with ease through the forest and even hunt at night.

A passing firefly lit up the scene with a brilliance that seemed to approach the light of day. My sense of hearing was also much more acute. I could separate the night sounds far and near. When a cricket buzzed nearby I could see him in the dark on a stem rubbing his legs against the sound box of his body. A group of small yellow frogs up in a nearby tree started an alternating exchange of a bell-like call, "chill-ing, chill-ing," echoing back and forth with the exquisite clarity of a small silver bell. From the treetops there drifted down on a descending air current the heavy musky fragrance of a night-blooming orchid. In my state of heightened sense perception, this was almost overwhelming in its intensity and it overflowed into indescribable sensations of taste.

The call of an owl, "whooo whooo," floated on the still night air and was answered in the darkness.

"You will learn to see and hear at night as clearly as the owl," was the chief's comment. And I felt that it was true.

With chants and the calls of the various animals, the chief evoked in my visions vivid episodes in the lives of the nocturnal forest animals. The chants, the calls and the visions they brought were all to become part of my own repertory.

The morning sunlight breaking through the forest canopy awakened me from a strange sleep that I could not remember falling into. Orientation with time and space returned, but only slowly. I felt as though I were coming back from a distant journey to unknown and unremembered places.

The chief offered me a calabash of thick fruit gruel to drink, which helped my senses return to reality. We soon walked, at Xumu's usual measured, deliberate pace, back to the village.

I was still kept on a strict diet, and it turned out that this was to be a period of intensive training for me. Once every eight days I would have a session of visions with the chief. These included examination of plants and their various uses both as food and as medicine, as well as further study of the animals. During the time between sessions I was taken often to the forest on both day and night trips with small groups of hunters. On these excursions I found to my delight that the intensified sense of perception and increased awareness of my surroundings originating in the sessions with the chief stayed with me. In the forest my companions would point out origins of sound and smell and continually test my progress in becoming completely one with the forest environment.

After each series of four sessions with the chief eight days apart, I would have an equivalent period to work with and absorb the new experience and knowledge. A strict diet was still kept up, and then another series of vision sessions would begin. At times during all this, which went on for months, I became nervous, high-strung and afraid of going insane. The chief and the old women noticed this. They took pains to explain and reassure me that as long as I followed the diets and instructions everything would come out well.

During my training I became aware of subtle changes in my

mental process and modes of thought. I noticed a mental acceleration and a certain clairvoyance in anticipating events and the reactions of the tribe. By focusing my attention on a single individual I could divine his reactions and purposes and anticipate what he would do or what he planned to do. This was all important to the way Xumu governed the tribe, and I began to see what lay under the surface in his management of their community life. The old man said my power to anticipate and know future events would improve and grow, also that I would be able to locate and identify objects from a great distance. All this, he told me, would help protect and control the tribe.

As the training process went on I began to sense a vague feeling of urgency on the part of the chief to impart his fund of knowledge and experience to me adequately. In actuality, I believe you could say that he was transmitting the accumulated tribal knowledge of, perhaps, centuries. The tribe could stand no rivalries in the chieftainship and it became clear that I was being prepared.

During the rest period between the vision sessions, in addition to going out with the hunters, Xumu himself often took me on short excursions to the nearby forest. There he would take great pains to show me and to explain the use of the plants, many of which we also saw in the visions. He would explain to me the secrets of their preparation for use and repeat the chants that should accompany both preparation and application. It was strongly believed among them that the chants helped in bringing about the desired effect of the treatment.

Joel
NORTH AMERICA/DOGRIB

Joel was twenty-one years old when he encountered the old and weathered Dogrib Indian shaman Adamie. The young Brooklynite, like many others in the early 1960s, seemed to be on a quest, but the direction of his journey was not clear. He had been to Mexico and eaten peyote. Now, working in a fishing camp near the Mackenzie range in

Canada, he found himself being drawn toward the Dogrib, who use the hallucinogenic mushroom *Amanita muscaria* as a sacrament.

One day, Joel was approached by Adamie, who invited him to his cabin. When Joel arrived, he discovered that a shamanistic healing séance was in progress. It was not long before the young man had fallen into a violent trance state, having been called by the spirits. Sometime later, Joel presented himself to Adamie and indicated that he wanted to learn the path of the shaman.

Before Joel's actual apprenticeship began, Adamie insisted on inspecting the young man's soul to see whether the potential apprentice was worthy and ready for the ordeals that were to follow. Again, Joel fell into a profound trance state, which he described to Steve and Robin Larsen years later: "Whatever [Adamie] had done, he had snatched me. I had no volition, I had no power of my own. I didn't eat, didn't sleep, I didn't think—I wasn't in my body any longer. Adamie had me, . . . looked at all the cracks in my soul, saw what he liked and what he didn't like."[12]

Joel endured many ordeals in the process of his apprenticeship. He was beaten and badgered, bathed in icy water and whipped. Finally, he was permitted the experience with the sacred mushrooms. In his first session with the visionary herb he experienced unmitigated violence and chaos, a terrible dismembering, a tearing, a shredding, a slaughter. In his second séance with the *Amanita,* he again encountered the animal spirits that tore him apart; yet, this time, he emerged from the ordeal strong and refreshed. In one of Joel's poems, he exclaims, "Cleansed and ripe for vision/I rise,/a bursting ball of seeds in space/ . . . I have sung the note that shatters structure./And the note that shatters chaos,/and been bloody./ . . . I have been with the dead and attempted the labyrinth."[13]

In the end, Joel had to leave Adamie and return to the ground of his own culture. He was not a Dogrib; the barrenness of the landscape and the strange, lonely life of a shaman were overwhelming. He had balanced his song against his sanity; he had pierced his tongue for the wind. And finally he could only return to his own world.[14]

My encounter with shamanism took place in the area near Great Slave Lake and the Mackenzie Range. I was working at a fishing camp, the kind rich men from the States fly up to for enormous sums of money. There was a group of Dogrib Indians there who worked as guides. I had heard that they were mushroom eaters and I became interested in them for that reason. I had been into peyote down in New Mexico and I was excited by the prospect of experiencing something new. I even allowed for the possibility of learning something.

The head man of the Indians was named Adamie. I had heard stories about him, and I became curious. I began checking with the guides every day to see if he had arrived yet at camp. While working on the boat dock one day I noticed an Indian I had not seen before watching me. He was about sixty years old and weather-beaten. His face was a dendritic river basin, deep furrows carved in almost perfect pattern. As he approached I felt my spine involuntarily quiver. I lost sight of everything except his deep-set black eyes. I heard his voice say to me, "You have been looking for me. I am at the house farthest north in the village."

Up till that moment my stay at this place had been a detached fantasy—a drifter's game to be played for two or three months until I had my fill of the river and its fish. Now, suddenly I began to feel a sweaty fear of survival urging me to get the hell out of that wilderness. But that was crazy. Just because an old Indian, tatooed by the wind and cold, had spoken to me was no reason to run. I did a lot of running then, but I usually had better reason than this.

The First Seance—The Call

I went to visit Adamie at his house. There was a seance going on. Adamie was shamanizing, curing a sick woman.

Suddenly the drumming seemed louder and louder. The pitch became unbearable. It screamed like thunder over the lake. Animal cries cut through the darkness as Adamie leaped up. The metal that hung from him rang like a thousand bells gone berserk. I was pulled into a state of turmoil. I saw great birds smash through the room. A force was pulling me into the dance and frenzy. Time was lost. I wanted to jump up from my place and scream wildly. Blood filled my head till I felt like it was bursting out of my eyes and mouth. I stared at Adamie and felt my body convulse violently. I turned my gaze on the others in the room. They were distant and embalmed. My bones began to lose their adhesiveness—swirling light passed through my body. My mind made one last grasp at validity. I screamed.

The chaos ended as suddenly as it had begun. Adamie fell by the woman's side and began murmuring. Then he was silent. Those around me started to get up and move towards the door. I couldn't move. The dirt floor held me like a cradle and swayed me gently. Someone lifted me with pleading and frightened sounds and half carried me to the door. Once outside I began to regain my footing. The ground shifted from the vertical back to the horizontal plane. It was almost daylight. I started back to the lodge, Eddie, one of the guides, giving me a hand. "Poor Joe, poor white man," he whispered. "All those good Indians there and you the one that gets called. Sometimes I wonder if those spirits know what they're doing. You don't even know nothing about it."

The days after the ceremony were days of shadows. Something had entered me and I felt as if I were being watched and motivated by some force outside myself. My will was being drained from my body, and I often felt the nauseating dizziness associated with loss of blood. It was like jumping up too fast after lying down too long—thrown off by the sudden shift in altitude.

A manic excitement eventually overtook me. I managed to get through my chores. All my excess energy was channeled into a "hash" pipe I was carving from a piece of hardwood. I became intensely concerned with every detail of its making. Each cut in the wood was carefully made and had to be exact. My fingers became sensitive to the precise needs of the wood. I felt its history run through the knife and into the palm of my hand. I took care with my work as I had never done before in my life. It seemed as if my very existence was tied to its outcome.

When the pipe was finished to my satisfaction I put it carefully into my leather pouch with some tobacco and went looking for Adamie. I didn't want to go, but something insisted on an answer to my present condition and it seemed that Adamie would have that answer. I worked my way slowly to his house like a fox trying to hide his tracks. I backtracked, dodged, and circumvented my destination till by a miracle of will I found myself at Adamie's door. I didn't knock, I just walked in.

Adamie was sitting in an old chair by a small wood stove in the center of the room. The room was almost barren except for a table filled with odds and ends of fishing tackle and a mattress on the floor in the corner. The hiss of two gas lanterns was the only sound that greeted me. Adamie looked up at me, and his face came alive with a gap-toothed, grandfather smile. He clapped his hands several times and began to laugh.

"How's that woman?" I blurted. "She's well," Adamie answered, continuing to laugh gently. His laugh was a feather on my feet; it tickled and was painful. "I . . . I brought you this," I said, offering the pipe from my pouch.

"Why have you come here?" he demanded.

"To learn," came out of my mouth without me wishing it.

I placed the pipe on the table to occupy myself in the fragile silence my words had created. I feared that something terrifying was about to smash that wordless world.

"What are you thinking now?" Adamie's voice cracked through the hiss of the lanterns.

"That you're an old, ugly Indian, and what the hell am I so afraid of." I stunned myself with my honesty.

Adamie smiled. He motioned me to sit down on the floor near his chair. He got out of the chair and sat down next to me.

We talked for a long time, or at least I did. Adamie asked me question after question: What was Edmonton like? And New York? Where had I fished? Where was my home? Who were my people? He kept me talking till he had emptied me of everything that had come to be my identity.

"You have been so many places and seen so much. What do you think I could show you?" he asked.

"You could show me how to fish the lake for a start, and maybe . . . well . . . how you healed that woman."

"And is that why you brought me the gift?"

"I don't know exactly," I answered.

The Inspection of the Soul

"I would look at your soul," Adamie said flatly and finally.

"Help yourself, Adamie." I was feeling too spaced-out to be taken aback by his request. . . .

Adamie instructed me to lie down with my hands at my sides. He began to chant, walking slowly around me. Lying there I felt pleasant, and trusting, perhaps slightly amused.

Adamie's chant was cool and smooth and felt like a lover's

body wrapped in silk. And as the chant fondled the mind, the silk grew warm and I threw the covering away and reached for the sources of heat inside the flesh of the lover, inside the flesh of the chant. Till my hand touched the fire—till I was the fire. A giant wind sucked the breath from the fire and I gasped in the darkness.

(Someone floated with no will, in black space. "I" no longer existed in the darkness that fell heavier than sleep. There are no recollections, no metaphors to express the suspended emptiness.)

I felt a gale blow across me, and a shiver which began at my mouth rippled my entire body. I heard Adamie chanting, and the sounds pulled my eyelids open.

"How long have I been asleep?"

A midday light entered the room.

"Hell." I tried to jump up but my body ached and I fell back. "The boss is going to kill me. I should have been to work hours ago."

"You have missed two whole days already," Adamie said grinning. "I told the boss you would stay with me now. You work with me, stay here."

Adamie moved towards the table and picked up the pipe. He carried it gently as if it were a small sleeping child.

He turned to me.

"I accept your gift.". . .

Then Adamie proceeded to teach me. The initiation consisted of ordeals. It was a preparation for what was to come. If I had a structure, the idea was to break down that reality, to take away my structures until I had none.

I was bathed in ice water, I was whipped, badgered continuously both physically and psychologically, and all the time being taught—being taught about the way of the spirits, about how the world was ordered in a different way than I had imagined.

It was a process of breaking down and reordering over and over again. . . .

I felt pushed past my limits. Kind of when you've been snowshoeing too long and you've really "had it." You can't stand it, but for some reason you keep on going through second winds and thirds. . . .

Something in me was saying "Why are you putting up with it?" But it didn't stop, a feeling like I had to go on. But after a while

I wanted to go into my first seance, I think mainly to get away from the other ordeals.

The First Mushroom Experience: Dismemberment

Adamie asked me if I was ready to meet the spirits. And I said "Yes." I ate mushrooms *(Amanita muscaria)* and there was drumming and a seance. It was a very frightening experience. The drug felt toxic and I didn't know how to deal with it. . . .

It was like eating belladonna. . . . Like there's no way out now because those things with big teeth are coming. Everything was chaos and disorder. I wasn't ready, I didn't know enough, I couldn't put any pieces together.

I was physically ill, psychically terrified, close to death, no control, no direction. It was hell, an endless chaotic battle with no real point. . . .

I just gradually came out of it, still alive physically, but that's about it. It just stayed at one level of confrontation, and then it went away eventually. . . .

Afterward Adamie asked me what had happened, and I explained to him what I'd experienced. He picked out each fear, each feeling, and he explained to me the spirit that controlled it. He told me spirit names, and what they did. . . .

Before the first one I had thought, "They'll stop badgering me now." Before the second one I no longer wanted to stop it. Somehow the first time I found out that I was fucking up. The way I was, the thing I was holding on to was just not real. I had to stop holding on to that identity. That had to be chopped away. It wasn't very central, it wasn't strong. . . .

I didn't want the vision, the dream to take me, to take me out of what I was. That had to be beaten out of me, psyched out of me. And then there was a moment. . . .

And after that moment, it was time to start to learn. What are these forces that are tearing you apart. Let's give them a name and see what to do with them.

The Second Seance: Meeting with the Spirit

The next seance started with dancing and drumming. And this time I participated. I started to dance wildly and more wildly, getting more ecstatic. And then I felt this wave going up my spine, exploding in my head, and then I hit trance.

In trance I had a vision, I saw a bear. And the bear motioned for me to follow it. This was the spirit, the force I was to follow, to take my journey with. As I was following the bear it turned into a woman. And then there was a whole series of sexual imagery, buttocks, thighs, breasts, a whole swirl of sexuality, of flesh.

I was swirling and whirling, and I felt like I was falling to the center of the earth. And as I was going down there were creatures on all sides of me. And they would rip and tear, take pieces from me as I went down. And when I hit bottom they all descended on me and tore me up: a falcon on my eyes, a many-toothed dog pawing my backbone.

I was torn and torn. But somehow this time I was not afraid in the same way. I accepted it all. I obeyed the fear and went with it. I was torn until some spirit—some force—cried *Stop!* . . . And then I began to be put back together again. And as I was coming together again I didn't recognize what I saw coming together as me. It wasn't exactly right. Something was there that wasn't there before, but as it put itself, molded itself, back together I began to understand that something had been added. Instead of being structured 1–2–3, I was structured 1–2–3 and 4. That 4 was very important, it made the whole thing more than it had been.

My feelings were of high ecstasy, shock waves of energy traveling through me. I felt I could see through things, hearts, bones, souls. There was a sound and it was coming up from within me. I was singing a song, the song of my experience, and I felt the song gave me new strength and power. I knew I must remember that song. It is my medicine song. . . .

Not long after that second trip, I realized this was going to take a long, long time. I was twenty-one years old and not ready to give up the world. . . .

One part said you are going to become an old man in the woods, you can't get an Indian woman, and everyone is going to be afraid of you. But no one is going to love you. Adamie is more respected than loved. But the other forces were calling me to continue the journey. . . .

I would be a second-rate shaman if I stayed . . . A sort of crazy man who hung out in the woods and went down to Edmonton in midwinter, because I wasn't Indian and couldn't stand the barrenness. That's pretty much where I'd be. I would have been between two cultures. . . .

I feel that the very flows of this culture can be used. It keeps making me sort through my values and doesn't provide any set package so that I have to keep sorting through till I say, "Aha, this is real for me. . . .

It's coming back into the world with a song after having a vision—but then there aren't many people to share it with, not like a primitive tribe where you can come back and say, "Here are my bear's teeth or my vision, this is what my name is, this is the spirit who guides me." I can't really do that here. . . .

[Staying with Adamie] would have been red suspenders and flannel shirts and taking out rich white men fishing. And going trapping in the winter . . . but that wasn't who I was, I wasn't a north woods Indian, and much as I could relate to the worlds of realities in their mythology, I couldn't adapt to their life style, make it mine, and stay there the rest of my life—let my hair grow down to my knees, wear an iron shaman's costume.

I felt I had to go back to my own culture, to work things out. I had to somehow take the little I'd mastered back to my own culture, and make it work there. There's no grounding mythology for me here, no strong physical presence of a human guide, but the song remains. The song is always there.

6 The Power to Transform

The title of this Eskimo Oonark drawing is *Shaman in Flight*. The caption to this pencil drawing is as follows: "When the moon rocket went to the moon and some of the young kids were trying to tell the old people about this, they were getting really frustrated because the old people were saying, 'Oh, that's nothing, my uncle went to the moon lots of times.'" (From: *Stones, bones and skin: Ritual and Shamanic Art,* edited by Anne Trueblood Brodzky, Rose Daneswich, Nick Johnson. The Society for Art Publications, Toronto, 1977, p. 122.)

Willidjungo
AUSTRALIA/MURNGIN

The shaman Willidjungo was a renowned healer among the Murngin of northeastern Arnhemland. Described by anthropologist W. Lloyd Warner as a large, heavyset man with a mop of straight hair, he was not different from other men of his tribe except perhaps for his unusually good disposition. He had six wives and numerous children, and he was a hunter, a fisherman, and an active participant in the ceremonial life of his people.

Warner, who knew Willidjungo and collected the narrative that follows, maintained that the "white magic" practiced by Australian shamans was "an effective force used to cure sickness, heal wounds, take away the malignant effect of a snake bite, and, in general, to remove from the individual any feeling of dysphoria and to give him a sense of well-being and adjustment to his community."[1]

According to Warner, the shaman can remove foreign objects that have been shot into the body of the afflicted one and can perform diagnostic procedures on the principle that the illness is caused by the intrusion of a foreign object. But if the patient's soul is stolen, the shaman can do nothing to alleviate suffering or delay death.[2]

Here is how Warner introduces Willidjungo's initiatory experience:

> One day when Willidjungo was a mature man having several wives and children he was out in the bush looking for wild honeybees' nests. After a time he decided to return home. On his way back to camp he felt a pain in his right leg near the hip. He knew afterwards that the familiars which he later acquired had given it to him. His leg became very stiff and stayed that way for over a week. During this time he lay in the camp and covered himself with paper bark to keep warm. One of Willidjungo's wives slept by him. The two familiars, who were a little boy and girl, started talking to him underneath the paper bark. They talked in a rhythmic chant: "Dul! dul! dul!—ter ter ter."

Said Willidjungo, "The sound was like a small frog out in the lilies."

Willidjungo woke up his wife. "You better sleep among the women tonight," he said. His wife left their hut and went over to her mother's and father's. She was very frightened of these two spirits. The two continued talking. They went back into the bush and Willidjungo followed them. . . .[3]

I kept listening to that noise they [the spirit familiars] were making. I listened but I did not look, and followed them. The two things came back to camp and I came with them. They sat down by my fire and talked. When it was night and dark those two spirits flew in the tops of the trees. They had the sound of a quail flying. They sat on the top of my head and on my shoulders. They had white feathers, but I did not know that at that time. I could only feel them on my head.

They did not come back for me then but I went out to look for them. I saw them out in the bush then for the first time. Their bodies looked like jabirus. Their eyes looked like your glasses. Their face and stomach looked like a man and their legs looked the same way. They had big stomachs like children. Their arms were like wings and had little feathers on them. Their wings had big feathers. They were standing on a tree. I took my spear-thrower. I put the hooked end under my arms and put sweat on it. I took it out then to reach for those two spirits. I caught them and put them under my arms. I held them in my hands like you would a small bird when you catch a wild one. They left me before I came back to camp. Before they left they said to me, "You have a wife. It is better that you go back by yourself."

[I replied], "Oh, no, I don't want to do that. . . . What are your names?"

"We are two *na-ri* [familiars]. Don't you try to cure people yet. If people are sick you let them alone and tell some other doctor to try to cure them."

Then I came back to camp. Dorng's daughter was sick. I did nothing but look at her. She had a big hole in her chest. It had cracked open. I kept on looking. One of the old doctors tried to fix her but he couldn't do anything, but I didn't do anything. Afterwards I took the flesh and put it together and she became better right away the first time I tried. I made her well when she was half dead. Those two spirits talked to me then. They said, "The first time you have tried you have done a good job. The next time anyone is sick you treat them. That is your work. We gave this to you and it will help you, but there are some things you cannot do. You must not go in the salt water and get covered with it. You must go alone near the shore. If you go down under the salt water, we two will be dead."

If I should dive in the ocean these spirits would die. These two spirits come around at night, usually in the middle of the night. Yesterday I carried a kangaroo on my shoulder and pressed hard on my armpits. I hurt one of my familiars, and I am sore under my arm. Last night the little one that was not hurt left me and went into the bush to look for another spirit. The other one followed him. The sick one said, "My master is sick now like me. You come and we will fix him."

The well one took something out of the sick one and they came back. They found something hard in my chest and took it out.

When I was getting these spirits I went around very quietly and said nothing. I did not smoke very much. I only ate vegetable food and stayed in one place. I made an old doctor my friend. I fed him and gave him tobacco. One of the spirits left him and came with me.

*   *   *

When I treat people those two go right inside a man. That bone which is inside the man sticks right straight in him. I keep rubbing on the outside. Those two children of mine take hold of that bone and when I suck they jump right out with it. Sometimes I can look right through a man and see that he is rotten inside. Those two go inside but they can do nothing. Sometimes when people steal a man's soul in the bush he comes here to my camp. I go look; he is empty inside. I say, "I can't fix you up. Everything is gone. Your heart is still there, but it's empty. I can't fix you up." Then I tell everybody he is going to die.

Sometimes people carry a sick man to me and I see them coming a long way down the beach. I call out to those people, "You people stand each side of him," and I look in that man. Soon the souls of the two men who killed this sick man half dead come

out. When I see this I call out the names of those two men who
stole this man's soul.

Before this, men and women have gone in the bush and have
played with each other and one man's wife will be with another
woman's husband. They say, "We are going to spear kangaroo."
The man goes to spear kangaroo and then goes to find that woman.
They come back. My spirit children come to me and say, "That
man and woman have played together out in the bush. You go tell
that woman's husband." I say, "Oh, no, I won't do that. That will
make trouble." I do not tell their husbands and wives because that
would make too much trouble in the camp.

Sometimes I am sitting with a man and I look at his head and
I can say to him, "You think so and so." The man says, "How do
you know that?" and I say, "I can see inside your mind."

Mun-yir-yir
AUSTRALIA/MURNGIN

**Mun-yir-yir started to become a doctor when he was pulled down into
a water hole by one of three soul children who were his "doctor spirits." After several initiatory experiences, which he describes in the
narrative that follows, he slowly began to develop his abilities as a
curer.**

**Although Mun-yir-yir had been a proficient healer and had cured
many people, he lost his power after breaking a taboo. According to
tradition, those who have the power to heal will destroy their helping
spirits if they fall into salty water. Mun-yir-yir was on the Goyder
River side of Millingimbi Island when another canoe struck his small
one, and he fell into the ocean. His helping spirits, the opossum children, fell from his head and into the water with him. As a result, he
lost his spirit allies and his power.[4]**

I found my doctor spirits in my country, in the snake country.
I was hunting for bandicoot and I had caught one and was cooking
him. I think perhaps that those doctor spirits smelled that bandicoot cooking. I went down to a creek to get some water to drink.
I leaned over and drank out of the water hole. When I did that a

doctor soul caught my nose and made me sink down in the water. I was in a coma and fell in the water. The doctors, they were two boys and a girl, took my hand and put it in a dry place. . . . They took out something from inside my body when I was sick after falling in the water and they opened my eyes and nose and mouth and made me well. They blew in my mouth. I got up and took my stone axe. I hit one of those doctor souls on the nose and I hit the others, too. They looked like opossums. When I caught them, one of the men doctor souls said, "You make us well now."

I blew on the man and made him well, then I made the others well. They said to me, "Now you go back to camp. Don't you eat dog any more, but you eat cold food and don't sleep near the fire."

When I got near the camp those opossums called out to me. They made a loud noise. The people said, "Look out for Mun-yir-yir. He has found some familiars." These familiars hit their arms against their sides and made a popping noise. I came and sat down in my camp. I slept. I slept a little while in the night and went out in the bush. Those two took me to the bush with them. I did not try to make anybody well.

I went to Elcho Island from the Naladaer country and then came back again to the mainland. Some of the people said to me, "We are sick here in the chest. We don't feel well. Please, Mun-yir-yir, help us." I went then and took a shell and filled it with water and washed my hands. I felt over their chests and took out a bone and showed them. A man came from another country. He had a sore back. He said, "I can't walk." I looked from a long way and I saw that little hard thing inside him. I blew on his back and this thing came out a long way. I showed it to him. The other man was hunting for kangaroo then and his back didn't hurt him and he was very pleased.

Those two spirits sit down on my shoulders. Sometimes they sit on my head. I call them my children. Sometimes they used to come to me in the night. They would say, "There is a man sick over there."

In the early morning I would say, "Where is that man?" and they would show me and they would say, "He has got something inside him," and they would show me where. Sometimes I used to take bushes and brush against the man and now blow on him and that hard thing would fall a long way from him.

When I first started some of the people said, "You are lying and not telling the truth." I said to them, "You look at my mouth." I opened my mouth and let them see I had nothing in there.

* * *

I had been down . . . to the ocean. It was on the Goyder River side of Millingimbi Island. Those doctors of mine were sitting on my head and shoulders. I was out in a canoe standing in it when another canoe came along and hit our small one. I fell in the ocean and I was covered with the salt water. I heard those opossum children make noises. I put my hand on my head and they fell down inside the water when I came up. A little after that an old man was sick. "I am sick inside here," he said. [He touched his chest.] I looked to see what was inside him but I could see nothing now. My eye was too dark. I had lost my doctor children. I can't see anything now inside people. Everyone says that I have lost my very good thing that I had. It's too bad. I said to all the people then, "I can't look out for you people any more. I fell down in the salt water and it covered me and I can't cure any more." If I had fallen down in fresh water it would not have hurt those doctor children of mine.

ESKIMO/IGLULIK

The origins of shamanism among the Iglulik and, most particularly, of out-of-the-body travel, are found in this unusual narrative. The tale was given this introduction by its narrator:

In the very earliest times, men lived in the dark and had no animals to hunt. They were poor, ignorant people, far inferior to those living nowadays. They travelled about in search of food, they lived on journeys as we do now, but in a very different way. When they halted and camped, they worked at the soil with picks of a kind we no longer know. They got their food from the earth, they lived on the soil. They knew nothing of all the game we now have, and had therefore no need to be ever on guard against all those perils which arise from the fact that we, hunting animals as we do, live by slaying other souls. Therefore they had no shamans, but they knew sickness, and it was fear of sickness and suffering that led to the coming of the first shamans. The ancients relate as follows concerning this:

"Human beings have always been afraid of sickness, and far back in the very earliest times there arose wise men who tried to find out about all the things none could understand. There were no shamans in those days, and men were ignorant of all those rules of life which have since taught them to be on their guard against danger and wickedness. The first amulet that ever existed was the shell portion of a sea-urchin. It has a hole through it, and is hence called itɛq (anus) and the fact of its being made the first amulet was due to its being associated with a particular power of healing. When a man fell ill, one would go and sit by him, and, pointing to the diseased part, break wind behind. Then one went outside, while another held one hand hollowed over the diseased part, breathing at the same time out over the palm of his other hand in a direction away from the person to be cured. It was then believed that wind and breath together combined all the power emanating from within the human body, a power so mysterious and strong that it was able to cure disease.

"In that way everyone was a physician, and there was no need of any shamans. But then it happened that a time of hardship and famine set in around Iglulik. Many died of starvation, and all were greatly perplexed, not knowing what to do. Then one day when a number of people were assembled in a house, a man demanded to be allowed to go behind the skin hangings at the back of the sleeping place, no one knew why. He said he was going to travel down to the Mother of the Sea Beasts. No one in the house understood him, and no one believed in him. He had his way, and passed in behind the hangings. Here he declared that he would exercise an art which should afterwards prove of great value to mankind; but no one must look at him. It was not long, however, before the unbelieving and inquisitive drew aside the hangings, and to their astonishment perceived that he was diving down into the earth; he had already got so far down that only the soles of his feet could be seen. How the man ever hit on this idea no one knows; he himself said that it was the spirits that had helped him: spirits he had entered into contact with out in the great solitude. Thus the first shaman appeared among men. He went down to the Mother of the Sea Beasts and brought back game to men, and the famine gave place to plenty, and all were happy and joyful once more.

"Afterwards, the shamans extended their knowledge of hidden things, and helped mankind in various ways. They also developed their sacred language, which was only used for communicating with the spirits and not in everyday speech."[5]

Only the greatest of the *angakoq* are able to make the out-of-body journey to the Land of the Day, the afterlife realm that lies toward the east of the dawn.* The *Pavungnartuts,* flying shamans who can voyage to this paradise of the dead, often make their celestial journeys for pure pleasure. The shaman's preparation for the trance voyage of the spirit is complex and involves a party of assistants. First, the shaman seats himself in the back of his house on the sleeping bench, where a skin curtain hides him from view. His hands are then tied behind his back, and his head is lashed to his knees. The men who have bound him take a glowing ember on the point of a knife and draw rings in the air above his head. As they are doing this, they cry out, "Let him who is now going a-visiting be fetched away."[6]

The lamps in the hut are then extinguished, and all sit in a deep silence, their eyes closed. After a while, strange throbbing, hissing, and whispering sounds seem to emanate from different parts of the house. The shaman loudly cries, *"Halala—halalale, halala—halalale!"* And he is answered by his friends, "Ale—ale—ale!"

When a rushing sound is heard, all who are in attendance know that the shaman's soul is leaving his body, and flying up to the Land of the Day. His ecstatic flight is assisted by stars who were men in an earlier time.

While the shaman is away, his friends below entertain themselves with ancient songs. When the wizard returns, although exhausted from his efforts, he recounts his adventures in paradise.[8]

However, the journey out of the body is not always made for pleasure. At times, the *angakoq* must leave his mortal form to retrieve the lost soul of one who has been abducted by the spirit of a sorcerer; or he must travel to other worlds to seek for the soul of one who is ill or injured. If the community is afflicted with misfortune, the shaman must descend to the sea's depths in order to appease the Mother of Sea Beasts.[9]

---

*It is said that the People of the Day, those who have been drowned or murdered, live there joyfully laughing, singing, and playing ball with a walrus skull. Those who have not been purified by a violent death go first to the Narrow Land to do penance for their sins.[7]

The shaman's soul voyage to unearthly realms, whether for pleasure, during a healing ceremony, to escort the dead, allay the gods, or during an initiatory crisis, is a constant feature of shamanism in all parts of the world. Aua's account is particularly interesting in comparison with the narratives by Ramón (pp. 135–137, 169–173, and 233–237) and !Kung healer K"xau's (pp. 54–62) and Sereptie (pp.39–49).

The great shamans of our country often visit the People of Day for joy alone; we call them pavuŋnArtut (those who rise up into heaven). The shaman who is about to make the journey seats himself, as in the case of nak·a·j₂q, at the back of the sleeping place in his house. But the man who travels to the Land of Day must be bound before he is laid down behind the curtain; his hands must be fastened behind his back, and his head lashed firmly to his knees; he also must wear only breeches, leaving legs and the upper part of the body naked. When this is done, the men who have bound him must take an ember from the lamp on the point of a knife, and pass it over his head, drawing rings in the air, and say: "ni₂ᴿuniArt₂q aifa·le": "Let him who is now going a-visiting be fetched away".

Then all lamps are put out, and all visitors in the house close their eyes. They sit like that for a long while, and deep silence reigns throughout the house. But after a time, strange sounds are heard by the listening guests; they hear a whistling that seems to come far, far up in the air, humming and whistling sounds, and then suddenly the shaman calling out at the top of his voice:

"Halala—halalale, halala—halalale!"

And at the same moment, all visitors in the house must cry: "Ale—ale—ale!"; then there is a sort of rushing noise in the snow hut, and all know that an opening has been formed for the soul of the shaman, an opening like the blowhole of a seal, and through it the soul flies up to heaven, aided by all those stars which were once human beings. And all the souls now pass up and down the souls' road, in order to keep it open for the shaman; some rush down, others fly up, and the air is filled with a rushing, whistling sound:

"Pfft—pfft—pfft!"

That is the stars whistling for the soul of the shaman, and the guests in the house must then try to guess the human names of the stars, the names they bore while living down on earth; and when they succeed, one hears two short whistles: "Pfft—pfft!" and afterwards a faint, shrill sound that fades away into space. That is the stars' answer, and their thanks for being still remembered.

Often a shaman will remain away for a long time, and his guests will then entertain themselves by singing old songs, always with closed eyes. It is said that there is great joy in the Land of Day when a shaman comes on a visit. They do not perceive him at first, being occupied with their games and laughter and football. But then there is heard the cry: "niɔʀuᴀrzuit, niɔʀuᴀrzuit!" ringing out over the ground: "Visitors, visitors." And at once people come running out of the houses. But the houses have no passage ways, no entrances or exits, and therefore the souls come out from all parts, wherever they fancy, through the wall or through the roof. They shoot right through the house, and though one can see them, they are nevertheless nothing, and there are no holes in the houses where they passed through. And they run towards the visitor, glad to greet him, glad to bid him welcome, for they believe it is the soul of a dead man, like themselves. But then when he says: "pu-ᵈla·liuvuŋa" "I am still of flesh and blood," they turn away dissappointed.

Up in the Land of Day, the thong with which the shaman was bound falls away of itself, and now the dead ones, who are always in high spirits, begin playing ball with it. Every time they kick it, the thing flies out into the air and seems to take the shape of all manner of beings, now a caribou, now a bear, now a human being. They are fashioned by a mass of little loops, which form of themselves at a mere kick from one of the dead.

When the shaman has amused himself a while among all the happy dead, he returns to his old village. The guests, who are awaiting him with closed eyes, hear a loud bump at the back of the sleeping place, and then they hear the thong he was tied with come rushing down; this does not fall behind the curtain, but down among all the waiting members of the household. Then the shaman is breathless and tired, and only cries: "Pjuh—he—he—he."

Afterwards he tells of all that he has seen and heard.

Ramón Medina Silva
MESOAMERICA/HUICHOL

For the Huichol, illness is always attributed to a supernatural cause. As such, the *mara'akáme* must go beyond the symptoms of the affliction and must seek out the ultimate source of the calamity in order to undertake a cure. If this is not done, Peter Furst explains, there will surely be a recurrence of the illness, if not death.[10] The shaman then must reenact or retrace precisely the events and circumstances that pertain to the affliction or loss of the individual's life energy. Only in this way is he or she able to retrieve that precious life that is weakened or has slipped out of the body.

The loss of an individual's soul is a constant danger to the Huichol. The soul may wander away from the body during sleep and be captured by a sorcerer or animal spirits, or the *kupúri* (the life essence of the individual) may spill out from the top of the head and be abducted or consumed by malign entities that are under the influence of a sorcerer.[11]

In the case of the loss of soul, if the person is still alive, then the *kupúri* is not necessarily permanently ruptured from the body, and there might still be time to avert death. The shaman must then prepare to look for this delicate essence.

The *kupúri* is envisioned as a tiny energy body, small as a fly or a tick, and making a high-frequency hissing or whistling sound. When searching for the soul, the *mara'akáme* listens intently as he travels the route that the afflicted one had taken. When he hears the whirring sound of the *kupúri,* he communicates to the subtle body by whistling to it, much as the Mazatec shamans do. After he has located the little luminous soul, he contacts Tatéi Niwetúkame, the Goddess of Children, who instructs the *mara'akáme* to lift up the *kupúri* in order to protect it from hungry animals or sorcerers. The shaman then wraps the soul in a wad of cotton. When he returns to side of the patient, he inserts the soul, cotton wad and all, into the top of the patient's head.[12]

Although Ramón did not indicate to Peter Furst whether he physically retraced the patient's route or whether his spirit went in lieu of his body, this narrative has many parallels in other cultures and in other out-of-the-body soul voyages in Huichol culture.[13]

All during the life of the person, the soul lives in the head. It is the soft spot, the crown of the head. It is the same thing, the crown and the life, that which we call *kupúri. Kupúri,* that is the crown, the life of the soul.

The life of the soul of the man lives in the head. And the same for the woman. Because that is where we think. If one receives a blow on the head one cannot think. One becomes unconscious. Because we carry everything in our heads. Because everything that is communicated to us is given through the head. The one that has lost his thinking does not know what to do. He does not know that his life has been lifted from him, from up there in the crown of his head. He does not know what he is doing.

That life force, it is as though it were connected to one by a fine thread. It is like spider's silk, this thread. That is what it is like, like the web of the spider. When one is asleep the life can leave the body. It can leave one and roam about. It roams about in this way and that. But it does not wander far away. But even if it does not wander far away it is possible for a sorcerer, or some animal which has been sent by the sorcerer, to capture that soul. Then the man wakes up ill in the morning. He does not know what happened. Then they call the *mara'akáme.* He goes about searching for that soul to bring it back. If he does not find it, that man dies.

We have many barrancas in our country. When one goes to cut firewood or to clear the brush from the fields for planting, it happens that one can trip over a stone. One falls there and then goes rolling down, down, down.

One falls there and one hits one's head on a rock. Then that *kupúri,* that which is the soft spot on the head, the crown of the head which is the life of the soul, falls to one side. The *kupúri* falls and is frightened.

One lies there and cannot think. One is not dead and one is not asleep. But one lies there, not moving. Then after a while one gets up from there, feeling bad. One feels very ill. Because one does not know what happened. One does not know about one's head. One cannot think properly. One has no thoughts. One is out of one's mind, as one says. One walks off-balance. It is because everything fell.

One gets up after a time but one does not feel well. One walks and walks, one climbs up there, not feeling well. One's head aches. One returns home but one cannot do anything. One lies there, feeling ill, ill.

Then the relatives go to the *mara'akáme*. They say to him, "Well, this and that happened to our relative. This man fell. This one fell in such and such a place."

The *mara'akáme* follows that life,* to see where that life was lost. To see where it is lying, frightened. Where it is in danger. The *mara'akáme* goes walking along that trail, where that man walked. He listens with his arrows, with his plumes. He goes searching, searching. He goes listening, listening, to see where that life was dropped. . . .

The *mara'akáme* goes looking and looking, searching and searching, listening and listening, until he arrives where that man tripped and rolled over into the barranca. Where that man fell down. And even if it is a perilous place full of sharp rocks, full of dangerous animals, with scorpions and snakes, the *mara'akáme* is not afraid. He goes looking down there, looking and looking.

Even if he could fall down and hurt himself, that *mara'akáme* must not be afraid. Even if there are dangerous animals there, he must not be afraid. He goes looking, listening, listening with his arrows, in his heart.

He goes looking to see where he can hear it. Because the life of that man begins to cry as we cry. As one cries when one is lost, lost far away in the barranca where one cannot find his way back. There one says, "Oh, oh, where am I? What am I doing here? What shall I do? Where shall I go? I am lost here."

One cries and one whimpers. That is how the life, the life of the soul of that man, also cries.

And the *mara'akáme*, he listens for all that. He comes closer and it begins to whimper. It hisses and whistles like a soft wind. It hisses softly, in the same manner in which *Tatewarí* hisses when he is first lit, when the wood that is his food is not dry. It hisses and whistles like that.

Then the *mara'akáme* listens to this sound with his feathers, with his arrows. Then he goes there very carefully, very slowly. He may find that life under a branch, or under a leaf, or under a small stone as he walks there on the ground. That life, it is only

*"That life" refers to *kupűri*, the life energy or vital essence that could be described as consciousness, spirit, or soul.

as small as the smallest insect, the smallest tick. That is how small
it is.

So the *mara'akáme* comes close, there where that life is whistling. And he whistles back, very softly, so that the life can hear
him. That is how they call out to one another. Wherever that life
is, that is where the *mara'akáme* goes to look for it.

Then with his feathers, with his power, he calls out to *Tatéi
Niwetúkame.* He calls to her and asks if it is possible to lift him up.
To lift up that life. He calls to *Tatéi Niwetúkame* because she is in
charge of all the children. It is she who put that life into that
person.

Then she says, "Yes, why not? Of course." She tells the
mara'akáme, "Lift him up quickly before some animal comes and
eats him up. Lift him up before some sorcerer comes and takes
him." Because if an animal eats it up, that man dies. Or if a sorcerer
comes to take it, he becomes sick, each day he becomes more sick
and then he dies.

Then the *mara'akáme* takes a little wad of cotton. He has
brought this wad which is like cotton to lift up that life, to protect
it. He lifts the life up with his plumes, carefully, carefully. On the
tip of his feathers, very slowly, very carefully, he lifts it up. It is
very small, that life, tiny, tiny. So small one can hardly see it. He
takes that life and wraps it up in the cotton.

He has a small reed, a piece of bamboo that is hollow. He puts
the *kupūri* inside, he puts that life inside there, in the center. Then
he closes it up with cotton. Each end he closes up in this manner.
Then he places it inside his *takwátsi.* * He puts that life inside the
takwátsi and closes it up. Very carefully he ties it. Then he takes
it away.

Then the *mara'akáme* goes walking, walking. He returns to the
house where the sick man is lying. He brings him into the
xíriki. ** There he lies inside the *xíriki,* that man who has lost his
life. Then the *mara'akáme* takes out the life from the hollow reed.
He puts it on the man. He puts that life on the crown of the head,
there where one had the soft spot. He puts it there, inside the head.

*The *takwátsi,* or shaman's tool kit, is an oblong container woven in the design of
  a rattlesnake.
**The *xíriki* is the temple.

And that little wad of cotton, that which contains the life, that also goes inside. The cotton disappears inside the head with that life. And that man comes back to life again.

Petaġa Yuha Mani
NORTH AMERICA/SIOUX

Petaġa Yuha Mani, He Walks with Coals of Fire, is a Sioux medicine man. Arthur Amiotte, who apprenticed with Petaġa, describes him:

> His face is noble, deep-lined with age and bold with wisdom tempered with hard work, weather and uncompromising devotion to living out his vision.
>
> His large rough hands tell the story of a man whose youth was spent in labor yet who in his time has touched and guided saint and sinner to enlightenment with gentle and self-sacrificing effacement."[14]

Petaġa Yuha Mani, also known as Pete Catches, was chosen for his work by the Thunder Beings: "I am compelled to live this way that is not of my own choosing, because they [the Thunder Beings] chose me. . . . My whole life is to do the bidding of the Thunder Beings and of my people and to pay heed to what the Grandfathers tell me."[15]

His flesh pierced in thanks and devotion to the Sun, Petaġa Yuha Mani has danced the traditional Sioux Sun Dance many times. He has taught, guided, and healed his people. And as a person who recognizes the source of his body and spirit, he is moving into a state of deep absorption with the gentleness and wildness of the solitudes, the place of the Ancient Ones.[16]

I live in an age that has passed. I live as though it is fifty years ago, a hundred years ago. I like it that way. I want to live as humbly, as close to the earth as I can. Close to the plants, the weeds, the flowers that I use for medicine. The Great Spirit has seen to it that man can survive in this way, can live as he is meant to live. So my wife and I are dwelling in a little cabin—no electricity, no tap water, no plumbing, no road. This is what we want.

This simple log cabin knows peace. That's how we want to be for the rest of our lives. I want to exist apart from the modern world, get out, way out, in the sticks, and live much closer to nature, even closer than I am doing now.

I don't even want to be called a medicine man, just a healing man because this is what I am made for. I don't ask for anything. A white doctor has a fee; a priest has a fee. I have no fee. A man goes away from me healed. That is my reward. Sometimes I do not have the power; it makes me sad. When I have the power, then I am happy. Some men think of money, how to get it. That never comes into my mind.

We live off nature, my wife and I; we hardly need anything. We will somehow live. The Great Spirit made the flowers, the streams, the pines, the cedars; he takes care of them. He lets a breeze go through there, makes them breathe it, waters them, makes them grow. Even the one that is down in the crags, in the rocks. He tends to that, too. He takes care of me, waters me, feeds me, makes me live with the plants and animals as one of them. This is how I wish to remain—an Indian—all the days of my life. This does not mean that I want to shut myself off. Somehow many people find their way to my cabin. I like that. I want to be in communication, reach out to people everywhere, impart a little of our Indian way, the spirit's way, to them.

At the same time, I want to withdraw farther and farther away from everything, to live like the ancient ones. On the highway you sometimes see a full-blooded Indian thumbing a ride. I never do that. When I walk the road, I expect to walk the whole way. That is deep down in me, a kind of pride. Someday I'll move my cabin still farther into the hills, maybe do without a cabin altogether, become part of the woods. There the spirit still has something for us to discover: an herb, a sprig, a flower, a very small flower, maybe. You can spend a long time in its contemplation, thinking about it. Not a rose, yellow, white, artificial, big. I hear they are breeding black roses. That's not natural. These things are against nature. They make us weak. I abhor them.

So as I get older, I burrow more and more into the hills. The Great Spirit made them for us, for me. I want to blend with them, shrink into them, and finally, disappear in them. As my brother

Lame Deer has said, all of nature is in us, all of us is in nature. That is as it should be.

Thunder Cloud
NORTH AMERICA/WINNEBAGO

A great healer and an adept poisoner, Thunder Cloud knew well the ways of the ancestors. With startling clarity, he was able to recall his past lives, the "in-between-life-time" states, and his experiences of his own births. His people loved and revered this holiest and most powerful of shamans. And they feared him, too, because of his reputation as a poisoner and his remarkable abilities as a healer.

He was described by his brother-in-law, Crashing Thunder, as a good and virtuous man, disliking no one. He never stole or fought. He adhered strictly to the duties he was to perform as a member of the sacred Medicine Rite. Crashing Thunder reports that "after reaching a ripe old age, . . ." [Thunder Cloud] died. Properly and humbly he had progressed along the Road of the Sacred Rite. That now was finished. Up above, where all go who have heeded the injunctions of the Rite he went. There in his new home, he lived and there he married.

"After living there for some time, he prepared to come back to earth. Once a month he fasted and all the different spirits whom Earthmaker had created, gave him their blessings. And so, in the course of time, he was born again, born as a human being. Here on this earth he fasted again and the spirits above, who dwelt where Earthmaker sits all bestowed their blessing upon him. Thus he became a holy man, a shaman, in fact the reincarnation of the North-Spirit."[17]

A traditionalist, Thunder Cloud was a member of the Medicine Dance Secret Society. Its members were said to possess the knowledge of killing one another and then restoring each other to life. This ritual of death and rebirth increased the power of those who went through it and gave them special knowledge of death. Among the Winnebago, only prominent people and members of the Medicine Dance could be reincarnated. Thunder Cloud's vivid recollection of his deaths and afterlife bespeaks of his privileged status in this group.[18]

I once lived with a small group of Indians numbering about twenty camps. When I had grown up to be a lad, although still not large enough to handle a gun, a war-party attacked us and killed us all. I did not know, however, that I had been killed. I thought that I was running about as usual until I saw a heap of bodies on the ground and mine among them. No one was there to bury us, so there we lay and rotted.

My ghost was taken to the place where the sun sets. There I lived with an old couple. The land of the spirits is an excellent place and the people have the best of times. If you desire to go anywhere all that you have to do is to wish yourself there and you reach it. While there I thought I would like to come to the earth again so the old man with whom I was staying said to me, "My son, did you not speak about wanting to go to the earth again?" I had as a matter of fact only thought of it yet he knew what I wanted. Then he said to me, "You can go but you must ask our chief first." Then I went and told the chief of the village of my desire, and he said to me, "You may go and obtain your revenge upon the people who killed your relatives."

Then I was brought down to earth. I did not enter a woman's womb but I was taken into a room. There I remained conscious at all times. One day I heard the noise of little children so I thought I would go outside. Then it seemed to me that I was going through a door but I was really being born again from a woman's womb. As I walked out I was struck by a sudden gust of cold air and I began to cry.

At the place where I was brought up I was taught to fast a great deal. Afterwards I did nothing but go to war and I certainly took my revenge for my own death and that of my relatives, thus justifying the purpose for which I had come to this earth again.

There I lived until I died of old age. All at once my bones became unjointed, my ribs fell in and I died a second time. I felt no more pain at death then that I had felt the first time.

This time I was buried in the manner used then. I was wrapped in a blanket and laid in the grave. Sticks were placed in the grave first. There I rotted. I watched the people as they buried me.

As I was lying there some one said to me, "Come, let us go away." So then we went toward the land of the setting sun. There we came to a village where we met all the dead. I was told that I would have to stop there for four nights, but, in reality, I stayed there four years. The people enjoy themselves here. They have all sorts of dances of a lively kind. From that place we went up to where Earthmaker lives and I saw him and talked to him, face to face, even as I am talking to you now. I saw the spirits too and, indeed, I was like one of them.

Thence I came to this earth for the third time and here I am. I am going through the same that I knew before.

* * *

At the very beginning those above taught me the following. All the various spirits who live up above in the clouds, in a doctor's village, came after me and instructed me in what I was to do. They taught me and told me the following. "Here let us try it," they said to me. There in the middle of the lodge lay a rotten log, almost entirely covered with weeds. They tried to make me treat this log. I breathed upon it and all those who were in this spirit lodge also breathed upon it. Then for the second time I breathed upon it and they with me. Then for the third and the fourth time I did it. After the fourth time the rotten log arose and walked away. Then the spirits said to me, "Human being, very holy indeed are you."

There from the middle of the ocean, from the shaman's village, they came after me. They blessed me, all the spirits in the middle of the ocean. They made me try my power. As many waves as exist, all of them as large as the ocean, upon these they asked me to blow; and as I blew upon them everything became as quiet as the water in a small saucer. So they became. Then I blew for the third time and it was the same. The fourth time the spirits made the ocean very choppy and the waves were piled, one upon the other. Then they told me to blow again and show my power. I blew, and the ocean, mighty indeed as it was, became very quiet again. "Now this, human being, is what you will have to do," they said to me. "Not anything will there be that you cannot accomplish. Whatever be the illness a person may have, you will be able to cure him."

All the spirits on the earth blessed me. "If any human being who is suffering from pain, makes an offering of tobacco to you, then whatever you demand, that we will do for you," the spirits told me.

Now at Blue Clay Bank (St. Paul) there lives one who is a dancing grizzly-bear spirit. Whenever I am in great trouble I was to pour tobacco, as much as I thought necessary, and he would help me. This grizzly bear gave me songs and the power of beholding a holy thing; he gave me his claws, claws that are holy. Then the grizzly bear danced and performed while he danced. He tore his abdomen open and, making himself holy, healed himself again. This he repeated. One grizzly bear shot claws at the other and the wounded one became badly choked with blood. Then both made themselves holy again and cured themselves. They had a front paw disappear in the earth and after a while pulled out a prairie turnip. Finally they grabbed hold of a small plum tree, breathed upon it and shook it, and many plums began to fall.

The Prayers to the Spirits

Here, O Fire, is the tobacco for you. You promised that if I offered you some, you would grant me whatever request I made. Now I am placing tobacco on your head as you told me to do when I fasted for four days and you blessed me. I am sending you the plea of a human being who is ill. He wishes to live. This tobacco is for you and I pray that the one who is ill be restored to health within four days.

To you too, O Buffalo, I offer tobacco. A person is ill and is offering tobacco to you and asking you to restore him to health. So add that power which I obtained from you at the time I fasted for six days and you sent your spirits after me. They took me to your lodge which lies in the center of the earth and which is absolutely white. There you blessed me, you Buffaloes of four different colors. Those blessings that you bestowed upon me then, I am now in need of. The power of breathing with which you blessed me, I am now in need of. Add your power to mine as you promised.

To you, Grizzly Bear, I also offer tobacco. At a place called Pointed Hill there lives a spirit who is in charge of a ceremonial lodge, and to this all the other grizzly bears belong. You all blessed me and you said that I would be able to kill whomsoever I wished and that I would be able to restore any person to life. Now I have a chance to enable a person to live and I wish to aid him. So here is some tobacco for you. You took my spirit to your home after I had fasted for ten days and you blessed me there. The powers with which you blessed me there I ask of you now. Here is some tobacco that the people are offering you, grandfathers.

To you, O Chief of the Eels, you who live in the center of the ocean, I offer tobacco. You blessed me after I had fasted for eight days. With your power of breathing and with your inexhaustible supply of water, you blessed me. You told me that I could use my blessing whenever I tried to cure a patient; you told me that I could use the water of the ocean and you blessed me with all the things that are in the water. A person has come to me and asked me for life. As I wish him to live I am addressing you. When I spit upon the patient may the power of my saliva be the same as yours. Therefore do I offer you tobacco. Here it is.

To you, O Turtle, you who are in charge of a shaman's lodge, you who blessed me after I had fasted for seven days, you who carried my spirit to your home, to the home of birds of prey, to you I offer tobacco. You blessed me and you told me that should, at any time, human beings suffer from pain I would be able to drive it out of them. You gave me the name of *He-who-drives-out-pain*. Now I have before me a patient with a bad pain and I wish to drive it out of him. This the spirit told me I would have the power to do, when they blessed me before I was reborn. Here is tobacco.

To you, O Rattlesnake, you who are perfectly white, you who are in charge of the snake lodge, to you I pray. You blessed me with rattles to wrap around my gourd; you told me after I had fasted for four days that you would help me. You said that I would never fail in anything I attempted. So now when I offer you tobacco and shake my gourd, may my patient live and may life be opened out before him. That is what you promised to me, grandfather.

O Night Spirits, you also, I greet. You blessed me after I had fasted for nine days. You took my spirit to your village lying in the east, and there you gave me your flutes. You told me they were holy. My flute likewise you made holy. For your flutes I now ask you, since you know that I am speaking the truth. A sick person has come to me and has asked me to cure him. I want him to live and so I am speaking to you. You promised to accept my tobacco at all times. Here it is.

To you, too, O Disease-Giver, I offer tobacco. After I had fasted for two days you informed me that you were the one who gave disease; that if I desired to heal any one it would be easy to do so if I were blessed by you. So, Disease-Giver, I am offering tobacco to you and I ask that this sick person who has come to me, be restored to health again.

To you, O Sun, I offer tobacco. Here it is. You blessed me after I had fasted for five days and you told me you would come to my aid whenever I had something difficult to do. Now, some one is here who has pleaded for life. He has brought good offerings of tobacco to me, because he knows that you have blessed me.

To you, grandmother Earth, I also offer tobacco. You blessed me and promised to help me whenever I needed you. You said that I could use all the best herbs that grow upon you, and that I would always be able to effect cures with them. I beseech you for those herbs now and I ask you to help me to cure this sick man.

Dick Mahwee
NORTH AMERICA/PAVIOTSO

Like many Paviotso shamans, Dick Mahwee did not acquire his power until he was fifty years old. As a young boy, this future shaman from Pyramid Lake, Nevada, had had dreams about healing others, but he did not take these signs seriously. In his maturity, he decided independently to go to a sacred cave in order to seek the power that can come to curers.

The shaman Mahwee has said that one who is ready for power must go alone to a cave that is known to be the locus for the acquisition of knowledge. He may take with him enough food for a midnight and a morning meal. Upon entering the cave, and with little ceremony, the aspirant asks simply and directly for the particular kind of power that he desires. He then makes preparations to spend the night. Power comes only if the request is sincere and the mind is focused on the desire.

Mahwee's power to heal came from the primordial Spirit of the Night. He also had access to the power of the Sun, the spirits of Eagle and Crow, and the ghost of a Pit River Indian. The nocturnal curing ceremonies that he and other Paviotso shamans undertook occurred only in the blackness of the night, for only then does the "second night," the invisible night of the universe of spirits, appear to the shaman.

An adept trancer, Mahwee's curing songs came to him through the eagle feathers attached to the wand that he planted in the ground next to the head of the sick one. Because of his ability to enter profound trance states and travel in the world of the spirits, Dick Mahwee was considered to be a powerful shaman-curer.[19]

When I was a young man I had dreams in which I doctored people. I did not take those dreams seriously. My uncle was an Indian doctor. He knew what was coming to me. He told me to be careful in talking, not to speak harshly [in order not to offend the supernatural spirits]. I did not become a doctor from these dreams. Finally, I decided to go to the cave near Dayton. I was about fifty then. My uncle did not tell me to go there. I just decided to do this myself.

I went into the cave in the evening. As soon as I got inside, I prayed and asked for power to doctor sickness. I said, "My people are sick. I want to save them. I want to keep them well. You can help me make them well. I want you to help me to save them. When they have died give me power to bring them back [return the lost soul]." I said this to the spirit in the cave. It is not a person. It comes along with the darkness. This is a prayer to the night.

Then I tried to go to sleep. It was hard to sleep there. I heard all kinds of noises. I could hear all the animals. There were bears, mountain lions, deer, and other animals. They were all in caves in the mountain. After I went to sleep I could hear people at a doctoring. They were down at the foot of the mountain. I could hear their voices and the songs. Then I heard the patient groan. A doctor was singing and doctoring for him. A woman with a sage-brush shoot in her hand danced. She moved around the fire jumping at every step. Each time she jumped she said, "hə', hə', hə'." Then the shaman sprinkled water on the patient with sage-brush. The singing and dancing went on for a long time. Then the singing stopped. The patient had died and the people began to cry.

After a while the rock where I was sleeping began to crack like breaking ice. A man appeared in the crack. He was tall and thin.

He had the tail-feather of an eagle in his hand. He said to me, "You are here. You have said the right words. You must do as I tell you. Do that or you will have a hard time. When you doctor, you must follow the instructions that the animals give you. They will tell you how to cure the sickness. I have this feather in my hand. You must get feathers like it. You are also to find the things that go with it. Get dark beads. Put them on the quills of the feathers and tie a strip of buckskin to the quills. Also get a hoof of a deer, and down from the eagle. With these you can go to people to cure them. These are your weapons against sickness. You must get three rolls of tobacco. You can use them to tell your patients what made them sick and then you can cure them. The tobacco will also help you if you are choked with clots of saliva when you suck out the disease. With this you are beginning to be a doctor. You will get your songs when you doctor. The songs are now in a straight line [ready for use]. Bathe in the water at the foot of the cliff and paint yourself with i·bi [white paint]."

Then I woke up. It was daylight. I looked around but I could not see anyone. The man was gone and there was no sign of the animals or the people who had been singing and doctoring. Then I did as the spirit had ordered and waited to become a doctor. In about six years I had received enough instructions to begin to cure.

* * *

The Indian doctor gets his power from the spirit of the night. This spirit is everywhere. It has no name. There is no word for it. The Indians hold this spirit so sacred that they are afraid if they had a name for it the spirit would be angry. No one has ever dared give it a name.

Eagle and owl do not give a shaman power. They are just messengers that bring instructions from the spirit of the night. Some doctors have water-babies for their messengers. They are called when the shaman doctors. They do not give him his power; they only carry messages from the spirit of the night. When the shaman is treating a patient he calls for the water-babies and they bring him instructions from the spirit.

At the time that the spirit of the night gives power for doctoring, it tells the shaman to ask for help from the water-babies, eagle, owl, deer, antelope, bear or some other bird or animal.

When shamans get power it always comes from the night.

They are told to doctor only at night. This power has nothing to do with the moon or stars. I knew one woman who used the sun, moon, and stars for her power. I saw her fill her pipe and just as the sun came up she puffed and started to smoke. I saw her do this several times. I watched her closely but she did not use matches. Her power lighted her pipe.

* * *

I smoke before I go into the trance. While I am in the trance no one makes any noise. I go out to see what will happen to the patient. When I see a whirlwind I know that it caused the sickness. If I see the patient walking on grass and flowers it means that he will get well; he will soon be up and walking. When I see the patient among fresh flowers and he picks them it means that he will recover. If the flowers are withered or look as if the frost had killed them, I know that the patient will die. Sometimes in a trance I see the patient walking on the ground. If he leaves footprints I know that he will live, but if there are no tracks, I cannot cure him.

When I am coming back from the trance I sing. I sing louder and louder until I am completely conscious. Then the men lift me to my feet and I go on with the doctoring.

Isaac Tens
NORTH AMERICA/GITKSAN

When Isaac Tens, a Gitksan Indian, was thirty years old, he found himself repeatedly falling into deep and disturbing trances. Terrifying visions appeared to him on these occasions: visions of great, fierce animal spirits; tall, serpentlike trees chasing him; flies crawling over his face, and a noisy crowd pursuing him. Once, he felt himself drifting in a whirlpool; another time, his very flesh seemed to boil. Things appeared and disappeared in a frightening fashion. Frequently, he awakened from the trances to discover that he was injured and bleeding.

Later, songs began to force their way out of him. Realizing at last that he was to become a shaman, he withdrew into semisolitude for a year as more songs awakened within him. At the end of this period, his father called other medicine men to his son's aid in order that they might "strengthen" him for the next phase of his initiatory journey.

Another year was spent fasting and dreaming. All the while, the middle-aged apprentice was training with the *halaait* doctors. After these years of preparation, he was finally ready to attempt a curing. This he did so successfully that his fame quickly spread throughout the area.

Medicine men such as Tens usually own between fifteen and twenty songs. However, Tens himself owned three groups of songs, totaling twenty-three. These chants were the heart of healing séances, emerging only after the shaman had fallen into a trance.

When Marius Barbeau collected this astonishing narrative in 1920, the old medicine man had abandoned his profession and converted to Christianity.[20]

Thirty years after my birth was the time when I began to be a *swanassu* (medicine-man). I went up into the hills to get firewood. While I was cutting up the wood into lengths, it grew dark towards the evening. Before I had finished my last stack of wood, a loud noise broke out over me, ch^u_____, and a large owl appeared to me. The owl took hold of me, caught my face, and tried to lift me up. I lost consciousness. As soon as I came back to my senses I realized that I had fallen into the snow. My head was coated with ice, and some blood was running out of my mouth.

I stood up and went down the trail, walking very fast, with some wood packed on my back. On my way, the trees seemed to shake and to lean over me; tall trees were crawling after me, as if they had been snakes. I could see them. Before I arrived at my father's home, I told my folk what had happened to me, as soon as I walked in. I was very cold and warmed myself before going to bed. There I fell into a sort of trance. It seems that two *halaaits* (medicine-men) were working over me to bring me back to health. But it is now all vague in my memory. When I woke up and opened my eyes, I thought that flies covered my face completely. I looked down, and instead of being on firm ground, I felt that I was drifting in a huge whirlpool. My heart was thumping fast.

The medicine-men working over me were Kceraw'inerh (*Kceraw'inerhlorhs:* the sun shines out, in the morning) of the household of Lutkudzius, Gyedemraldo, and Meeky. While I was in a trance, one of them told me that the time had arrived for me to become a *halaait* like them. But I did not agree, so I took no notice of the advice. The affair passed away as it had come, without results.

Another time, I went to my hunting grounds on the other side of the river here, opposite Temlarham (the Good-land-of-yore), at the foot of Rocherdéboulé. After I reached there, I caught two fishers in my traps, took their pelts, and threw the flesh and bones away. Farther along I looked for a bear's den amid the tall trees. As I glanced upwards, I saw an owl, at the top of a high cedar. I shot it, and it fell down in the bushes close to me. When I went to pick it up, it had disappeared. Not a feather was left; this seemed very strange. I walked down to the river, crossed over the ice, and returned to the village at Gitenmaks. Upon arriving at my fishing station on the point, I heard the noise of a crowd of people around the smoke-house, as if I were being chased away, pursued. I dared not look behind me. Then I wheeled round and looked back. There was no one in sight, only trees. A trance came over me once more, and I fell down, unconscious. When I came to, my head was buried in a snowbank. I got up and walked on the ice up the river to the village. There I met my father who had just come out to look for me, for he had missed me. We went back together to my house. Then my heart started to beat fast, and I began to tremble, just as had happened a while before, when the *halaaits* were trying to fix me up. My flesh seemed to be boiling, and I could hear S^u_____. My body was quivering. While I remained in this state, I began to sing. A chant was coming out of me without my being able to do anything to stop it. Many things appeared to me presently: huge birds and other animals. They were calling me. I saw a *meskyawawderh* (a kind of bird) and a *mesqagweeuk* (bullhead fish). These were visible only to me, not to the others in my house. Such visions happen when a man is about to become a *halaait;* they occur of their own accord. The songs force themselves out complete without any attempt to compose them. But I learned and memorized these songs by repeating them.

During the following year I composed more songs and devoted all my time to my new experience, without doing any other work. I would lie down in my father's house, for I felt sick. Four people looked after me all the time in order to hear me sing my new songs, and they were not satisfied until they had learned them too.

My attendants were Kaldirhgyet (Split Person), Andawlerhsemhlorhs pistaei (The Grouse-warms-itself-in-the-sun), Waral-sawal (Crazy or idiot, a *narhnorh* or spirit), and 'ArhkawdzemTset-sauts (the Tsetsaut-is-thoughtless, also a *narhnorh*). They were cousins of mine; all four were, like me, members of the Wolf *(Larhkibu)* clan. All the time they kept watching over me.

One day a year later, my father summoned the *halaaits* in the village to come down and act over me. The first thing they did was to *sedarhgyætu* (to strengthen me), that is, they raised me from my couch and walked me round the room. Then I was really strengthened. To pay for their services my father distributed a great amount of property to all those who had assembled there to witness the event.

That was the time when I became a *swanassu* (medicine-man). This was the fasting period, when one aspires to become a *halaait*. I had to have dreams before being able to act. This period lasted a year, in seclusion at my father's house, out of touch with other folk excepting the four attendants.

The instructions which the medicine-men gave me were: "We look at the patient and diagnose his ailment. Sometimes, it is a bad song within him or her, sometimes a *narhnorh* (a spirit)."

When later I attended a patient for the first time, on my own, I had a new vision. The *halaait* doctors were still training me, teaching me. For this reason I was invited to all the *swanassu* activities. As soon as I was able to go out by myself, I began to diagnose the cases by dreaming (*wawq:* sleeping, or *ksewawq:* dreaming), with the help of my instructors. I acquired charms, that is, things I would dream of: the *Hogwest* (snare for the bear), *Hlorhs* (the Moon), and *Angohawtu* (Sweat-house). And besides, I had also dreamed of charms: the Mink *(nes'in),* the Otter *(watserh),* and Canoe *('mal).*

I acquired charms when I attended a patient. I used a charm *(aatirh)* and placed it over me first, then over the body of the person from whom I was to extract the disease or illness. It was never an actual object, but only one that had appeared in a dream. In a dream I once had over the hills, I saw a canoe *('mal).* Many times it appeared to me in my dreams. The canoe sometimes was floating on the water, sometimes on the clouds. When any trouble occurred anywhere, I was able to see my canoe in visions.

My first patient was a woman, the wife of chief Gitemraldaw.

Her full name was Niskyaw-romral'awstlegye'ns (Small-wooden-box-to-gather-berries; the grizzly has a bladder like it). She was seriously ill, had been for a long time, and she had been treated before by various *halaaits* in turn, but without avail. I was called in to see whether I could undertake to do something for her. So I went into her house and instructed the people there to light a fire first. As I began to sing over her, many people around me were hitting sticks on boards and beating skin drums for me. My canoe came to me in a dream, and there were many people sitting in it. The canoe itself was the Otter *(watserh)*. The woman whom I was doctoring sat with the others inside this Otter canoe. By that time, about twenty other *halaaits* were present in the house. To them I explained what my vision was, and asked, "What shall I do? There the woman is sitting in the canoe, and the canoe is the Otter."

They answered, "Try to pull her out."

I told them, "Spread the fire out, into two parts, and make a pathway between them." I walked up and down this path four times, while the other *halaaits* kept singing until they were very tired. Then I went over to the couch on which the sick woman was lying. There was a great upheaval in the singing and the clapping of drums and the sticks on the boards. I placed my hand on her stomach and moved round her couch, all the while trying to draw the canoe out of her. I managed to pull it up very close to the surface of her chest. I grasped it, drew it out, and put it in my own bosom. This I did.

Two days later, the woman rose out of bed; she was cured. My prestige as a *halaait* gained greatly. This, because the others had failed to accomplish anything with her, and I had succeeded. More demands came to me from other parts, as far as the village of Gitsegyukla. Everything usually went well in my work. The fees for doctoring might be ten blankets, prepaid, for each patient, or it might be as little as one blanket. But if the doctored person died afterwards, the blankets were returned. The fees depended upon the wealth of the family calling for services, also upon the anxiety of the relatives of the sick person who wanted to urge the doctor to do his utmost. Should a *halaait* or *swanassu* refuse to doctor a patient, he might be suspected of being himself the cause of the sickness, or of the death should it occur. In this eventuality, the relatives would seek revenge and kill the one suspected. This was the hard law of the country. But the doctors were not known to decline any invitation to serve the people in need.

Swanassu Songs

First song. . . . The spirit Salmon weakens when I do. . . .

. . . The large village shall be cured when my Salmon spirit floats in.

. . . The chief of the Salmon is floating in the canyon underneath me.

. . . The She Robin has flown away with me.

This cannot be explained rationally because it is a vision, and visions are not always intelligible. In my vision I dreamt that I was very sick, and my spirit became sick like me; it was like a human being but had no name. In the same dream I saw that there had been a heavy run of salmon headed by a large Salmon. This would bring relief to the people who were starving. The huge Salmon appeared to me in my vision, although he was way down deep in the canyon. The She Robin came to me, and she lifted me out of my sickness. That is how I was cured.

Second song. Wahawhala . . . iyaw yaw'ehehe. (Burthen):

. . . The Grizzly shall go a long way from here behind the sky.

Singing this, the actual words were not uttered, only the meaningless syllables of the burthen. But their meaning was kept in the thoughts, although they were not considered a secret.

. . . The *halaait* . . . in his vision sees the fires of the common people through the ground.

When getting ready for the songs, I fell into a trance and saw a vast fine territory. In the middle of it a house stood. I stepped into it, and I beheld my uncle Tsigwee who had been a medicineman *(halaait)*. He had died several years before. Then another uncle appeared—Gukswawtu. Both of them had been equally famous in their day. The songs above are those I heard them sing. While they were singing, the Grizzly ran through the door, and went right round. Then he rose into the air behind the clouds, describing a circle, and came back to the house. Each of my uncles took a rattle and placed it into one of my hands. That is why I always use two rattles in my performances. In my vision I beheld many fires burning under the house. As soon as I walked out of the house, my trance ended. From then on I sang those chants just as I had learned them in my vision.

Third song:

. . . My feet are held fast in the large spring.

. . . It is the mussel-shell that is holding my feet.

In the vision for this chant, I dreamt of a lake or a large pool, and I put my feet into it. I sank down, way over my knees, and I was unable to get out.

Fourth song: heyuwaw haye . . . hayawa'nigwawhs . . . *eyiwaw!* (Exclamation):

. . . The bee-hives' spirit stings my body.

. . . Grandmother is making me grow, in my vision.

It is as if she were looking after a small boy. In my vision, I went round in a strange land which cannot be described. There I saw huge bee-hives, out of which the bees darted and stung me all over my body.

Fifth song:

. . . The mountains were talking to each other, as I was walking about.

. . . I went into the river where it makes the noise of the canyon.

. . . I walk about on my trail down a steep incline.

In my vision of this part, I was standing on the brink of the canyon, and I could not draw away from its edge, because behind me stood the steep mountain. A great noise was rising out of the canyon. I fell into the water, but I landed in the canoe that was there. I drifted in it further; then it rose with me into the mountain. Two mountain peaks stood there. I drifted between them. These peaks made a noise like bells, and I knew that they were speaking to each other. Now I found myself on a steep incline on the side of one of the mountains. I made a trail down for myself to the bottom.

Sixth song:

. . . Whose canoe is it where I stand with a stranger?

. . . It floats about among the whirlpools.

In my vision, I was taken in my canoe to many places, among the trees where I was left; but they were receding from under my canoe. My canoe kept floating about, on land or in the water.

When I am called to treat a patient, I go into something like a trance, and I compose a song, or I revive one for the occasion.

As a last resort, I would use my charms *(hogwest)*, only when in great difficulties. Then I put on a bear robe, I use a bear-claw head-dress, and I pass a snare *(hogwest)* round my neck. I suspend myself by the neck with it. That is, I would not actually hang by it, but I would be tied by this collar, and the cord would be held in hands by the people present. We would fall down side by side. And I would throw my weight on my neck. Four *halaaits* together are in action, one at each corner. The chief *halaait* would take water and throw it over my head. Then the four of us stand over the pool of water and hold a consultation among ourselves; this is called *silin*. While this happens, another *halaait* performs over the patient. After we have stepped over the pool of water, we cover ourselves up with a mat. If the patient is very weak, the chief doctor captures his spirit into his hands and blows quietly on it to give it more breath. If weaker still, the *halaait* takes a hot stone from the fire-place and holds the spirit over it. Perhaps a little fat is put on the hot stone to melt. The hands turn from one side to the other, thus feeding the sick spirit. After this is done, the *halaait* sits the spirit, then places it on the patient's head.

When a *halaait* is himself the patient, the treatment is called "Returning-the-catch" or "Returning-the-man" *(guksmugu'e)*, or "Causing-the-man-to-recover." A cedar collar *(luirh)* is placed around the neck of the sick medicine-man. All the other doctors get together and intone their chants. In the middle of their songs, they raise the sick man, pulling him by the *luirh* (red cedar-bark collar). In time the patient may be able himself to sing; that is, after he has fully recovered. All the medicine-men eventually die a very hard death, because they are not truly human. They are bad spirits.

Now I use a different method in treating my patients. I employ nothing but prayers which I have learned at the church. I pray like the minister—the Lord's Prayer. It has been translated into Gitksan by the Rev. Mr. Price of Kitwanga. I have entirely given up the practice of the *halaait*. My two children became sick—Philip *(Piyawsu)* and Mary *(Tsigumnæq)*. The folk around here agitated me and urged me to use the *halaait* over them. They blamed me for my refusal and declared that they would consider me responsible for their deaths. So I tried to revive one of my old charms—the Sun or the Moon *(hlorhs)*. But my body was altogether different from what it used to be. I was sure that I had lost my powers as a *swanassu*. I was unable to act on my children. Being too weak, I had to quit. Then I spent $50 on medicine-men *(halaaits)* to assist me in my trial. But like me they could do nothing. My charms were of no use to them. So I have finally trusted my children to the treatment of the white man's doctor. One of the two is still sick at the hospital. But the other has recovered.

7 Singing into Life

The Ancient Ones or Anasazi when they departed from their cliff shelters some 600 years ago left behind awesome friezes on the rock walls of Utah's Barrier Canyon. The walls of this sanctuary are covered with fantastic anthropomorphic wizard creatures, one of which is redrawn here from an artist's rendering. *(From: Douglas Mazonowicz, Voices from the Stone Age, New York, Thomas Y. Crowell, 1974, p. 181.)*

María Sabina

On the night of July 12, 1958, María Sabina performed a *velada* (night vigil) on behalf of Pefecto José Garcia, a seventeen-year-old who was seriously ill. Pefecto had been brought to the shaman by R. Gordon Wasson, Thomas Davis, and Allan Richardson in order that they might fully record an authentic healing ritual involving the sacred psilocybin mushroom. The chanting and interaction that occurred in the course of the mushroom ceremony covered more than 100 pages of translated text. This has been edited into a continuous chant, greatly abbreviated and without the comments of the others assisting in the ceremony. The complete text can be found in R. G. Wasson's monumental work *María Sabina and Her Mazatec Velada.*[1]

Two hundred years of Catholicism have left a deep imprint on this archaic Mesoamerican sacred canticle form. The Mazatec cosmos and Christian symbolism are here forged into a single numinous metaphor of many levels. The two traditions do not vie for supremacy. Those who have ingested the sacred mushrooms must have understood the fundamental unity that underlies both religious traditions. The mushrooms were "known to the ancient Meso-Americans as the Flesh of God," wrote Henry Munn, "called by her [María Sabina's] people, the blood of Christ. Through their miraculous mountains of light and rain, the Indians say that Christ once walked—it is a transformation of the legend of Quetzalcoatl—and from where dropped his blood, the essence of his life, from there the holy mushrooms grew, the awakeners of the spirit, the food of the luminous one."[2]

And it is from within this divine medicinal food that the ecstatic language of the chant emerges. It is said that the mushrooms speak. The shaman is merely the vehicle for the Word. Furthermore, the mushroom is the embodiment of many who are, at the same time, the mushroom. Christ, his spittle, his blood, bishops, nuns, clowns, dwarfs, little children, children of the morning star, children of the moon: "Thirteen superior whirlwinds. Thirteen whirlwinds of the atmosphere. Thirteen clown, says. Thirteen personalities, says. Thirteen white lights, says. Thirteen mountains of point, says. Thirteen old hawks, says, thirteen white hawks, says. Thirteen personalities, says. Thirteen mountains, says. Thirteen clowns, says. Thirteen peaks, says. Thirteen stars of the morning."[3] All, all are the mushroom, the embodiment of Logos.

It is the mushroom that knows the source of Pefecto's illness, and it is the mushroom that announces his fate. The mushroom sings out, "There's no cure now." "It's true, [the mushroom] says."[4] There is nothing to be done. Some six weeks later, Pefecto dies.

> *Daughter of Mary am I,*
> *Humble woman am I,*
> *Poor woman am I,*
> *Humble woman am I,*
> *Clean woman am I,*
> *Woman of clean spirit am I,*
> *Woman of good spirit am I,*
> *Woman of the morning am I,*
> *Woman of the day am I,*
> *Woman of 13* breeches am I,*
> *Woman of 13 shirts am I,*
> *Woman of clean spirit am I,*

*THE COWANS: The word *te³jan²* is the number 13, the number of *brujeria* or witchcraft, the number that brings *buena suerte,* good luck or power, according to María Sabina. In contrast, the number 53 means *mala suerte,* bad luck, and is used by another class of witchdoctors who work to bring about harm as well as good. María Sabina, as a shaman, only works to do good, she says.

RGW: Both Borhegyi and Weitlaner attributed importance to this reference to 13. Borhegyi pointed out that the ancient Middle American pantheon consisted of 13 abodes in the Heaven ruled by thirteen gods. Weitlaner saw in this reference to thirteen that the ancient calendar system, called in Nahuatl the *tonapohualli,* still either functions among the Mazatec soothsayers or figures at least subconsciously in the minds of some *curanderas.* Weitlaner's note continues: "The association of trousers and shirts with 13 is not clear to me. Consulting with Dr. Alfonso Caso, we agreed that the number 13 brings good luck. More so is the number 52 ($= 4 \times 13$), important in the Aztec calendar; 53, the following number, would by contrast or in opposition to 52, be an unfavorable number. . . . The calendar enjoyed magical prestige among Mesoamerican Indians.

RGW: Here María Sabina begins to present her "credentials" to the deity. This continues intermittently and repetitiously for a long time. (Mr. López . . . refers to a similar practice in the early 17th century as the *autopresentación.*)

Woman of good spirit am I,
Yes, Jesus Christ, Father Jesus Christ,
Hail, most holy Mary, hail Mary
Hail, most holy Mary, oh Jesus Christ,
Hail, Mary, oh Jesus
Woman who waits am I,
Woman who divines am I,
Oh, Jesus Christ, hail Mary,
Well thus I am known. . . .
Thus I am known, for the son of God says so, yes
You, Christ . . . . . Christ says.

* * *

Father who art in heaven
For I am a daughter of Christ
Jesus. . . . . .
Woman of justice, am I,
Woman of law, am I,
God knows me,
The saints know me.
Woman of the Southern Cross am I,
Woman of the first star am I,
Woman of the Star of God am I,
For I go up to the sky [heaven].
Woman of the big star am I,
Woman of the Southern Cross star am I,
Jesus. . . . .
I am a daughter of Christ, a daughter of Mary
Lawyer woman am I, *

*RGW: Here and later María Sabina refers to herself as a lawyer woman, as a woman of affairs, as a Mexican woman; she speaks of the Mexican flag. These are simply terms of self-enhancement, as she with candor explained to me. In her circle the great world outside is represented by "the law" and lawyers, by what she calls in broken Spanish *trámites* (for her the "paper work" of Governmental affairs), by events involving the Mexican flag. She gives luster to herself by proclaiming that she is master of these, for her, confusing practices. Her broken Spanish, which she herself hardly understands, impresses her monoglot Indian clientèle. Alfredo López Austin, relying on Ruiz de Alarcón's text, reports that already in the beginning of the 17th century the Nahuatl shamans were having recourse to Christian religious terminology. . . .

This refrain in multiple variations recurs throughout the text. On this night María Sabina has trouble in hitting her stride, preoccupied as she is with her "enemies," and I think she has recourse to the law, the Mexican

Woman of transactions am I,
Mexican woman am I,
Woman like a clock am I,†

Woman like the big eagle am I,
Woman like the opossum am I,
Woman who examines am I,
Woman like the hunting dog am I,
And woman like the wolf am I,
Woman like the hunting dog am I. . . . .
I'll show my power.

* * *

Woman of justice am I,
Woman of law am I,
Clean [pure] woman am I,
Woman of justice, woman of law am I.
Woman of justice am I.

* * *

The law which is pure,
The law by which we live,
The law which is good,
Lawyer woman am I,
Woman of paper work am I,
I go to the sky [heaven],
Woman who stops the world am I,
Legendary woman who cures‡ am I.
Father Jesus Christ,
I am truly a woman of law,
I am truly a woman of justice,§
My poor child, my dear humble child,
My poor child, my dear humble child,

---

†THE COWANS: As María Sabina continues her chant, the following that she declares she is, is a list of things she is seeing in her vision, according to what she affirmed during the transcription.

‡RGW: Herlinda and the Cowans did not recognize this word, which is not in current use. From an elderly informant we learned that it means *mujer legendaria que sabe curar; manda a los médicos de las manos sabias,* "a legendary woman who knows how to cure; she directs the hands of the skillful physician." References to her recur often. . . .

§THE COWANS: Upon inquiry María Sabina brought out the fact that she relates the idea of "justice" to the curing of the patients.

My patron mother, mother Conception,
Poor woman am I, humble woman am I
Father Jesus Christ, Father Jesus,
I am a woman of law,
I am a pure woman,
Father Jesus Christ,
Poor child, dear humble child,
Woman of justice am I,
Woman of law am I,
Pure woman am I,
and good woman am I,
My thinking is very good,
and my heart is very good.
My thinking is rare, and of great value,

Woman of justice am I,
And woman of law am I,
Poor child, humble child,
I am going to rub with my hands,
I walk with the pure doctor, the good doctor,
Brave woman am I,
And woman of beauty am I.
Father Jesus Christ, Father Jesus,
Woman saint [male] am I,*
And woman saint [female] am I,
Woman of pure spirit am I,
And woman of good spirit am I,
I am going to meet,
I am going to disenchant,
I am going to bring air,
Because a doctor woman am I,
Medical woman am I,
Good medical woman am I,
Father Jesus Christ,
Lawyer woman am I,
Woman of affairs am I, Father Jesus Christ,

* * *

Father Jesus,
Woman who waits am I,

---

*WEITLANER: María Sabina refers to herself here and in a number of later places as a male and female saint. This reminds me of the bi- or ambi-sexuality of certain gods in the pantheon of the Loxicha (Zapotec) calendar.

Woman who tries am I,
Woman who scatters am I,
Woman who uproots am I,
Woman doctor am I,
Father Jesus Christ,
My poor child, my dear humble child,
My poor child, my dear humble child,
A woman of justice am I,
A lawyer woman am I,
There it is being shown him, that he will be cured, that he will have
    herbs,
I will place myself poor and humble
Poor child, dear humble child,
Father Jesus Christ,
For with calmness, with care, I go
Before your sight [eyes], before your glory,
Before your eyes, mother,
Before your eyes, before your mouth,
My mother patron, mother Conception,
Father Jesus Christ, oh Jesus.
[There] goes [a] young man,* [a] well developed man,
Man who remains, who stands,
Father Jesus Christ.

* * *

Man who remains, who stands,
Woman [of a] root below the water am I,
Father Jesus Christ,
Tender root woman am I,
Luxurious [leafy] root woman am I,
Begonia woman am I,
Woman of pure spirit am I,
Woman of good spirit am I,
Woman of the air, of the day, am I,
Father Jesus Christ,
Eagle woman am I,
Opossum woman am I,
Woman who examines am I,

---

*RGW: The adjectives apparently applied to Jesus Christ seem unusual: he is
    "young" and "well developed." But may we not be seeing here a case of
    religious syncretism? María Sabina is perhaps speaking of a pre-Conquest
    deity, el Joven, whom Mr. López identified as Tezcatlipoca in the Nahuatl
    pantheon. . . .

Hunting dog woman am I,
Father Jesus Christ,
Woman of a sacred, enchanted place† am I,
and opossum woman am I,
Clock woman am I,
Pure woman am I,
Good woman am I,
Father Jesus Christ,
Thus as you stood, Father,
Thus as you stood, papa,
Father Jesus Christ, oh Jesus,
Saint woman [male] *am I,*
and woman of pure spirit am I,
Oh Jesus, oh Jesus Christ,
Oh most holy Mary, oh Jesus,
Legendary healing goddess am I,
Lowly woman am I,
Poor, lowly am I,
Jesus, oh Jesus Christ,
Saint woman [male] *am I,*
Woman of pure spirit am I,
Woman of good spirit am I,
Eagle woman am I,
Important [holy] *eagle woman am I,*
Clock woman am I,
Whirling woman of the whirlwind‡ am I,
Yes, Jesus Christ says,
Saint woman [male] *am I,*
Woman of pure spirit am I,
Oh Jesus, clock woman am I,
Eagle woman am I, oh Jesus,

* * *

†RGW: This word has fallen out of use and neither María Sabina nor Herlinda our
translator recognized it. From an old woman of Huautla I learned that it
means *un lugar sagrado, encantado, delante de Chilchotla, en la sierra mazateca;* "a holy
place, enchanted, in front of Chilchotla," a town in the Sierra Mazateca. This
holy ground will be invoked repeatedly.

‡RGW: The word *tso¹tji³* is no longer used and María Sabina did not recognize it,
though she made use of it in her singing. According to Herlinda it means
"woman of the round *(tji³) huipil (tso¹),*" that is, the woman who whirls like
a whirlwind when dancing. *Huipil* is the tunic-like garment that many Indian
women wear in Vera Cruz, Oaxaca, Guerrero, Chiapas, and the Yucatán
peninsula. This word recurs often. . . .

Now our son has died, because the lion has eaten him up,
By his **soerte** *has he been eaten up,*
The lion has eaten him up.
Lawyer woman am I, woman of affairs am I,
No one frightens our son,
No one frightens our people,
Lawyer woman am I, woman of affairs am I,
Pure woman am I,
Good woman am I,
The lion ate up our son,
By his **soerte** *has he been eaten up,*
By his **soerte** *has he been eaten up,*
The lion ate up our son,

                *   *   *

There's no cure now. [There's nothing left to do]
                    *   *   *

With calmness, with care,
With breast milk, with dew,
With freshness, with tenderness,
With breast milk, with dew,
Saint Peter, Saint Paul
Shout, you! whistle, you!
I am going to thunder, I am going to sound,
Even below the water, even the sea,
No one frightens you, no one is two-faced,
No one comes between, no one passes,

                *   *   *

No one comes between, no one passes,
No one frightens us, no one is two faced,
Lord Saint Peter, Lord Saint Paul,
Justice that is good, law that is pure,
Law that is fine [climate] . . .
Cheer up!
With constancy . . .
With breast milk, with dew,
With freshness, with tenderness,
No one who frightens, no one who is two-faced.
I am going to do justice even unto the house of the sky [heaven],
Even before your eyes, even unto your glory,
My patron mother, princess mother, heart of Jesus,
May she live!
Woman of law am I, woman of affairs am I,
No one intervenes, no one passes,

Woman of justice am I, woman of law am I,
Pure woman am I, good woman am I,

Woman of space am I,
Woman of day am I,
Woman of light am I,
No one frightens him,
No one is two-faced to me,
Lawyer woman am I, woman of affairs am I,
I give account to my Lord,
And I give account to the judge,
And I give account to the government,
And I give account to the Father Jesus Christ,
And mother princess, my patron mother, oh Jesus, Father Jesus Christ,
Woman of danger am I, woman of beauty am I,
He has my Book
My dear bishop, good, clean,
My good and clean prayer,
My good and clean nun, oh Jesus Christ,
No one frightens me, no one is two-faced to me,
Lawyer woman am I, woman of affairs am I,
I am going to the sky [heaven], *Jesus Christ,*
And the law knows me, the government knows me,
And the judge knows me, and God knows me, Father Jesus Christ,
Lawyer woman am I, woman of affairs am I,
I am going to the sky [heaven], *there is my "paper,"*
There is my Book,
Even in your sight, in your mouth, your glory,
Oh Jesus Christ, oh hail Mary, oh Jesus Christ,
No one frightens me,
No one is two-faced to me, oh Jesus Christ,
Gifted woman am I, privileged woman am I,
Woman of hunting dogs am I,
Woman who examines am I,
Whirling woman of the whirlwind am I, woman of a sacred, enchanted
*   place am I,*
Eagle woman am I, and clock woman am I,
Isn't that so now?

* * *

With breast milk, with dew,
The world can be cheered up, let's cheer up, let's be enlightened.
Let our Father come out to us, let Christ come out to us,
We wait for our Father, we wait for our Father, we wait for Christ,

With calmness, with care,
Man of breast milk, man of dew,
Fresh man, tender man,
Woman of justice am I, and woman of law am I,
Pure woman am I, good woman am I,
Woman of law am I,
Law that is good, justice that is good,
Oh Jesus Christ, oh Mary most holy, oh Jesus Christ,
Oh hail most holy Mary, oh hail Mary,
Oh hail most holy Mary, oh Jesus,
And I give account now to my good, clean [pure] *bishop,*
My good, clean bishop,
My good, clean prayer,
My good, clean nun,
And there I give account, [the mushroom] *says,*
There I give account to him face to face, before your glory, [the mushroom] *says,*
There I give him account, [the mushroom] *says,*
Jesus says, for I have an owner, [the mushroom] *says,*
Yes, Jesus Christ says, there I have an owner, [the mushroom] *says,*

Jesus Christ says,
The government controls us, [the mushroom] *says,*
The judge controls us, [the mushroom] *says, Father Jesus Christ says,*

Woman lord of "clowns" am I, [the mushroom] *says,*
Woman lord of the holy clown am I, [the mushroom] *says,*
Yes, Jesus Christ says, yes Jesus says,
Woman of the clock am I, he says,
Woman lord of the eagle am I, he says,
Woman Jesus Christ am I, he says,
Yes, Jesus Christ says . . . [repeated]
Yes, Jesus Christ says, Jesus says,
It's holy, he says, Father Jesus Christ says, says,

* * *

It's a holy man, [the mushroom] *says, it's a holy woman,* [the mushroom] *says,*
It's true, [the mushroom] *says,*
The thing is true, [the mushroom] *says,*

* * *

Woman who waits am I, woman who tries am I, [the mushroom] *says,*

Father Jesus Christ says [so]

*   *   *

Cheer up, cheer up, cheer up . . .
Cheer up, don't be concerned.
Look at the world.
The world is pretty.
You my patron Mother, mother Conception . . .
My little Virgin doll, Holy Rosary, Mother Mazatlán
My father Holy Rosary,
Woman of the whirlpool* in the lake am I, woman who waits
 am I,
Woman who tries am I, clean woman am I,
Oh Jesus, my patron Mother, look at this world,
Look how it is, dangerous world, dark world,
I'm going to free this, [the mushroom] *says, I'm going to dry it*
 out in the sunlight, [the mushroom] *says,*
Woman of the hunting dog am I,
My patron Mother, Mother Conception
My Virgin Magdalene, Mother Guadalupe . . .
By your heels, by your hands, Father Christ,
I am going there where you spat, Christ,
That's how I am going there to the sky,
There before your eyesight, before your mouth, your glory,
Heart of Jesus, may it live, lawyer woman am I,
Woman of affairs am I, Mexican woman am I,
Woman of the principal star am I, woman of the star of God am I,
Woman of the star of the [Southern] *Cross am I, woman of the*
 star of the [Southern] *Cross am I,*
Clean woman am I, woman of the clock am I,
Eagle woman am I, eagle woman am I,

Lawyer woman am I . . .
And woman of affairs am I,
Woman who is than more *human am I, Father Jesus Christ says,*
Woman of the principal star am I, woman of the star of the [Southern]
 Cross am I,

---

*RGW: There are numerous beliefs in Mazatec and Chinantec folklore about the existence, contrary to fact, of a lake on top of the Cerro Rabón above Jalapa de Díaz. In this lake there exists a putative fauna of *marine* animals such as whales. Around this lake there blows constantly a strong whirlwind that makes it impossible to approach the lake. On the water floats a *jícara* (gourd) in the seven colors of the rainbow.

Woman of the star of God am I, woman who waits am I,
Woman of the shooting stars am I, lawyer woman am I,
Woman of affairs am I, I am going to the sky,
Yes, Jesus Christ says.
There my paper is, there my Book is
My clean Book, my good Book,
I am going, because it is clean for me, yes, Jesus Christ says,
There the paper is, then, there my Book,
A clean woman am I, a good woman am I,
Woman of the hunting dog am I,
Yes Jesus Christ says, oh Jesus Christ says,
My patron Mother, Mother princess,
I have very good thoughts,
My little prayer, my little nun,
My good, clean nun, my good, clean Christ,
Woman of the principal star am I, and woman of the star of God am I,

Woman of the Star of the [Southern] *Cross am I, yes Jesus Christ says,*

Woman who stops the world am I, legendary woman who cures am I,
Woman of paper of smoke am I, yes Jesus Christ says,
There where my little prayers are,
And where my little nuns are,
And I go to the sky, yes Jesus Christ says,

Woman born thus am I,
Woman who came into the world thus am I,
Clock woman am I, yes, yes, Jesus Christ says,
Woman who was born thus am I
and quick woman am I
Woman above am I, yes, Jesus Christ says,
Woman general am I, yes, Jesus Christ says,
Saint woman am I,
Woman of clean spirit am I,
Woman of good spirit am I, [he] *says,*
I merely throw here and there, I merely scatter, [the mushroom] *says,*

I merely throw here and there, I merely scatter all
*   that is dirty, all that is useless, [the mushroom] says,*
I give account to him who is my chief, [the mushroom] *says,*
Woman who was born thus am I, [the mushroom] *says,*
And woman who came into the world thus am I, [the mushroom] *says,*

Yes, Jesus Christ says, woman, Jesus Christ says,
Yes, Jesus Christ says [so]
Woman drummer* am I, he says,
Woman musician am I, he says,
Yes Jesus Christ says,
Woman who thunders* am I, he says,
Woman who uproots am I, he says,
Woman doctor am I, he says,
Yes Jesus Christ says,
Woman of the principal star am I, he says,
Woman of the Star of the [Southern] *Cross am I, he says,*
No one will frighten us, he says,
No one will be two-faced to us, he says, yes Jesus Christ says,
I throw about and scatter, he says, yes, Jesus Christ says,
Woman of the clock am I, he says, eagle woman am I, he says,
Yes, Jesus Christ says, . . . [four times]
I merely throw about, I merely scatter he says, yes, Jesus Christ
  says,
Woman general am I, he says, yes, Jesus Christ says,
Woman musician am I, he says,
Woman drummer am I, he says, yes, Jesus Christ says,
Woman [male] *saint am I, he says, woman* [female] *saint am*
  I, he says,
Spirit woman am I, he says, illuminated woman am I, he says,
Woman of the day am I, he says, yes, Jesus Christ says,
I am going to the sky, he says,
And I am going even into your presence, even into your glory,
No one will frighten me, he says,
Woman who is than more *human am I, he says,*
Lawyer woman am I, he says,
Woman of affairs am I, he says, yes, Jesus Christ says,
Yes, Jesus says, I only throw about, I only scatter, he says,
Woman of Puebla am I, he says,
Woman who examines am I,
Important eagle woman am I, he says,
Clock woman am I, he says,
I am going to show my valor, he says, I am going to show my valor,
  he says,

*RGW: As Borhegyi and Weitlaner pointed out, there is a link between drumming
and thunder; to which I would add a link between them and the sacred
mushrooms. . . .

Even before your eyesight, your glory, he says, (woman who waits
  am I, he says,)
When I shall show my valor, he says,
I am a woman who is than more human, he says,
Yes Jesus Christ says, yes Jesus says,
No one frightens me, he says,
No one is two-faced to me, he says,
Yes Jesus says, yes Jesus says,
Music woman am I, he says,
And drummer woman am I, he says,
Woman violinist am I, he says,
Yes, Jesus Christ says,
Woman of the principal star am I, he says,
Woman of the star of God am I, he says, woman of the star of the
  [Southern] Cross, he says,
Launch [canoe] woman am I, he says, yes, Jesus Christ   says,
Woman chief of the "clowns" am I, hesays, yes Jesus Christ says,
No one frightens me, he says, no one is two-faced to me, he says,
Woman who is than more human am I, he says,
Lawyer woman am I, he says,
And I am going to the sky, he says, yes Jesus Christ says,
Woman [male] saint am I, he says,
I am going to burn the world, he says, yes Jesus Christ says,
I am going to burn the world, he says, yes Jesus Christ says,
Woman of shooting stars am I, he says,
And Saint Peter woman am I, he says,
Whirling woman of the whirlwind am I, he says,
Woman of a sacred, enchanted place am I, he says, yes Jesus Christ says,

Woman [male] saint am I, he says, spirit woman am I, he says,
Illuminated woman am I, he says, yes Jesus says,
I am going to burn the world, he says, yes Jesus Christ says,
Woman who examines am I,
No one frightens me, he says,
No one is two-faced to me, he says,
I'm not surprised, he says, I'm not frightened, he says,
I give account to the judge, he says, I give account to the government,
  he says,
And I give account to my bishop, he says,
The good, clean bishop, he says, the good, clean nun, he says,
Yes Jesus Christ says, yes Jesus says,
Yes Jesus says, yes Jesus Christ says,

I throw about, I scatter, he says,
Yes Jesus Christ says, yes I am going to spread out in the main trail
  ["Royal Road"], he says
Only ounces, only pounds, he says, yes Jesus Christ says,
Woman who thus was born no less am I, he says, woman who thus came
  into the world no less am I, he says,
. . . clock woman am I, he says,
Yes Jesus says, I am going to burn the world, he says,
Saint Peter woman am I, he says, whirling woman of the whirlwind am
  I, he says,
Woman of a sacred enchanted place am I, he says, yes Jesus Christ
  says,
Woman of the hunting dog am I, he says,
Wolf woman am I, he says,
Woman who thunders am I, he says, yes Jesus Christ says,
No one frightens me, he says,
No one is two-faced to me, he says,
Yes, Jesus Christ says,
Yes, I am going to throw [it] away there, he says,
Yes, I am going to put it out to dry there, he says,
Only ounces, only pounds, he says, yes, Jesus Christ says,
Woman [male] saint am I, he says, woman who came to the world thus
  am I, he says,
Woman who thunders am I, he says, yes Jesus Christ says, yes Jesus Christ
  says,
Woman [male] saint am I, he says, spirit woman am I, he says,
Yes, Jesus says, there is still God, he says,
There are still saints, he says, there is still God, he says,
Yes Jesus Christ says, I am going to burn the world, he says,
Yes Jesus Christ says, I am a woman who waits, he says,
Yes, Jesus Christ says, Saint Peter . . . says,
I am going to accuse everything, he says, yes Jesus says,
Yes Jesus Christ says . . .

*   *   *

He was eaten up in the fangs of the lion, I tell you for sure. . . . he was
  eaten up by the lion, I'm not going to hide it from you.
He was eaten up by the lion, he was eaten up in his soerte.

*   *   *

Can't he be left?
Only Saint Peter, Saint Paul,
Only God who does what is right, God knows what he does,
And if he doesn't know God, let him seek Him out then.

He was eaten up only in his soerte, *he was eaten up only by
the lion. . . .*

* * *

Why should I tell you that he was bewitched?
He was merely eaten up in the fangs of the lion.
This person was not bewitched.

* * *

With breast milk, with dew.
Work! [Shamanize!] *. . . nothing will happen to you.*
He knows how to think over what happened to these people.
There now, it is fitting that he answer the call of nature and urinate.
Only by performing his necessities and urinating, will this sickness
    apparently come out of the skin.* [How indeed?]
Only performing his necessities and urinating, this is not dangerous.

Christ. . . . . Jesus. . . . .
I am a Saint Peter woman, you Father Christ,
Most Holy Mary, my patron Mother, Mother Conception,
As you did, you Father,
As you did, you Christ,
Thus am I doing also, with the heel, with the feet, Father,
With the heel, with the hands,
With the heel, with the feet,
As you did, you Father,
As you did, you Christ,
Most holy mother, mother holy Rosary, our Father Sanctuary,
Mother princess, my little doll Virgin, Saint Rose Ojitlán,
Father . . . , thus is how I am going, Christ,
With the heel, you, with the hands, you,
As you rested, you Father,
As you rested, you Christ, thus I am going

There where the light and the day are, I go, Father,
Even unto your presence, unto your glory,
My patron Mother, Mother Conception . . .
Humble woman am I, I, my patron Mother,
Because I carry your heart, patron Mother,
Mother princess, because I carry your heart, Mother,
Because I carry your heart, Father,
Because I carry your features,

---

*BORHEGYI: Passing sickness by urinating has wide currency among the Indians of
    North America.

Just as my thoughts are clean,
Just as my heart is full of greatness, though small,
As my sentiments and my heart feel greatness,
As my thoughts are clean,
There is where I am with you, mother,
There is where I am before your sight, before your mouth,
    mother.
I am not eating many tortillas, mother, yes,
I am not eating many tortillas, mother, nor heavy things,
I am not two-faced, mother, [I am not fickle]
I do not eat much, nor heavy, I, oh Christ,
As I am very satisfied, I,
As my heart gives me no pricks,
My patron Mother, Mother princess, holy Christ child of
    Atocha,
Mother Guadalupe, Mother Conception,
Because I carry your heart, heart of Jesus,

They are many, my little nuns,
My pure nuns, my clean prayers,

My heart is very satisfied,
It is your pure Book,
It is your clean pen,
That I have, Father, that I have, Father,
Before your sight, before your mouth, until your glory,
Look, I feel as though I'm going to the sky,
I am a woman lord of the sea which ends, I feel,
Woman who came blessed am I, I feel,
Woman serpent am I, I feel,
Serpent woman am I, I feel,
I am not eating much,
I am not eating heavy, Father,
Just as you are resting, you, Christ,

Father
Look, I have your pure cane, your fresh cane, you,
My patron Mother, look how poor I am,
Look how humble I am,
Poor woman am I, humble woman am I,

Tender woman, abundant woman am I,
Woman of big roots am I, woman rooted below the water am I,

Woman who sprouts am I, woman like a begonia am I,
I am going to the sky, in your sight, before your glory,
There my paper, my Book remains, *
Woman who stops the world am I, legendary woman healer am I,
My feelings are satisfied,
My heart is satisfied,
Because I carry your heart, I,
Because I carry your heart, Christ,
Because I carry your heart, Father.

* * *

Woman who thunders am I, woman who sounds am I,
Spider woman am I, hummingbird woman am I,
Eagle woman am I, important eagle woman am I,
Whirling woman of the whirlwind am I, woman of a sacred, enchanted
*   place am I,*
Woman of the shooting stars am I, yes Jesus Christ says,
Clock woman am I, yes Jesus Christ says,

* * *

We're going to be able to place the complaint.
I am humble, he says, I pass below the earth, he says,
There are my little nuns below the earth, he says,
There is my little nun, Jesus Christ says,
Look now, isn't that so?

* * *

Lawyer woman am I, he says, woman of affairs am I, he says,
I burn the world, he says, Father Jesus Christ says,
I winnow and throw away everywhere, he says, yes Jesus Christ says,
Woman chief of "thousands of little children" am I, he says, woman of
*   "thousands of holy children" am I, he says,*
Woman chief of the "clowns" am I, he says, woman of the holy "clown"
*   am I, he says,*
Woman of the whirlpool in the lake am I, he says, woman who waits am
*   I, he says,*
Yes, Jesus Christ says, I pass below the earth, he says,
Yes, Jesus Christ says, my words join with the Santo Domingo river,
Yes, Jesus Christ says, woman of the big [morning] *star am I, he says,*
Woman of the star of God am I, he says, woman of the [southern]
*   star cross am I, he says,*

*RGW: Again we read of the paper, the Book. The paper is clearly the magic beaten bark of pre-Columbian days, still being made and used by the Indians.

Yes, Jesus Christ says, my pure little moon, he says,
Yes, Jesus Christ says, my children of the moon, children of star, he
  says,
Yes, Jesus Christ says, my pure [clean] *children, he says,*
My prepared [good] *children, he says,*
Look now . . . isn't that so?

*   *   *

Jesus oh Mary, holy child, the arm and the hand of the lord of the
  world.
Dangerous things are being done, tragedies are being worked out.
We are left only perplexed, we mamas.

*   *   *

Who can stand all these things?
It's the same there, it's the same here.
Really this thing is big.

Balu Asong Gau
MELANESIA/KENYAH DYAK

Balu Asong Gau, a Kenyah Dyak *bali dayong* ("one who enters a
trance state to seek the spirits") was the head shaman of spirit medium activities that still survived in the longhouse. Although she
had met and become devoted to Jesus Christ of the new religion in
her middle years, her shamanistic experiences persisted as they had
since early childhood. When she was a young girl, the ancient spirits had possessed her and spoken through her, and she did not
know why this had happened. Nor would they leave her, in spite
of her adoration of Christ. In 1972, she told the American poet
Carol Rubenstein that she suffered a terrible anguish from the conflict between the old religion of her people and the new religion of
Jesus.

Christ does not appear as an animating figure in her healing
chants. Instead, the archaic spirits of the flowing rivers and dense
green jungles—the Spiderhunter, the hawk in human form, the tiger,
the spirit of the cloud, the young dragon spirit of the river, the spirit
of the crocodile—cry and sing through her. These and many, many
more live within her, move through her as she chants,

214 SINGING INTO LIFE

> *I am Laeng,*
> *the* plaki *bird come circling,*
> *the hawk in human form which has entered my body.* [5]

A *dayong* can only come to his or her profession through a summoning. Frequently, that call comes during a dream. And suffering and madness are frequently part of the *dayong's* calling, as they are for shamans the world over. This agony does not necessarily abate, but the *dayong* learns to control and direct the powerful energies that seize him or her.

Although she came from an aristocratic family, Balu Asong Gau was still regarded with fear and jealousy by the people of the longhouse. Rubenstein wrote that the children hurried past her and that the women "like herself drying and pounding the *padi* or weaving baskets, are in their attitude toward her careful—a mixture of jealousy, caution, and sarcasm—and minimally friendly as well."[6]

This Borneo shaman, a widow in her sixties, shared her suffering with Carol Rubenstein so great were her pain and despair over Christ's displeasure with her, that she wished to die.[7]

> *E-e-e-e-e-e-e-e!*
> *I am young Lagong,*
> *the light swift* isit *bird*
> *which has taken human form and entered into my body.*
> *I am young and brave—*
> *swift, light is this* isit *bird flying across the path.*
> *I am the Spiderhunter, this swift* isit *bird.*
> *The spirit of the* plaki *bird has come, the hawk*
> *which takes flight thru clouds that turn into rain,*
> *and then the clouds are gone.*
> *I am Laeng,*
> *the* plaki *bird come circling,*
> *the hawk in human form which has entered into my body.*
> *Only briefly do I come.*
> *I am the tiger Laeng on Weng plateau,*
> *the tiger leaping, lightly springing,*
> *leaping and springing lightly in the rain on Weng plateau.*
> *Here come I, Batong Asang,*
> *spirit of the cloud,*
> *now in human form come within my body,*
> *the cloud that dissolves, turning into water.*
> *I am the young dragon,*

Bali Sungei, the spirit of the river—
it is within my power to drain the riverbed dry.

My dear people, human beings, all of you,
for what reason have you called upon me?
My dearest lover is shouting for me,
loudly his voice calls me to come.
I feel a weakness overwhelming me.

I am Bali Sungei, the dragon, spirit of the river.
Of men, I am the leader of Weng plateau,
the model that all the people copy—
in the world, I am the chief source of all that rises.
Now I am the tiger, he who can stop the wind—
I who am the tiger can halt all currents,
can even make the flowing of the water of the river
  cease.
We grandsons of the tiger roam thruout the world.
For what reason have you come in search of me?

Now come I, Ingan Jalong,
spirit of the light of day—
I, Ingan Jalong,
who stay on Puong plateau during the daylight hours,
I am the spirit of spirit mediums—
along the path I dance.

Hoi! With the speed of the tiger,
to lunge and clasp with power to lunge and clasp,
lunging and clasping that which is best, I always the
  first.
But now is not as it was before, now is not as it was.
I like to dance circling, I like to go circling
on the floor made of the lueng *tree,*
on the floor made of the lueng *tree,*
whose fruit is bitter to eat.
With the speed of the tiger, with the speed of the tiger
come I, Jalong, leaping past the moon.
I, Jalong, can defeat ten people, leaving them all behind.

E-e-e-e-e-e-e-e!
Yes, you, my lover,

you are entering within my voice.
I am Lian, dumb spirit,
unable to utter any but scattered sound.
None could ever defeat me as I used to be.
Come, let us go circling, dancing
on the floor made of the lueng *tree,*
whose fruit is bitter to eat—
dancing, circling on the floor made of hard stone.

I come, I, Lawai, spirit of the crocodile,
the man who can halt the whole river in its coursing.
Only for a short while do I come.
Wearily, wearily I come,
I, Jalong Balan, tiger who has always been foremost.
We are omens sent by the spirits of the padi.
I am Lawai, spirit of the crocodile,
wearing my tough garment.
Our garments are the toughest of all the kinds in the
*   world.*
Weng plateau is always lonely—
there are many clusters of beads
at the end of Weng plateau.
I, Kareng, come out, along with Laeng Ingan,
the hawk who has taken human form within my body.
We are the chief fathers of the spirits of the padi.
What a pity, pity for you!

We people of the stream make loud music;
we of the stream make music that is so loud
the sound keeps striking within one's head.
I am Sagon Lawai, king of the frogs.
I, the frog king, stay at the mouth of the river,
wearing my special design, spotted freely everywhere.
All we spirits are friends, sharing the same feelings,
come from the same birth.
This is Tama Sagon, father of the frogs,
who is always calling for rain,
the man who calls the greatest clouds
which turn into the heaviest rain.
I am Irang Taja, spirit of taboo,
I am Irang Taja, spirit of taboo.
I am Irang Taja, who lives on the bright plateau,

I am Irang Taja, who lives on the bright plateau.
The bright plateau is continually a lovely vision,
the bright plateau is continually a lovely vision,
the plateau which is completely bare,
which no one is allowed to see.
Here comes Lenjau Laeng, who lives on Weng plateau,
my great friend who comes from the mouth of the river.
No one can defeat me, making me fall behind.
I want to visit my mother, the Shining Moon.
Always has he been my friend—
however cruel you are,
young man, spirit of the padi, eh-yeh!
You living at the mouth of the river of the moon.
I am on my way to see Lenjau Laeng,
who stays at Weng plateau, near the source of the
  rain.
I am able to stop the enemy in their tracks.

E-e-e-e-e-e-e-e!
Dear people gathered, all of you,
do not play senselessly.
I truly pity you,
you who are spinning,
chief of those who spin the most.

This year has been dry,
a bad spirit has shriveled everything.
I am Padan Jalong, whose house at the mouth of the
river
is covered with foam,
that mouth ushering forth life forever.
I am the young leopard,
whose coat is designed like rain.
I await the arrival of those people
who live on an island surrounded by water,
those people surrounded by water because of heavy rain.
The clouds you people live beneath
are the source of the tears dropping from our eyes.
Truly, I pity you, as I see into your eyes,
my dear people living on this earth.
We are the dragons, the spirits of the river,
who can cause dryness.

Mostly it is we who make the long dry spell,
we are the spirits who make the season long and dry.

Be careful, my grandson,
the enemy is coming up the Maradian river.
Now I can see the sign—
this is the war party come to strike down the moon.
I am Lusat Jalong, this is Lusat Jalong,
I stay in the deepest pool of the river.
Grandson, my grandson,
do not play senselessly.
We worry about you, my grandson.
For a long time I have wanted to meet you,
my young friend who sways and circles in his dancing—
Lusat Jalong, who stays within the deepest of the river's pools.

Kabon Tiri Tiri, Kabon Tiri Tiri—
all of you young men—
Kabon Kujan Kujan, Kabon Kujan Kujan—
all the young girls are likely to be caught,
scooped up like a bunch of beads cut from their string.
Lawai, the crocodile, wears a tough garment,
a garment made entirely of beads.
Do not play senselessly.

We are the spirits of the spirit mediums, we are many.
Truly these are the spirits who make my luck.
We come from the bare plateau, which no one is allowed to see,
the bare plateau where we have many enemies.
We have nothing to share with you,
with you, my young first-born one,
my son whose father is dead.
You, Chinese visitor, who have come from downriver;
you, high-born woman, you of royal blood;
there is nothing I can share with you,
to share with you to eat,
no food to give you from my fingertips.
This is how our spirits, those of the spirit medium, live,
the spirits of the spirit medium dancing along the path,
along the plateau on which the raindrops fall.
Rain is beating on my river mouth,
sounding like a metal drum.

I am sorry we can stay only so brief a time.
We are the true spirits of the spirit medium—
that is the gift given me, the prohibited gift.
The spirits of the spirit medium sometimes dance
on the bare plateau, the place that is forbidden,
the bare plateau where many of the enemy live.
We live in separate places,
we each stay in a different river.
How I pity all of you!
Slowly we must go back, back we go into the clouds.
Bali Lingai, spirit of shadow, slowly, slowly
do we return to you, our mother.
This is truly the way of spirit mediums—
the prohibited gift that is my share,
that spirits may enter into me entirely.
But this is improper to be done at this time.
We can stay for only a short while.
My mother is the Shining Moon.

I am anxious to purify the feelings in your body,
by the help of Sio, the spirit who grants all wishes.
I am but this particle of dust—
I, Liang, spirit of the burial ground,
which is mainly dust,
surely to pile overhead, to cover our knees.
My son, slowly I return to my mother—
that is my parting word.
My grandson, and all of you,
slowly, slowly we spirits must go back,
fading fast as if we flew.

A curse on you young people!
I am Lian, dumb spirit,
who utters only scattered sound with no meaning.
You died when you were still young.

E-e-e-e-e-e-e-e!
We go away, we go back,
we spread out in flight, a crowd of hornets,
many hornets spreading out and wheeling.
Back we go to our mother.

We are the true spirits of the spirit medium, we are many.
Eyes open naturally at the light of day.
Because we are so many, thousands thronging among us,
because we are as many as fronds on the late palm.

8 The House of Dreams

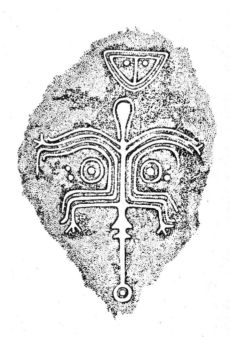

This stylized figure is redrawn from an artist's rendering of a rock engraving at Nyí, near Meyú Falls, Pira-paraná in the Vaupes territory of Colombia. The Meyú Falls are at the earth's equator, a zone of verticality in relation to the rising and setting constellations. The roaring, foaming falls, according to anthropologist Reichel-Dolmatoff, would be precisely the environment that the mythological Sun Father would have chosen to mate with the feminine earth in order to create the human race. The anthropologist states that the Vaupes' Indians interpret the triangular face as a vagina and the styled human figure below it as a winged phallus. *(From: Gerardo Reichel-Dalmatoff, The Shaman and the Jaguar, Philadelphia, Temple University Press, 1975, Figure 26.)*

Desana Shaman
SOUTH AMERICA/DESANA

The development of the powers of the Desana shaman requires a long and systematic learning process. Unlike most shamans in other parts of the world, the *payé* does not usually receive a call to the vocation through a psychological, spiritual, and physical crisis. Rather, the healer-priest "develops his personality slowly and steadily," according to anthropologist Reichal-Dolmatoff, "the driving force being a truly intellectual interest in the unknown; and that not so much for the purpose of acquiring power over his fellowmen as for the personal satisfaction of 'knowing' things which others are unable to grasp."[1]

The *payé* is a humanist who is vitally interested in the archaic traditions of his people. He is also concerned with the social dynamics in the community and consequently often finds himself assuming the role of sacred politician, resolving social conflict. Shamanistic trance, frequently induced by powerful hallucinogens, demonstrates the divine origin of the rules regulating social relationships.[2] This is the means whereby the *payé* restores harmony to the community.

The myths of the Desana center on the institution of the sacred drug séances and endow both the plant and the rituals associated with the ingestion of these potent snuffs and infusions with a deep sense of order, of coherence.

In the narrative that follows, the Origin myth of Yajé, Yajé Woman seems to be the first woman on earth and the House of Waters into which she came was the first *maloca*.*Her appearance in the midst of the men after giving birth to the Yajé Child, which is then rudely dismembered, is extraordinarily dramatic. When the men see her, they feel like "drowning." The Desana use the word *drown* to describe the sensations experienced during sexual intercourse. To the Desana, see-

---

*The Desana live in large communal houses called *malocas*.

ing visions, drowning, sinking into a coma, confounding oneself, and being saturated are all conditions that are related to sexual intercourse.[3]

Yajé Woman produces the powerful visions, and yajé is female.[4] Reichel-Dolmatoff explains that "during coitus the person 'drowns' and 'sees visions'; the act is described as a state of intoxication *(niaróre),* of drunkenness, a state of rapture in which anxiety and bliss combine and transport the male into another dimension of physical and spiritual consciousness. . . . To the Tukano, this close association between sex and hallucinatory trance is quite natural; these two experiences, because of their intensity and rapture, have much in common, and the myth simply explains how they came into being."[5, 6]

It was a woman. Her name was *gahpi mahsó*/Yajé Woman. It happened in the beginning of time. In the beginning of time, when the Anaconda-Canoe was ascending the rivers to settle mankind all over the land, there appeared the Yajé Woman. The canoe had arrived at a place called *dia vii,* the House of the Waters, and the men were sitting in the first maloca when the Yajé Woman arrived. She stood in front of the maloca, and there she gave birth to her child; yes, that was where she gave birth.

The Yajé Woman took a *tooka** plant and cleaned herself and the child. This is a plant the leaves of which are red as blood on the underside, and she took these leaves and with them she cleaned the child. The leaves were shiny red, brilliant red, and so was the umbilical cord. It was red and yellow and white, shining brightly. It was a long umbilical cord, a large piece of it. She is the mother of the yajé vine.

Inside the maloca the men were sitting, the ancestors of mankind, the ancestors of all Tukano groups. The Desana were there, and the Tukano proper, the Pira-Tapuya, and the Uanano; they were all there. They had come to receive the yajé vine. To each one the yajé vine was to be given, and they had gathered to receive it.

Then the woman walked toward the maloca where the men were sitting and entered through the door, with the child in her arms. When the men saw the woman with her child they became

---

* *Tooka* is a small unidentified plant with round, blackish berries, often mentioned in rituals.

benumbed and bewildered. It was as if they were drowning as they watched the woman and her child.

She walked to the center of the maloca and, standing there, she asked: "Who is the father of this child?"

The men were sitting, and they felt nauseated and benumbed; they could not think anymore. The monkeys too, yes, the monkeys were sitting and were chewing herbs; they were *bayapia* leaves.* The monkeys could not stand the sight either. They began to eat their tails. The tapirs, too, were eating their tails which, at that time, were quite long. The squirrels, too, were eating their tails and were chewing herbs. The squirrel made a little noise— kiu-kiu-kiu—as it was chewing. "I am in a bad way," the squirrel said; "I am eating my tail." "What is going on?" the monkeys said and touched their tails, but the tails were gone. "We are in a bad way," the monkeys said; "Poor me!" said one of the monkeys; "I shall go mad eating my tail! Poor me!"

The Yajé Woman stood in the center of the maloca and asked: "Who is the father of this child?"

There was a man sitting in a corner and saliva was dripping from his mouth. He rose and, seizing the child's right leg, he said: "I am his father!" "No!" said another man; "I am his father!" "No!" said the others; "We are the child's fathers!" And then all the men turned upon the child and tore it to pieces. They tore off the umbilical cord and the fingers, the arms, and the legs. They tore the child to bits. Each one took a part, the part that corresponds to him, to his people. And ever since each group of men has had its own kind of yajé.

[At this point the tale was interrupted and the question was asked how the woman had become pregnant.]

It was the old man, the Sun Father; he was the phallus. She looked at him and from his appearance, from the way he looked,** the seed was made because he was the Yajé Person. The Sun Father was the Master of Yajé, the master of the sex act. In the House of the Waters she was impregnated through the eye. By looking at the Sun Father she became pregnant. Everything happened through the eye.

Bayapia, an unidentified plant that is probably a hallucinogen, seems to be related to the Desana words *bayí* (spell) and *bayarí* (dance).

**Fertilization through the eye is mentioned in several Tukano myths.

The Yajé Woman had come with the men. While the men were preparing *cashirí* the woman left the maloca and gave birth to the yajé vine in the form of a child. It was night. The men were trying to find a way to get drunk. The Yajé Child was born while the men were trying to find a way to become intoxicated. They were just beginning to sing; their song rejected the child. They rejected it with a stick rattle of *sëmé* wood.* The animals that were eating their tails were cohabiting because they had become intoxicated. The yajé should have produced only pleasant visions, but some became nauseated and so they rejected it.

The woman had walked to the center of the maloca. There was a box of feather headdresses; and there was a hearth. When she walked in, only one of the men had kept a clear head and had not become dizzy. The men were drinking when she had her child, and at once they became dizzy. First they became dizzy; then came the red light and they saw red colors, the blood of childbirth. Then she entered with her child, and when she stepped through the door they all lost their senses. Only one of them resisted and took hold of the first branch of yajé. It was then that our ancestor acted like a thief; he took off one of his copper earrings and broke it in half, and with the sharp edge he cut the umbilical cord. He cut off a large piece. This is why yajé comes in the shape of a vine. They all tore off bits and pieces of the child. The other men had already taken their parts of the child's body when at last our ancestor, *boréka*,** took the part corresponding to him. Our ancestor did not know how to take advantage of yajé; he became too much intoxicated.

Warao Shaman
SOUTH AMERICA/WARAO

The 15,000 Warao of eastern Venezuela live in the labyrinthian waterways and inaccessible swamps of the Orinoco delta. Because of the

Sëmé is a leguminous tree with edible seeds.
**Boréka* is the name of the highest-ranking sib of the Desana.

remoteness of their habitat, they have remained more or less culturally and genetically free from any admixture with other races or tribes, and their traditions have remained unusually pure.

Johannes Wilbert, the collector of this myth, states that the myth of the House of Tobacco Smoke gives the origin for the "history of consciousness" of the Warao people. The Creator Bird of the Dawn was a divine bird spirit who, in an ancient and mythological past, was a radiant youth from the East. Merely thinking of a house, *Domu Hokonamamana Ariawara,* the Bird of the Dawn, manifested a house, round and white and made of shining tobacco smoke. It was in this house that "light" shamanism was born.[7]

The "light" shaman *(bahanarotu)* presides over an ancient fertility cult called *habisanuka.* In dream or a tobacco-induced trance state the *bahanarotu* travels to the eastern part of the cosmic vault. The celestial bridge of tobacco smoke that he maintains and on which he travels to the eastern Supreme *Bahana* (spirit) ensures all in the tribe an abundant life on earth. An aggressive *bahanarotu* can cause sickness or death among his enemies. Such misfortunes can be averted by a friendly *bahanarotu* who will suck out the magic arrows or cure with tobacco smoke those who are afflicted.[8]

Wilbert goes on to say that "this myth is the origin tradition of the *bahanarotu* shaman. It is the charter by which he orders his conscious existence and his supernatural experience. It is taught to him by his master in long and arduous initiatory training, and so firmly does it become fixed in his psyche that, when he is considered ready for his initiatory tobacco ecstacy, the novice shaman himself relives the primordial shamanic existence."[9] Thus, myths are the maps for the voyage of transformations that the shaman makes time and time again in the course of his or her life.[10]

The House of Tobacco Smoke

One day the youth who had arisen in the East spread out his arms and proclaimed his name: *Domu Hokonamana Ariawara,* "Creator-Bird of the Dawn." With his left wing he held a bow and two quivering arrows, and his right wing shook a rattle. The plumes of his body chanted incessantly the new song that was heard in the East.

The thoughts of the Bird of the Dawn fell now on a house—and immediately it appeared: a round, white house made of tobacco smoke. It looked like a cloud. The singing Bird walked inside whirling his rattle.

Next he wanted to have four companions; four men and their wives. Rooms were already provided for each couple along the eastern wall of the House of Smoke.

"You, Black Bee," said the Bird of the Dawn. "Come share my solitude." And the Black Bee arrived with his wife. They transformed into tobacco smoke and chanted the song of the Bird of the Dawn.

"Wasp is next," called the Bird. The red Wasp arrived with his wife, transformed into smoke, and joined in the singing.

"Termite, now you," said the Bird of the Dawn. Termite's body and that of his wife were yellow. They took the room adjacent to Wasp, transformed into smoke, and learned the new song.

"Honey Bee, you are the last to be called." The Bees' bodies were blue. They occupied the room next to Termite. Like the others they transformed into tobacco smoke and joined in the chanting.

"I am the Master of this House of Smoke," exclaimed the Creator-Bird. "You are my companions. Black Bee is your chief, Wasp the constable, Termite and Honey Bee are workmen." Consenting to this, each companion approached the Master and stroked his head, shoulders, and arms so as to know him well. They chanted and smoked cigars. Thus they became the *bahanarao*, those who blow smoke.

The thoughts of the Bird of the Dawn fell now on a table draped in white and set with four dishes in a row—and there they stood in the middle of the house, all made of smoke. The Bird laid his weapons on it and said: "Now let us finish the Game of *Bahana*."

On Black Bee's dish there appeared a sparkling rock crystal. On Wasp's dish there was a ball of white hair. On Termite's plate white rocks appeared, and on Honey Bee's there gathered smoke of tobacco—the fourfold set of the Game of *Bahana*. *

Such is the House of Smoke of the Creator-Bird of the Dawn. This is how it became the birthplace of *bahana*, the shamanistic practice of blowing smoke and sucking out sickness. The House

---

*Crystal, hair ball, rocks, and tobacco smoke, each identified with a specific insect and color, are the principal agents of the shaman's power. Like arrows and other objects, they can be dispatched through the air as magical carriers of sickness.

of Smoke is situated to the East, halfway between the junction of earth and sky and the zenith of the cosmic vault. It came about long before there lived any Warao.

Then one day there appeared in the center of the earth a man and a woman. They were good people but their minds were unformed. However, they had a four-year-old** son who was very intelligent. He put his thoughts on many things. This way he came to think about the *Hoebo* place in the West with its stench of human cadavers, its blood, and its darkness. "There must be something in the East as well," reasoned the boy, "something light and colorful." He decided to go and explore the universe.

Now, although the young boy's body was relatively light, it was far too heavy for flight. The boy thought much about this until one day he asked his father to pile up firewood under his hammock. For four days he abstained from food and drink. In the evening of the fifth day he lit the wood with virgin fire and went to sleep. Then with the surging heat and smoke of the new fire the boy's spirit ascended to the zenith. Someone spoke to him, saying, "Follow me. I will show you the bridge to the House of Smoke in the East."

Soon the boy found himself on a bridge made of thick white ropes of tobacco smoke. He followed the invisible spirit guide until, a short distance from the center of the celestial dome, he reached a point where marvelous flowers began meandering alongside the bridge in a rainbow of brilliant colors—a row of red and a row of yellow flowers on the left, and lines of blue and green flowers on the right. A gentle breeze wafted them back and forth. Like the bridge they adorned, the flowers were made of solidified tobacco smoke. Everything was bright and tranquil. The invisible guide ushered the boy toward the House of Smoke. From a distance he already perceived the chanting of the *bahanarao.*

The bridge led right to the door of the House of Smoke in the East. The boy arrived there, listened to the beautiful music, and became so elated that he desired nothing more than to enter at once.

"Tell me who you are," demanded a voice from inside.

**Four is the sacred number of the Warao, a concept they share with numerous North and South American Indian tribes.

"It is I. The son of Warao."

"How old are you?"

"Four."

"You may enter," consented the Creator-Bird. It was he, the Supreme *Bahana*, who had questioned the boy. "You are pure and free of women," he said.

The boy set foot into the House of Smoke. He saluted the Creator-Bird of the Dawn and his four companions who came out of their quarters. The boy stood in front of the table with its four-part Game of *Bahana* and the weapons on top. He wanted to learn all about them.

"Which one would you rather possess?" the Supreme *Bahana* wanted to know.

"I take them all: the crystal, the white hair, the rocks, the smoke, and the bow and arrows as well." The boy was very wise.

"You shall have them."

"Now teach me your beautiful song."

And emerging from below the floor of the House of Smoke the boy beheld the head of a serpent with four colored plumes: white, yellow, blue, and green. They chimed a musical note like a bell. Projecting its forked tongue, the plumed serpent produced a glowing white ball of tobacco smoke.

"I know *bahana!*" exclaimed the youth.

"Now you possess it," said the *Bahana*. "You *are* a *bahana-rotu.*"

The serpent retreated. The insect-companions returned to their chambers and the boy awakened from his ecstatic trance. He rejected his mother's food for four days and more.

"You will die," she warned.

But he only appeared dead. He no longer desired *moriche* flour, fish, and water. He longed for the food of *bahana:* tobacco smoke.

On the fifth day the young *bahanarotu* experienced a strange transformation. His hands, his feet, his head began to glow. His arms and legs and finally his entire body turned brilliantly white. Then people appeared around his house: ten couples of Black Bee people, ten couples of Wasp people, ten couples of Termite people, and ten couples of Honey Bee people. And there were also many beautiful children among them.

"He is alive," they said.

"My name is *bahanarotu,*" said the youth. This was the first time the name *"bahana"* was uttered on earth. The *bahanarotu* built a small house, put his four-part Game of *Bahana* into a basket, and placed next to it his bow and arrows. The smoke of his cigars formed a path from the center of the earth to the zenith, where the bridge commences that leads to the House of Smoke in the East.

The *bahanarotu* kept his body light by eating very little. Tobacco smoke remained his principal food. His parents died, and, with no fellow Warao on earth, he married a beautiful Bee girl, a child like himself. They lived together but did not sleep together.

The young *bahanarotu* observed in the palms of his hands four dark spots right below each of his fingers. From there, through the arches of his arms, led paths of smoke into his breast to his four sons, the insect-companions, who were gradually taking form. Elder Brother Black Bee above Younger Brother Wasp was living on the strong right side of his chest. Elder Brother Termite above Younger Brother Honey Bee on the left. They were growing firmer while the *bahanarotu* kept feeding them smoke. In the tube of his cigar he rolled four portions of tobacco, one for each of his sons. Had he slept with his wife while the sons were still feeble, the spirit children would have died, and *bahana* would have vanished from this earth.

Instead the young couple abstained for four times four years, until the *bahana* sons had grown strong from the rich tobacco food. Then the time had come for the *bahanarotu* to talk to them.

"My sons," he said, "I will give you a mother. Do not be alarmed. Tonight I will show you your mother."

When the *bahanarotu* slept for the first time with his Bee wife he was very gentle. Only the head of his penis entered her vagina. The four spirit sons saw their mother and liked her. Also the mother beheld her white-smoke sons in a dream and found them pleasing and handsome. During each of the succeeding nights the *bahanarotu* penetrated further and deeper. Thus the first *bahana* family was established.

The insect-people who had been living about the *bahanarotu's* home returned now to the House of Smoke.

"We should go there too," said the *bahanarotu* to his wife. "It is lonely here."

They began to fast so as to lighten their bodies. They smoked and smoked and after eight days the *bahanarotu* ascended. His wife followed shortly, but when she entered the House of Smoke, the Supreme *Bahana* suffered a seizure.

"I know how to help him," said the woman. Walking up to the Supreme *Bahana* she transformed herself into a beautiful black sea bird.* She spread out her wings, shook them like rattles, and, while blowing tobacco smoke on the epileptic body of her patient, soothed him gently with her plumes. The Supreme *Bahana* recovered.

"You are a *bahanarotu* indeed," said he. "Remain here, *Sinaka Aidamo,* spirit of seizures."

So there they are, the *bahanarotu* and his wife, smoking, rattling, and chanting in unison with the *bahanarao.*

Much time elapsed, and when many people appeared in the center of the earth, they knew nothing about *bahana* and the bridge that reached from their village to the House of Tobacco Smoke. For this reason the *bahanarotu* rolled a cigar with two *bahana* inside and aimed it at a young man whom he had chosen to receive them. He sent Smoke for the right side of the youth's chest and Rocks for his left side. Smoke became the Elder Brother, Rocks the Younger. When they struck the youth he fell over as if dead. The *bahana* spirits entered his body and became his helpers. But when he woke up displaying his weapons and rattle of tobacco smoke, the people vanished from sight. They were transformed into River Crab people and became the Masters of Earth.

Finally many Warao appeared in the center of the earth. Again the young *bahanarotu,* who was himself a Warao, shot the same pair of *bahana* spirits down to earth from the House of Smoke. The young man who received them survived and learned how to travel the bridge of tobacco smoke in the sky. Here he received much advice on how to preserve his *Bahana* spirits and how to use them.

That is why *bahana* continued on earth to the present day. It is not so perfect or so powerful as it was long ago, when the first *bahanarotu* received four spirit helpers. Nevertheless, *bahana* prevails. And it is still very strong among the Warao.

---

*Probably the Magnificent Frigate Bird, *Fregata magnificens,* also known as the Man-of-War Bird, with a wingspread of seven or eight feet.

Ramón Medina Silva
MESOAMERICA/HUICHOL

The work of the Huichol shaman is extraordinarily complex and demanding, requiring vast knowledge, aesthetic abilities, abundant physical resources, and keen social skills. The body of myth is ramified and elaborate, and the chants and rituals emerging from these ancient stories are a frequently occurring element in Huichol life. Physical health, great stamina, and will must, of necessity, be cultivated by the *mara'akáme,* who officiates at ceremony after ceremony, all night, night after night, when the sacred tales of life's origin and meaning are recounted in song or narrative.

Barbara Myerhoff's experience with Ramón's presentation of myth material provides a notion of the special role the stories of the ancients play in the life of these people: "At first Ramón dictated texts only in Spanish, but after a time, he gave them first in Huichol, followed by a Spanish version. The former were always longer, more intense, involving gestures, weeping, rejoicing, jumping about, whipping out objects for illustration, often using violin and song. When recording the Huichol texts, he would don full ceremonial attire and dictate only in the semidarkness of the windowless hut or in the empty countryside."[11]

The myths represent one aspect of the culture's science. They are the cartographies that give coherence and direction to the people's lives. They teach every man, woman, and child, "how one goes being Huichol." The myths are the repository of the culture's sacred history and, as such, are in the realm of truth. They are mythic fact.

"When the *Mara'akáme* Plays the Drum and Flies the Children to the Land of Peyote" is the mythological map that is chanted in the course of the *wima'kwan* (drum ceremony). Just as the Siberian shaman's drum becomes the vehicle of flight for the visionary's disincarnate soul, the drum played by the Huichol *mara'akáme* and his assistants guides the children along the cosmic geography that is traditionally traveled by those who are peyote pilgrims making their way to the Sacred Land of Peyote, the place of paradise. This is where the gods and goddess, Our Mothers and Our Fathers, first came in original times and where they are still to be found. The dangerous sacred journey replicates the adult peyote hunt in its most important aspects. As anthropologist Barbara Myerhoff observed, it is an "impressive and subtle blending of the actual, the magical, the symbolic, and the anticipatory."[12]

When the *Mara'akáme* Plays the Drum and Flies the Children to the Land of the Peyote

"Look," he tells them, "it is this way. We will fly over this little mountain. We will travel to Wirikuta, where the sacred water is, where the peyote is, where Our Father comes up."

And from there they fly, like bees, straight, they go on the wind as one says, this way. As though they were a flock of doves, very beautiful, like the singing turtle doves. They fly evenly. You can see that they become as little tiny bees, very pretty. They continue from hill to hill. They fly from place to place as the *mara'akáme* tells them. The *mara'akáme* goes with Kauyumari, Kauyumari who tells him everything. He protects them all. A little girl is missing a wing because the father or the mother have committed many sins. If they are missing a wing, the *mara'akáme* puts it back on. Then she flies with the rest of them.

So they continue to travel. As they come to a place, the *mara'akáme* points it out. So that they will know of it, how it was when Our Grandfather, Our Father, Our Great Grandparent, Our Mothers, when they went to Wirikuta, when Elder Brother Deer Tail, Maxa Kwaxí-Kauyumari, crossed over there and the children of the first Huichols went there, so that they became cured.

That is what the drum says on our rancho. When it is beaten. There the children fly. The *mara'akáme* leads them on the wind. They land on one of the rocks. It is as though they were clinging to the rock, very dangerous. The *mara'akáme* tells them, "Look, children, you are not familiar with these paths. There are many dangers, there are many animals that eat children, that threaten people. You must not separate, you must stay close together, all of you." And the children are very glad, very happy.

They fly on to Tokuari, to Where the Arrows Are. They fly past there. *Xiuwa, xiuwa, xiuwa,* so goes the sound of their flying. Their wings. They arrive at Tskata, the Volcanic Place, where in Ancient Times, the First Mara'akáme, Our Grandfather, blessed the sacred water in the caves, so that everyone could go there, our relatives, the Huichols, everyone. The *mara'akáme* takes a gourd bowl and with it sprinkles the sacred water over them. He tells them, "I bless you in the Four Winds, to the right and to the other side, to the north, to the south, and up above." So he says to them. He prays, "Let us feed them. There where Our Grandfather is, there on the south, there on the north. You, Our Aunt, Our Mother who are there. You, Kumúkite, gather yourselves together. You, Our Grandparents, who are kept in our houses as rock crystals, gather yourselves together. Your votive bowls are in their places, there they are."

He offers them on his right, he offers them on his left, he offers them to his east, he offers them above. Also he offers them to his west, where Our Mother Haramara dwells, where Our Mother Hamuxamaka dwells. So at last he says, "We will fly on." They land at Wakanarixipa. This is a terrible mountainous country. Here the *mara'akáme* explains to them, "That is the way we must travel, the symbols we must follow. For when someone dies, there is always someone who comes after." Then he flies on. The children fly on, to Where the Star Lives. Then they fly to a place they call Hukuta (La Ocota, Pine Grove, the Place of Kindling Wood). Now they say, "*Mara'akáme* tell us, how will we cross that river there?" "Well," he says, "I know how." And he takes them safely.

"At last," he prays, "Our Mothers, Our Fathers, all you who are in Wirikuta, those who are eaten as peyote, we are on our way to Wirikuta." He says to the children, "Act and feel like eagles. You will go there on your wings." They give instructions to one another, they learn. One tells the other, "Light your candle," and he answers, "Yes, very well." The *mara'akáme* takes tinder, he takes flint, he takes steel for striking fire. They do this five times and they light the candles and worship there and go on their way. They travel and come to a place they call Las Cruces, where the cross is. They exclaim, "Oh, look, we really have come far, yes we have come far. And how will we be able to go on?" And they say, "Well, it is because we are going to Wirikuta, where the peyote grows, where our ancestors traveled. We have to get rid of our sins, everything."

The *mara'akáme,* he travels on Kauyumari, who is the Deer, the Deer of the *mara'akáme,* Tatewarí, he leads them all, he is the one taking care of them all. They travel to a place called Irons Flying

Up and after they have passed there they arrive at Teapari. They get to know it in the daylight. Here Kauyumari grinds the roots for the colors with which the Huichols paint their faces. It is the peyote paint, the paint which they get from the yellow roots they find growing in the country of the peyote. To get to know that place, that is why Our Grandfather, Our Father, Our Mother Haramara takes hold of them as they are. This is where they painted their faces, so that they could go across. There they pick up the root, carry it with them, so that they bring it to their homes. Our Grandfather passed by here in Ancient Times; it is he who placed it here, it is in Ancient Times that it was given its name, when Our Grandfather passed by here, when Kauyumari passed by here. It is a very beautiful place, very grand. Very sacred. So they learn all that from the *mara'akáme.*

Now comes the most mysterious thing of all the great things on that journey. They arrive at the place called Where the Vagina Is, where it is called La Puerta, the Door, the Gate, in Spanish. Kauyumari opens it with his horns and he tells the *mara'akáme,* "Here, the way is open, we may proceed." It is a very sacred place. Where the *peyoteros* sit in their places around Our Grandfather, close to Our Grandfather, while the *mara'akáme* tells them to name all the women they have enjoyed, one by one. They must name them by their right names, even though all the other things are transformed. Where the knots are untied, the sins are taken away by Our Grandfather.*

They travel on to the place called Where the Penis Hangs.** Here the *mara'akáme* speaks to Our Mothers, Our Grandparents. "Let us see what the deer tail plumes say."

They descend holding on to one another. This place is called the Breast, that is the name it was given in Ancient Times. There, they go on. They come to the place called Where the Arrows Stand. Then to Witsexuka, where they sit in a circle. "What is this place here named?" he asks the children. So they learn. He goes on and on, until all can sleep there.

---

*This is exactly what occurs on the peyote trip. . . . The statement concerning the need for "right names" despite the fact that everything is transformed refers to the reversals instituted during the peyote hunt. "Confession" in this version occurs much later than that witnessed in the actual ceremony.
**No explication or identification of this place was possible.

We are not eating anything to speak of on this journey. Just a few watermelons, squash, green roasting ears of maize, just something, one thing and another. Oh, we carry a real load of life! If Our Mother is thus, if Our Father there is thus, they will give it to us, they will feed us. And he goes on, to the place where Wirikuta lies, that which they call Real Catorce, there they travel. He beats the drum.

Where it is called Wirikuta, where Our Mother Peyote dwells, there they arrive. When he has beaten the drum, when he stands by the sacred pools, when he has spoken to the Mothers and the Fathers, to Our Father, to Our Grandfather, to Our Great Grandparent, when he has laid his offerings down, when their votive bowls are in their place, when their arrows are in their place, when their wristbands are in their place, when their sandals are in their place, then it will be good, then we will have life.

The children are happy, all, they are contented. Because now they are blessed. The offerings are made, the deer tail plumes are in their place, the arrows are to the south, to the north, to the east, up above. He holds them out. The horns of the deer are in their place, no matter what kind.* The *mara'akáme* says, "Oh, Our Father, Our Grandfather, Our Mothers, you all who dwell here, we have arrived to visit you, to come and see you here. We have arrived well." And when they arrive, they kneel and Our Father, Our Grandfather, Our Elder Brother, embrace them.

"What did you come for, my children?" they ask. "You have come so far, why did you travel so far?"

They answer, "We came to visit you so that we will know all, so that we will have life."

"All right," they say, "it is well," and they bless them. And there they remain but ten minutes, a very few minutes, to speak with Our Father, Our Grandfather, with all of them there. And then the Mother gives them the blessing and they leave.

---

*This refers to the growing scarcity of deer in the Sierra, which often necessitates substitutions. Here it is made clear that above all location and usage determine what is really proper. Thus bull horns "become" a kind of deer horn if "they are there, in their proper place."

Prem Das
NORTH AMERICA/HUICHOL

In the fall of 1973, I met Prem Das, Lupe, María, José, and two other Huichols in Big Sur, California. It was our first meeting. With several others, we partook of the peyote sacrament and enacted a ritual that had powerful consequences in relation to my life. Ramón Medina Silva explained the significance of the peyote ceremony to Barbara Myerhoff and Peter Furst: "It is one, it is a unity, it is ourselves." As I looked into the eyes of Prem Das and his Huichol friends that day in Big Sur, I realized that my life was to be transformed in a way I could never have anticipated.

Even today, years later, many, many ceremonies later, I still find it difficult to describe my friend Prem Das. We have run in the high mountains like deer, fasted, climbed to the summit of *Kakauyaríxi* (the ancient gods or power spots); we have taught together and traveled together. He, my little brother, tested my strength of body, strength of mind, and strength of will. Without him, my interest in shamanism would have remained academic.

Prem Das's first experiences with visionary consciousness came at the age of nine, when he volunteered to participate in a series of hypnosis sessions for Dr. Ernest Hilgard at the hypnosis laboratory at Stanford University. An excellent subject, he was invited back for several days at a time, year after year, until he was fifteen.

Soon he began to study self-hypnosis, giving particular attention to the technique of age regression. This led him back through time, beyond the transition of birth, to the experience of previous lifetimes. But the past lives he encountered were not of greatest interest to him. Rather, he was drawn to explore the state or zone in between, known by the Tibetans as bardo.

At the age of eighteen, he met Ram Dass, who taught him various techniques of raja-yoga. After exploring these practices intensively over a period of six months, he was suddenly overwhelmed with the ecstasy induced by an activated kundalini. Realizing he needed guidance, Ram Dass sent him to his teacher in India, Baba Hari Das. From this master of ashtang-yoga, he received his name (which means "servant of love") and further instruction in raja- and kundalini-yoga.

After returning from India, Prem Das went to Mexico, where he could quietly practice the yoga techniques he learned in India. Quite unexpectedly, he met the Huichol shaman Ramón Medina Silva, and they became friends. Later, he followed Ramón back to his village high in the mountains of west central Mexico. It was there he met the elder shaman Matsúwa, who initiated him into the path of the Huichol shaman over a five-year period.[13]

After an all-night ceremony in which we did the deer dance around an open fire and listened to the sacred chants of my "grandfather," Don José, [Matsúwa] I returned to my grass hut totally exhausted, expecting to fall asleep. It was morning, so I had to pull my blanket well up over my head to cut out the light that partially illuminated the hut. I could still hear the children down below in the patio playing and the wind blowing through the rock-bamboo walls of my dwelling, but what at first was faint and then became louder and louder were Don José's chants, still echoing in my mind:

> Listen, my children, we are the ones
> The path is clear, the danger is gone
> Káuyumari will guide us, only he knows the way
> Light your candles, the gods have come.
>
> They were people, yet they were gods
> Follow the eagle, see where she goes
> From there they come, and the path unfolds
> So then the example is set, we must follow along.
>
> Look to the sky, to our Father above,
> We are all his children, dance to the song.
> As the Ancient Ones knew, the time has come,
> The nieríka is opening, and we pass on to the Sun.

The breeze passing through the hut somehow seemed to be coming and going in exact rhythm with the chant. My body had fallen asleep, yet my mind was ascending on a breeze-chant that had now turned into a jet stream upon which I was ascending higher and higher into the sky. From far above, I could see my hut and the village below. I was free and flying with such a feeling of exhilaration and joy that I wanted to cry, for now I was experiencing the real meaning of Don José's song. This was death to the person I believed I was, the life that I had lived in the body left far below. As the jet stream accelerated my ascent, I lost view of the village as well as all memories of who or what I was. How I could see and fly without any kind of body did not concern me at all, nor did I think, for all thoughts had vanished as well. Awareness and complete clarity remained as if all else had been blown clear by the extreme speed of acceleration.

Various kinds of light and forms passed; they looked like luminous clouds. Was I dreaming? Only now can I ask. Never have I dreamed (and recalled it) with such total awareness. The cloud forms were singing, and I was riding on their song. Each song lifted me still higher toward a warm, blissful, and radiant light. As I came closer to the great brilliant sphere, time was slowing to a stop. Intuitively, I knew I was dead and had absolutely no knowledge of who I was or where I came from. Yet, I *knew* and felt totally at home, as if I had returned from a journey in a faraway land. This knowing self I knew myself to be was ancient, existing in all time, for his residence was in the eternal, in a star, the sun, at the center of my universe.

Unfortunately, I recall very little of the experience. As I approached the Great Sun, I vanished completely. How can I say how long I was there? It seemed like forever. The last thing I remember was orbiting the sun, within it, and then vanishing.

Don José was sitting on my bed next to me when I awoke; he was smiling. He pulled a pack of cigarettes out of his bag and handed them to me. I sat up, lit one for him, placed it in his mouth, and then lit one for myself.

"Did you enjoy my chant?" he asked innocently, but with a mischievous grin.

"What can I say? It was—"

But before I could say anything—and all I was going to say was "incredible"—he said, "Let's go eat dinner."

I had been "traveling" all day; it was just then getting dark. Whether I had been out all day or for weeks or years, it would have been the same day. The power that took me to the sun realm had returned me to the same day, month, year, and location that I had left. I do not know how my descent occurred because I do not remember returning from that first journey.

The next day, I went with Don José down the mountainside to work with him on the slopes clearing jungle growth. This is done in the bright sunlight and heat with a machete, slashing the growth that will be burned at the end of the dry season. It is very hard work, and one sweats profusely. Don José believes sweating eliminates impurities from the body, thus promoting health and long life. He says it's not so much a matter of what you do (eating, making love, smoking, drinking coffee, and so on) as of what you don't do (hard exercise, long pilgrimages on foot to the *Kakauyaríxi,* * performing and dedicating ceremonies to the gods) that determines health and well-being. Anyone and almost everyone can enjoy the things of the first category. The second category is so much harder that its tasks are avoided and left undone; illness then finds weak bodies and minds that make easy prey.

During our first rest break, I told him of my flight the day before. He listened very attentively as I explained to him the details I could remember.

"The luminous clouds," he said, "these are the *urucate.* ** They change size and form freely, which is what you saw and is why they appear as clouds. When I chant, such clouds surround me, and it is they that sing through me; I only listen and repeat what I hear."

He reached into his beautifully embroidered *kutsiuri* † and took out a pack of cigarettes, offering me one. "Look at the smoke," he said. He then gestured to the ascent and expanding movement of the cigarette smoke as it ebbed and flowed, making invisible air currents apparent. "When the *mara'akáme* passes through the *nieríka* [visionary tunnel], he moves just as this smoke moves; hidden currents carry him up and in all directions at once. Just as the smokes from your cigarette and my cigarette rise, merge, and pass through each other, so, too, the *mara'akáme* rides as if upon waves, flowing into and through other waves; these other waves are the *urucate.* Constantly playing music and singing songs, they teach what no man knows or ever can know. For as the *mara'akáme* descends and begins to pass through the great *nieríka* on the return to his home and family, his memory of the *urucate* and their world fades; only a glimmer remains of the fantastic journey that he made.

"Why can't we remember?" I asked him.

*Natural monuments such as waterfalls and high, remote mountaintops that are places of the gods.
**Spirit beings.
†Bag or purse carried by most Huichols.

"It's really sad," he said with a twinkle as he lifted a water gourd and offered me a drink. "It's all Káuyumari's fault." And he farted. We both burst out laughing.

"Back in the first times, after the sun [Tayaupá] had a dream of a new world, he sent Káuyumari to find it. The Little Deer Spirit was informed by the sun where a great swirling tunnel of light existed, through which he was to pass. This is the *nieríka*. He was led by Tatewarí, Great Grandfather Fire, and quite a number of *urucate*. They traveled through the *nieríka*, arriving in *Heriepa*, the world in which we now live. They formed and created everything: the mountains, rivers, plants, animals, men and women. Of course, the story is very, very long, and this is just the general picture. So beautiful was the new world that even the sun traveled through the *nieríka* to take his place in the sky.

"The very first race were people, yet they were gods. They knew almost as much as the *urucate* and were able to travel back and forth through the *nieríka* at will. Great ceremonies were constantly being performed throughout the world, dedicated to the sun, celebrating the new life and world that had been dreamed of and discovered by the sun. The ceremonies of dance, music, and song that we still do to this day were passed down by our remotest ancestors, these men who were gods. This is our tradition and nothing of greater importance has been passed down from one generation to the next."

Don José and I both became enraptured as he continued to tell the story of Creation. We had forgotten not only the field clearing but also how or what had started us off into the legends and stories from the beginnings of time. Nothing pleased my "grandfather" more than to sit back, smoking, looking at the winding river below and the distant pine-covered mountain ranges, and recount that which had gone before us and had brought us to the present day.

"At one of these first ceremonies," Don José continued, "Káuyumari got drunk after drinking too much corn beer [*nawá*]. This is when all the trouble began. When he was leading the deer dance, he became attracted to one of the pretty Huichol girls dancing next to him. With the touch of his fluffy tail, a spell fell over her; and a little later that night, they wandered off and embraced while the ceremony was still in progress. He had broken the rule of ceremonial conduct that prohibits such activities before and during ceremonies, a law set down by the sun.

"Drunk, Káuyumari just couldn't help himself. The beauty of the girls overwhelmed him with such desire that he would sneak off with them into the darkness where he could feel them most intimately." This Don José explained laughing and shaking his head.

"Before long this became a habit. He would attend ceremonies, get drunk, and when dancing, tickle the girls with his soft little tail. He found the women enjoyed these spells and even began to seek him out. And then the women would get drunk and fight over who was to sneak off and enjoy embracing Káuyumari."

My "grandfather" could barely contain his laughter as he went on: "The Little Deer Spirit became notorious for the power of his spells over women throughout the Sierra. He was now using his shamanic powers for healing people in the daytime and for seducing women at night. Soon the shamans who were conducting the ceremonies became jealous of Káuyumari and his romantic affairs. They decided to use their sacred feathers and songs to enchant the women so that they, too, could have many women to enjoy.

"The ceremonies thus became a time of opportunity to sneak off with each other's wives, and the women also learned sorcery to gain the men that they desired to sleep with. It was not long before jealous fights broke out, and these occurred even during the ceremonies when corn beer and tequila were consumed.

"It was really terrible," Don José said. "No one cared about the ceremonies, and they turned into drunken brawls. The men's 'chilis' became so hot, all they wanted to do was push them into any hole that could be found, including animals'. The women as well only desired to be in heat and to embrace as many different men as they could.

"The great tradition of sacred, ceremonial celebrations that were dedicated to the sun ended and instead turned into a tradition of parties warmed up with lots of beer and tequila. The jealousy and fights got so bad, people started killing each other."

Don José pulled some tortilla bean tacos out of his bag, and we ate lunch sitting on some large boulders in the cool shade of several *capomal* trees. We had not cleared much jungle growth, but several of his sons had, and the sound of their machetes slashing through the dried vines and high brush was growing louder as they worked their way through the jungle toward us.

"The Sun, Tayaupá, was very saddened," he continued. "His children were forgetting their father. That they were making love with others than their spouses, especially during ceremonies, could have been a humorous and eventually curable situation. But getting drunk, fighting, leaving the sacred way of the ceremony, and killing each other was too disturbing for the Sun to contemplate. If his children were unhappy and suffering, the best thing to do would be to free them from their misery, return them to the Sky Realm, back to their real home.

"So this is exactly what the Sun did. He caused the rains to come and flood the entire world. Only one Huichol, *Watákame*, was saved. *Watákame* had never fought, gotten overly drunk, or run after other women. So the Sun saved him by informing him through *Nakawé*, Great Grandmother Growth, that the world was about to end with a flood and that he should gather seeds, build a canoe, and prepare himself. Thus, he survived the flood to become the forefather of all of us today."

Don José picked up his machete and began to sharpen it as he continued the story. "The world repopulated quickly after *Watákame* was given a wife. But he found that all his children, grandchildren, and great-grandchildren were born with a serious case of amnesia. They did not recall passing through the great *nieríka,* so they had no knowledge of their former home in Tateteima. Furthermore, they had no psychic powers such as their ancestors, the god-people [*urucate*] had possessed. Very curious about why this was the case, *Watákame* performed a ceremony and, while chanting, communicated with the Sun. He learned that the Sun no longer wanted all men to have psychic powers, and so it was to be except for those who were willing to suffer the rigors of self-sacrifice in order to know. These special persons would be known as *mara'akámte* (shaman-doctors) who would be allowed to use their powers only for healing, protecting, and guiding their people. If they used their knowledge or powers for casting spells to attract women or harm others, then the powers would be taken away, and they would fall ill, go insane, or die."

Don José's sons had cleared the jungle through to where we were sitting. Still sweating, they sat down with us to hear the end of the story. Don José offered everyone a cigarette and then went on.

"Káuyumari, although he never fought with anyone or caused any harm, was still to blame. Not being able to control his erotic nature created havoc when he got drunk. Father Sun reprimanded him severely and pleaded with him to set a better example for people to follow. The Little Deer Spirit was also to begin a new job with the second world, and that was to guard the access to the great *nieríka,* or doorway, between Heriepa and Tateteima."

Don José looked at me and said, "Here is the reason why we only remember a hazy fragment of our incredible journeys to the realm of the gods [Tateteima]. Káuyumari was allowed to let pass through only those who had met the Sun's requirement of self-sacrifice and devotion to helping, curing, and guiding the people. Once on the other side, they would be free to learn from the *urucate,* the gods, or the sun himself. Here again they would find and know their real home. Unfortunately, during the return trip back through the *nieríka,* they would have to pass Káuyumari. Unseen, our brother the Deer Spirit was under orders to fly by and steal any secret 'documents' the voyagers might be carrying. The documents, or memories, considered secret were those which contained knowledge that could be used as power once back in Heriepa. Of course, Káuyumari instantly knew who was going to use power for good purposes and who had other things in mind."

Julian, one of Don José's sons, looked at me, grinning, and said, "What happens if Káuyumari, prankster that he is, decides to steal the whole works, every memory he can get his hoofs on?" Don José buckled over with laughter, as we all did.

"Just think," little José, Don José's younger son added, "he wouldn't know what world he was awakening to; he wouldn't recognize his wife, family, or rancho!"

Don José said we should not be laughing, that it actually can happen, and that years ago he was asked to cure a Huichol that had spent several months in such a condition.

Again we all roared with laughter.

"Let's go," Don José said, picking up his machete and water gourd. "It's getting late."

As we followed him up the winding trail back to the village on the small mesa above, I would periodically look over my shoulder across the valleys and distant mountain ranges to the setting sun. There, in that flaming sphere which kindles all life on earth with its warm, luminous rays, dwell the Ancient Ones, the *urucate*, who, according to Huichol beliefs, helped create the world in the very beginning and have playfully worked to guide and teach mankind ever since.

9 Lifting up the Nieríka

Two shamans lift up the Nierka like a mirror that seems to invite the viewer to enter the worlds beyond surface appearances. *Elements from this drawing are from a yarn painting created by Ruturi and kindly lent by Ilana Rubenfeld.*

Matsúwa
MESOAMERICA/HUICHOL

*The shaman's path is unending. I am
an old, old man and still a nunutsi
[baby] standing before the mystery of
the world filled with awe.* [1]

Matsúwa, a renowned shaman among the Huichols, lives high in the
Mexican Sierras in the state of Nayarit in a small village called El
Colorín. According to him, his shamanic apprenticeship spanned a
sixty-four-year period. Today, Matsúwa, whose name means "pulse,"
says that he has at last completed his apprenticeship and can now
enjoy the fruits of old age.

A ceremonial shaman whose chants are of particular poetic
beauty, Matsúwa often sings for several days and nights in the course
of a single ceremony. While these sacred events are taking place, he
remains seated in his *uweni,* or shaman's chair, in order that the power
which has been manifested will not be lost.

He is also known for his ability to heal the sick. Sucking objects
out of the body and using his prayer arrows *(muviéri)* to adjust the
energy fields in and around the body, he offers prayers to the divine
forces that have the power to restore harmony and to increase the life
force *(kupúri)* of the one who is diseased.

Until some twenty years ago, this eighty-eight-year-old (perhaps
ninety-eight) shaman walked the 250-mile trip to Wirikúta, the high
desert in central Mexico which is the Sacred Land of Peyote. He still
makes pilgrimages to this sacred ground, although much of the journey is now made by bus and train because the path to Wirikúta has
been cut off by Mexican ranches.

Wild humor is one of Matsúwa's most endearing traits. At one
ceremony, in the midst of gales of laughter, he arranged an engage-
ment for marriage between me and the local sorcerer, Natcho Pistola.
Peter Furst told another story about him. During the ceremony in

which each peyote pilgrim must give a *complete* recitation of *all* past love affairs, Matsúwa, after disclosing several names, exclaimed, "I have led such a long life that my feet are already rotting in the earth; if I spoke here of all those whom I have enjoyed we would not leave here tomorrow or the day after tomorrow!"[2] In visions I have had during ceremonies, I have often seen him as an ancient eagle with the heart of a deer—a very playful and rascally deer!

Full of passion and vitality, Matsúwa expresses deep concern not only for the loss of tradition among his own people but also for the lack of balance in the lives of his North American friends. He came to New York and California in 1976 and 1977 so that we might "find our lives." During his visits, he often wept in the course of the ceremonies as he chanted about the catastrophies that plague the world. He said:

> In ancient times, when balance was lost on the planet, a great flood came to destroy all that which was on the earth so that the world could be reborn. A similar imbalance seems to be occurring in this generation; we have forgotten our life source, the sun, and the sacred sea, the blessed land, the sky, and all things of nature. Unless we remember quickly what our lives are about, unless we celebrate through ceremony and prayer, we will again face destruction, but this time, it will be by fire.[3]

I have pursued my apprenticeship for sixty-four years. During these years, many, many times I have gone to the mountains alone. Yes, I have endured much suffering during my life. Yet to learn to see, to learn to hear, you must do this—go into the wilderness alone. For it is not I who teach you the ways of the gods. Such things are learned only in solitude.

If you have the desire to learn the path of the shaman, the Fire will teach you, the Fire, Our Grandfather. You must listen to the Fire, for the Fire speaks, and the Fire teaches. And during the day, you learn from the Sun. The Sun will teach you, the Sun, Our Father. This is always best done with *hicuri*, peyote. From peyote comes forth Káuyumari, the Little Deer Spirit ally, and he will communicate that which you must learn. Káuyumari emerges like a mirror and shows you what you must do. The Little Deer knows. All the gods communicate with Káuyumari, and he teaches you.

The Fire (Tatewarí), the Sun (Tayaupá), Wirikúta (the Sacred Land of Peyote) can transmit the vision *(nieríka)* to you. The shaman can also transmit the *nieríka* to you, but you must not forget the gods. It is they who open your heart to the beauty of the *nieríka*. Your love of the gods—the Sun, the Fire, the Waters—brings forth the *nieríka*.

Yes, there are many ways to gain vision, many, many ways. Yet for me, the best is *hicuri*. When I eat *hikuri*, the world becomes radiant with glowing color. Káuyumarie, the Little Deer, comes to me to show me how it all is. When you hear me chanting the sacred songs, it is not I who sing but Káuyumarie who is singing into my ear. And I transmit these songs to you. It is he who teaches us, shows us the way. This is how it is.

The sacred feathers talk to me about why there has been no rain in this place [California]. In some places, Tayaupá burns your land; in other places, Tayaupá's face is hidden. This place that you live in and many other places in your country suffer from drought, too much rain, shortages, many problems. There is a reason for this misfortune, for you have not been doing ceremonies, gathering together, thanking the earth, the gods, the Sun, the sea for your lives. This is missing here. Without celebration, the gods are unhappy and bring misery to us. The ceremonies, gathering together, celebrating together—this is the love or energy that the gods live on. In the ceremonies, we come together to be as one. Those that do not want this in their hearts fall away.

The last time I was in your land, we did a ceremony. I chanted with my heart. And after the ceremony, a powerful rain came. Yes, we had purified ourselves at the ocean in the morning, after celebrating through the night; then the clouds began to gather, and within several hours, it was pouring rain. You should have told me sooner that you had such problems. I would have come earlier to do a ceremony in order to change the situation.

I see that many people here are so caught up in their own little lives that they are not getting their love up to the sun, out to the ocean, and into the earth. When you do ceremonies, sending out your love in the five directions—the north, the south, the east, the west, and the center—brings life force into you. That love brings in the rain. As it has been since human history began, people are wrapped up in their little worlds, and they forget the elements, forget the source of their life.

In my country, we anticipate disasters, and we do the ceremo-

nies to avoid the problems, working with the elements through the
ceremony. When the rains come in here, I will have to charge you
a hundred million dollars! [He was full of laughter.] I am lying. But
here it has been out of balance for a long time. It is difficult to
readjust the situation, to retune it. We will have to gather together
and, with the ceremonies, begin to tune ourselves with the environment, bringing it back into balance again. The ocean is telling
me that if it doesn't soon come into balance, terrible destruction
will come in the form of fire. It is very difficult what is happening
in your land. It almost makes me cry to feel the situation being so
out of harmony.

So, I ask you to go to the sea and make offerings. Take a
candle, chocolate, and money. Offer these things to Tateí
Haramara, Our Mother the Sea. Pray for her. Tune yourself to her.
But you do not believe; you have no faith. What if I ask you to
take all of your money and offer it to Tateí Haramara? What
would you do then? What if that was truly the only way? But only
a tiny bit is necessary. This is how it is.

You must study these things I am saying, and with understanding, your life will become stronger. You have your own way
of learning. Perhaps it is different from ours. But you have seen
the flower of my vision on my face, and you must know that it
is important to think of these things each day and each night.
Then, one day, the sea will give you heart; the Fire will give you
heart; the Sun will give you heart. And when you come to my
village, I will know. I will check you by lifting up the *nieríka,* like
a mirror, and I will see what you have done, how you have gone
in the world.

Sources
of the Narratives

Sereptie From Andrei A. Popov, "How Sereptie Djarroskin of the Nganasans (Tavgi Samoyeds) Became a Shaman," in *Popular Beliefs and Folklore Tradition in Siberia,* ed. Vilmos Diószegi and trans. Stephen P. Dunn, pp. 137–146. Bloomington: Indiana University Press, 1968.

Kyzlasov From Vilmos Diószegi, *Tracing Shamans in Siberia,* trans. Anita Rajkay Bubo, pp. 53–76. Oosterhout (Netherlands): Anthropological Publications, 1968.

Lizard's Son From Alfred W. Howitt, *The Native Tribes of South-East Australia,* pp. 406–408. London: Macmillan, 1904.

Old K"xau From Marguerite Anne Biesele, "Folklore and Ritual of Kung Hunters-Gatherers," pp. 154–173. Ph.D. dissertation, Harvard University, 1975.

Igjugarjuk From Knud Rasmussen, *Intellectual Culture of the Hudson Bay Eskimos,* trans. W. E. Calvert, pp. 52–55. Report of the Fifth Thule Expedition, 1921–1924, vol. 7. Copenhagen: Gyldendal, 1930.

Lame Deer From Lame Deer and Richard Erdoes, *Lame Deer: Seeker of Visions,* pp.11–16. New York: Simon and Schuster, 1972.

Leonard Crow Dog From Leonard Crow Dog and Richard Erdoes, *The Eye of the Heart.* New York: Harper & Row, forthcoming.

Brooke Medicine Eagle © Brooke Medicine Eagle, 1977.

Black Elk From John G. Neihardt, *Black Elk Speaks,* pp. 20–33. Lincoln: University of Nebraska Press, 1961.

Joe Green From Willard Z. Park, *Shamanism in Western North America,* pp. 16, 17, 24, and 25. New York: Cooper Square, 1975.

Rosie Plummer From Willard Z. Park, *Shamanism in Western North America,* pp. 16, 17, 30, and 31. New York: Cooper Square, 1975.

Autdaruta From Knud Rasmussen, *The People of the Polar North, A Record,* comp. and ed. G. Herring, pp. 305–309. Philadelphia: Lippincott, 1908.

Sanimuinak From Gustav Holm, "Legends and Tales from Angmagsalik," in *The Ammasalik Eskimo: Contributions to the Ethnology of the East Greenland Natives,* ed. William Thalbitzer and trans. Johan Petersen, pp. 298–300. Meddeleserom Greenland Series, Bind XXXIX and XL. Copenhagen: C. A. Reitzel, 1914.

Aua From Knud Rasmussen, *Intellectual Culture of the Iglulik Eskimos,* trans. William Worster, pp. 116–120. Report of the Fifth Thule Expedition, 1921–1924, vol. 7, part 1. Copenhagen: Gyldendal, 1930.

Gol'd Shaman From Lev Iakovlevich Shternberg, "Divine Election in Primitive Religion (including material on different tribes of N. E. Asia and America)," in *Congrès international des Americanistes,* pp. 176–178. Compte-Rendu de la XXIe

253

session, 2eme partie tenue à Goteborg en 1924. Xendeln (Liechtenstein): Kraus Reprint (Kraus-Thomson Organization Ltd.), 1968.

Tankli   From Alfred W. Howitt, *The Native Tribes of South-East Australia*, pp. 408–410. London: Macmillan, 1904.

María Sabina   From Alberto Ongaro, *"Interview with María Sabina,"* trans. R. Gordon Wasson and A. Alexander. *L Éuropeo*, November 25, 1971.

Ramón Medina Silva   From Barbara G. Myerhoff, *Peyote Hunt*, pp. 219-220. Ithaca, N.Y.: Cornell University Press, 1974.

Desana Shaman   From Gerardo Reichel-Dolmatoff, *The Shaman and the Jaguar*, pp. 150–151. Philadelphia: Temple University Press, 1975.

Manuel Córdova-Rios   From Bruce T. Lamb, *Wizard of the Upper Amazon*, 2d ed., pp. 86–97. Boston: Houghton Mifflin, 1975.

Joel   From Stephen Larsen, *The Shaman's Doorway*, pp. 188–199. New York: Harper & Row, 1976.

Willidjungo   From W. Lloyd Warner, *A Black Civilization*, rev. ed., 212–214. New York: Harper & Row, 1937.

Mun-yir-yir   From W. Lloyd Warner, *A Black Civilatiion*, rev. ed., pp. 215–218. New York: Harper & Row, 1937.

Ramón Medina Silva   Peter T. Furst, "Huichol Conception of the Soul," *Folklore Americas* 27, no. 2 (June 1967):52–56.

Petaga   From Lame Deer and Richard Erdoes, *Lame Deer: Seeker of Visions*, pp.137–138. New York: Simon and Schuster, 1972.

Thunder Cloud   From Paul Radin, *Crashing Thunder*, pp.5–13. Englewood Cliffs, N.J.: Prentice-Hall, 1926.

Dick Mahwee   From Willard Z. Park, *Shamanism in Western North America*, pp. 17, 27, 28, and 54. New York: Cooper Square, 1975.

Isaac Tens   From Marius Barbeau. *Medicine Men of the Pacific Coast*, Bulletin 152. National Museums of Canada, 1958, 1973.

María Sabina   From R. Gordon Wasson, George Cowan, Florence Cowan, and Willard Rhodes, *María Sabina and Her Mazatec Velada*, pp. 17–207. New York: Harcourt Brace Jovanovich, 1974.

Balu Asong Gau   From Carol Rubenstein, *Poems of Indigenous Peoples of Sarawak: Some of the Songs and Chants*, Parts 1 and 2, pp. 1305–1309. Special Monograph no. 2. Sarawak Museum Journal Series, vol. 21, no. 42, 1973.

Warao Shaman   From Johannes Wilbert, "Tobacco and Shamanistic Ecstacy Among to Warao Indians of Venezuela," in *Flesh of the Gods*, ed. Peter Furst, pp. 66–70. New York: Praeger, 1972.

Prem Das   From Prem Das [Paul Adams], *"Huichol Nierikaya:* Journey to the Realm of the Gods." Unpublished, 1977.

MatsúwaMatsúwa and Joan Halifax, 1977.

References

See Bibliography for complete publishing information.

I. Into the Nierika, pages 1–34.

1. Prem Das [Paul Adams], "Huichol Nieríkaya: Journey to the Realm of the Gods."
2. Henry Munn, "The Mushrooms of Language," p. 113.
3. Carmen Blacker, *The Catalpa Bow*, pp. 317–18.
4. Jerome Rothenberg, *Technicians of the Sacred*.
5. Knud Rasmussen, *The Netsilik Eskimos, Social Life and Spiritual Culture*, p. 500.
6. For a development of this theme see Stanislav Grof and Joan Halifax, *The Human Encounter with Death*.
7. Knud Rasmussen, *Across Arctic America*, p. 81.
8. Rasmussen, *Across Arctic America*, p. 385.
9. Gustav Holm, "Ethnological Sketch of the Angmagsalik Eskimo," pp. 88–89.
10. Frank B. Linderman, *Plenty-coups*, p. 302.
11. Natalie Curtis, *The Indian's Book*, pp. 38–39.
12. Curtis, *The Indian's Book*, pp. 38–39.
13. Rasmussen, *Across Arctic America*, pp. 82–84.
14. Rasmussen, *Across Arctic America*, pp. 85–86.
15. Rasmussen, *Across Arctic America*, p. 86.
16. Joseph Campbell, *The Masks of God: Primitive Mythology*, p. 252.
17. Barbara G. Myerhoff, *Peyote Hunt*, p. 33.
18. Myerhoff, *Peyote Hunt*, p. 34.
19. Andrei A. Popov, *Tavgijcy: Materialy po etnografii avamskich i vedeerskich targicev*.
20. Rasmussen, *Across Arctic America*, p. 34.
21. Andreas Lommel, *Shamanism*, p. 57. (with Lommel's translation of A. Friedrich and G. Buddness, *Schamanengeschichten aus Sibiriens*).

22. Mircea Eliade, *Shamanism*, p. 63.
23. See discussion by Mircea Eliade, "Spirit, Light, and Seed."
24. Knud Rasmussen, *Intellectual Culture of the Iglulik Eskimos*, p. 114.
25. Alan W. Watts, *The Two Hands of God*, p. 172.
26. Wenceslas Sieroszewski, "Du chamanisme d'après les croyances Yakoutes," p. 331, quoted by Eliade, *Shamanism*, p. 233; see discussion p. 173f.
27. John G. Neihardt, *Black Elk Speaks*, p. 28.
28. Niehardt, *Black Elk Speaks*, p. 276.
29. Sieroszewski, "Du chamanisme d'après les croyances Yakoutes," pp. 218–219, quoted by Mircea Eliade, "The Yearning for Paradise in Primitive Tradition," pp. 255–267.
30. Campbell, *The Masks of God, Primitive Mythology*, pp. 256–257.
31. Campbell, *The Masks of God, Primitive Mythology*, pp. 257–258.
32. Eliade, *Shamanism*, p. 4.
33. Barbara G. Myerhoff, "Shamanic Equilibrium: Balance and Mediation in Known and Unknown Worlds," pp. 100–101.
34. Myerhoff, "Shamanic Equilibrium," p. 102.
35. Neihardt, *Black Elk Speaks*, pp. 42–43.
36. Waldemar Bogoras, *The Chuckchee*, pp. 450–451.
37. Bogoras, *The Chuckchee*, pp. 450–451.
38. M. A. Czaplicka, *Aboriginal Siberia*, p. 253.
39. Eliade, *Shamanism*, p. 352.
40. Bogoras, *The Chuckchee*, pp. 450–452.
41. Bogoras, *The Chuckchee*, p. 451.
42. Waldemar Jochelson, *Religion and Myths of the Koryak*, p. 52.
43. Bogoras, *The Chuckchee*, pp. 450–452.
44. Weston La Barre, *The Ghost Dance*, pp. 306–307.
45. La Barre, *The Ghost Dance*, p. 221.
46. Rasmussen, *The Netsilik Eskimos*, pp. 303–304.
47. Johannes Wilbert, "The Calabash of the Ruffled Feathers," pp. 90–91.
48. Curtis, *The Indian's Book*, pp. 52–53.

49. Knud Rasmussen, *The Alaskan Eskimos as Described in the Posthumous Notes of Dr. Knud Rasmussen,* ed. H. Ostermann, p. 102.

50. Rasmussen, *The Netsilik Eskimos,* p. 321.

51. Ruth Murray Underhill, *Singing for Power,* p. 7.

52. Curtis, *The Indian's Book,* p. xxiv.

53. Rasmussen, *Across Arctic America,* p. 163.

54. Curtis, *The Indian's Book,* p. 324.

55. Rasmussen, *The Netsilik Eskimos,* p. 321.

56. Rasmussen, *The Netsilik Eskimos,* p. 16.

57. Leslie Spier, *Klamath Ethnology,* p. 239.

58. Rasmussen, *The Netsilik Eskimos,* p. 321.

59. Underhill, *Singing for Power,* p. 6.

60. Marius Barbeau, *Medicine Men of the Pacific Coast.*

61. Gauriil V. Ksenofontov, *Legendy i rasskazy o shamanach u yakutov, buryat i tungusov,* pp. 160–161, trans. and quoted by Joseph Campbell, *The Masks of God, Primitive Mythology,* p. 265.

62. Rasmussen, *Intellectual Culture of the Iglulik Eskimos,* pp. 118–119.

II. Journey to Other Worlds, pages 35–62.

1. Andrei A. Popov, "How Sereptie Djarvoskin of the Nganasans (Tavgi Samoyeds) Became a Shaman," p. 137.

2. Vilmos Diószegi, *Tracing Shamans in Siberia,* p. 58.

3. Diószegi, *Tracing Shamans in Siberia,* p. 61.

4. Discussion based on Diószegi, *Tracing Shamans in Siberia,* pp. 51–63.

5. Discussion based on Alfred W. Howitt, *The Native Tribes of South-East Australia,* pp. 406–408.

6. Marguerite Anne Biesele, *Folklore and Ritual of !Kung Hunter-Gatherers,* p. 151.

7. Biesele, *Folklore and Ritual of !Kung Hunter-Gatherers,* p. 151.

8. Biesele, *Folklore and Ritual of !Kung Hunter-Gatherers,* p. 152.

9. Biesele, *Folklore and Ritual of !Kung Hunter-Gatherers,* p. 153.

10. Discussion based on Biesele, *Folklore and Ritual of !Kung Hunter-Gatherers.*

III. The Quest for Vision, pages 63–91.

1. Knud Rasmussen, *Across Arctic America*, p. 87.
2. Rasmussen, *Intellectual Culture of the Hudson Bay Eskimos*, p. 155.
3. Rasmussen, *Across Arctic America*, pp. 85–86.
4. Rasmussen, *Across Arctic America*, p. 81.
5. Lame Deer and Richard Erdoes, *Lame Deer: Seeker of Visions*, pp. 157–158.
6. Lame Deer and Erdoes, *Lame Deer: Seeker of Visions*, pp. 157–158.
7. Discussion based on Lame Deer and Erdoes, *Lame Deer: Seeker of Visions*.
8. Discussion based on Richard Erdoes, personal communication, 1978.
9. Discussion based on Brooke Medicine Eagle, personal communication, 1977.

IV. Seeing in a Sacred Way, pages 93–125.

1. John G. Neihardt, *Black Elk Speaks*, pp. 279–280.
2. Black Elk, *The Sacred Pipe*, recorded and ed. Joseph Epps Brown, p. xxvii.
3. Discussion based on Neihardt, *Black Elk Speaks*.
4. Willard Z. Park, *Shamanism in Western North America*, p. 24.
5. Discussion based on Park, *Shamanism in Western North America*.
6. Discussion based on Park, *Shamanism in Western North America*.
7. Knud Rasmussen, *The People of the Polar North*, p. 305.
8. Rasmussen, *The People of the Polar North*, p. 305.
9. Discussion based on Rasmussen, *The People of the Polar North*, pp. 305–309.
10. Gustav Holm, *Ethnological Sketch of the Angmagsalik Eskimo*, p. 88.
11. Holm, *Ethnological Sketch of the Angmagsalik Eskimo*, p. 88–89.
12. Holm, *Ethnological Sketch of the Angmagsalik Eskimo*, p. 89.
13. Holm, *Ethnological Sketch of the Angmagsalik Eskimo*, p. 89.
14. Knud Rasmussen, *Across Arctic America*, p. 21.
15. Rasmussen, *Across Arctic America*, p. 21.

16. Knud Rasmussen, *Intellectual Culture of the Iglulik Eskimos,* p. 56.
17. Rasmussen, *Intellectual Culture of the Iglulik Eskimos,* pp. 92–93.
18. Rasmussen, *Intellectual Culture of the Iglulik Eskimos,* pp. 60–61.
19. Rasmussen, *Intellectual Culture of the Iglulik Eskimos,* p. 117.
20. Rasmussen, *Intellectual Culture of the Iglulik Eskimos,* p. 119.
21. Lev Iakovlevich Shternberg, "Shamanism and Religious Election," p. 75.
22. Shternberg, "Shamanism and Religious Election," p. 75.
23. Shternberg, "Shamanism and Religious Election," p. 77.
24. Discussion based on Shternberg, "Shamanism and Religious Election," pp. 61–85.
25. Discussion based on Alfred W. Howitt, *The Native Tribes of South-East Australia,* pp. 408–410.

V. Wondrous Medicine, pages 127–156.

1. R. Gordon Wasson, *The Wonderous Mushroom.*
2. Discussion based on Henry Munn, "The Mushrooms of Language," pp. 56–122; Álvaro Estrada, *Vida de María Sabina: La Sabia de los Hongos;* R. Gordon Wasson, George Cowan and Florence Cowan, and Willard Rhodes, *María Sabina and Her Mazatec Mushroom Velada;* R. Gordon Wasson, *The Wonderous Mushroom.*
3. Barbara G. Myerhoff, *Peyote Hunt,* p. 189.
4. Myerhoff, *Peyote Hunt,* p. 220.
5. Myerhoff, *Peyote Hunt,* p. 34.
6. Gerardo Reichel-Dolmatoff, *The Shaman and the Jaguar,* p. 67.
7. Reichel-Dolmatoff, *The Shaman and the Jaguar,* pp. 74–75.
8. Reichel-Dolmatoff, *The Shaman and the Jaguar,* pp. 74–75.
9. Discussion based on Reichel-Dolmatoff, *The Shaman and the Jaguar.*
10. F. Bruce Lamb, *Wizard of the Upper Amazon,* 2d ed., pp. 198–199.
11. Discussion based on Lamb, *Wizard of the Upper Amazon.*
12. Stephen Larsen, *The Shaman's Doorway,* p. 192.

13. Larsen, *The Shaman's Doorway*, p. 183.
14. Discussion based on Larsen, *The Shaman's Doorway*, pp. 188–199.

VI. The Power to Transform, pages 157–191.

1. W. Lloyd Warner, *A Black Civilization*, p. 210.
2. Warner, *A Black Civilization*, p. 210.
3. Warner, *A Black Civilization*, p. 212.
4. Discussion based on Warner, *A Black Civilization*, pp. 217–218.
5. Knud Rasmussen, *Intellectual Culture of the Iglulik Eskimos*, pp. 110–111.
6. Knud Rasmussen, *Intellectual Culture of the Iglulik Eskimos*, p. 129.
7. Knud Rasmussen, *Across Arctic America*, p. 28.
8. Rasmussen, *Intellectual Culture of the Iglulik Eskimos*, pp. 129–131.
9. Rasmussen, *Intellectual Culture of the Iglulik Eskimos*, p. 131.
10. Peter Furst, "Huichol Conception of the Soul," pp. 46–47.
11. Furst, "Huichol Conception of the Soul," pp. 51–52.
12. Furst, "Huichol Conception of the Soul," pp. 54–55.
13. For a complete discussion of this area read Peter Furst's article "Huichol Conception of the Soul."
14. A. Amiotte, "Eagles Fly Over," p. 29.
15. Amiotte, "Eagles Fly Over," p. 29.
16. Lame Deer and Richard Erdoes, *Lame Deer: Seeker of Visions*, pp. 126–127, 137–138.
17. Paul Radin, *Crashing Thunder*, pp. 2–3.
18. Radin, *Crashing Thunder*, pp. 6–7.
19. Discussion based on Willard Z. Park, *Shamanism in Western North America*.
20. Discussion based on Marius Barbeau, *Medicine Men of the Pacific Coast*.

VII. Singing into Life, pages 193–220.

1. R. Gordon Wasson, George Cowan, Florence Cowan, and Willard Rhodes, *María Sabina and Her Mazatec Velada*.
2. Henry Munn, "The Mushrooms of Language," p. 90.
3. Munn, "The Mushrooms of Language," p. 109.

4. Wasson, Cowan, Cowan, and Rhodes, *María Sabina and Her Mazatec Velada*, p. 93.
5. Carol Rubenstein, *Poems of the Indigenous Peoples of Sarawak*, p. 1305.
6. Carol Rubenstein, personal communication, 1977.
7. Discussion based on Carol Rubenstein, personal communication, 1977.

VIII. The House of Dreams, pages 221–246.

1. Gerardo Reichel-Dolmatoff, *The Shaman and the Jaguar*, p. 107.
2. Reichel-Dolmatoff, *The Shaman and the Jaguar*, p. 133.
3. Reichel-Dolmatoff, *The Shaman and the Jaguar*, p. 147.
4. Reichel-Dolmatoff, *The Shaman and the Jaguar*, p. 148.
5. Reichel-Dolmatoff, *The Shaman and the Jaguar*, p. 148.
6. Discussion based on Reichel-Dolmatoff, *The Shaman and the Jaguar*.
7. Johannes Wilbert, "Tobacco and Shamanistic Ecstacy Among the Warao of Venezuela," pp. 65–66.
8. Wilbert, "Tobacco and Shamanistic Ecstacy Among the Warao of Venezuela," pp. 58–60.
9. Wilbert, "Tobacco and Shamanistic Ecstacy Among the Warao of Venezuela," p. 70.
10. Discussion based on Wilbert, "Tobacco and Shamanistic Ecstacy Among the Warao of Venezuela."
11. Barbara G. Myerhoff, *Peyote Hunt*, p. 20.
12. Myerhoff, *Peyote Hunt*, p. 184.
13. Discussion based on Prem Das, personal communication, 1977.

IX. Lifting up the Nieríka, pages 247–252.

1. Prem Das, personal communication, 1977.
2. Peter Furst, "Peyote Among the Huichol Indians of Mexico," in *The Flesh of the Gods*, pp. 136–184, refer to p. 155.
3. Matsúwa, personal communication, 1977.

bibliography

Amiotte, A. "Eagles Fly Over." *Parabola* 1, no. 3 (September 1976): 28–41.

Barbeau, Marius. *Medicine Men of the Pacific Coast.* Bulletin 152. Ottawa: National Museums of Man, National Museums of Canada. 1958.

Biesele, Marguerite Anne. "Folklore and Ritual of !Kung Hunter-Gatherers." Ph.D. dissertation, Harvard University, 1975.

Blacker, Carmen. *The Catalpa Bow.* London: Allen & Unwin, 1975.

Bogoras, Waldemar. *The Chuckchee.* Jesup North Pacific Expedition, vol. 7 (American Museum of Natural History Memoirs, Vol. II), 1904.

Brown, Joseph Epes. *The Sacred Pipe.* New York: Penquin Books, 1971.

Campbell, Joseph. *The Masks of God: Primitive Mythology.* New York: Viking Press, 1972.

Curtis, Natalie. *The Indian's Book.* New York: Harper & Row, 1907.

Czaplicka, M. A. *Aboriginal Siberia: A Study in Social Anthropology.* Oxford: Oxford University Press, 1914.

Diószegi, Vilmos. *Tracing Shamans in Siberia.* Translated by Anita Rajkay Bubo. Oosterhout (Netherlands): Anthropological Publications, 1968.

————, ed. *Popular Beliefs and Folklore Tradition in Siberia.* Translated by Stephen P. Dunn. Bloomington: Indiana University Press, 1968.

Dunn, Stephen P., and Dunn, Ethel, eds. *Introduction to Soviet Ethnology.* Vol. 1. Berkeley, Calif.: Highgate Road Social Science Research Station, 1974.

Eliade, Mircea. *Shamanism: Archaic Techniques of Ecstasy.* Translated by Willard R. Trask (Bollingen Series 76). New York: Pantheon Books, 1964.

————. "Spirit, Light, and Seed." *History of Religions* 11, no. 1 (August 1971): 1–30.

————. "The Yearning for Paradise in Primitive Tradition." *Diogenes* 3 (Summer 1953): 18–30. Reprint. *Daedalus* 88, no. 2 (Spring 1959): 255–267.

Estrada, Álvaro. *Vida de María Sabina: La Sabia de los Hongos.* Mexico: Siglo Veintiuno Editores, 1977.

Furst, Peter T. "Huichol Conception of the Soul." *Folklore Americas* 27, no. 2 (June 1967): 39–106.

————, ed. *The Flesh of the Gods.* New York: Praeger, 1972.

————, and Anguiano, Marina. " 'To Fly as Birds': Myth and Ritual as Agents of Enculturation among the Huichol Indians of Mexico." In *Enculturation in Latin America: An Anthology,* edited by Johannes Wilbert, pp. 95–181. Los Angeles: UCLA Latin American Center Publications, 1977.

263

Grof, Stanislav, and Halifax, Joan. *The Human Encounter with Death*. New York: Dutton, 1978.

Hand, Wayland D., ed. *American Folk Medicine: A Symposium*. Berkeley: University of California Press, 1976.

Harner, Michael J., ed. *Hallucinogens and Shamanism*. Oxford: Oxford University Press, 1973.

Holm, Gustav. "Ethnological Sketch of the Angmagsalik Eskimo." In *The Ammasalik Eskimo: Contributions to the Ethnology of the East Greenland Natives*, Part 1, edited by William Thalbitzer. Meddelesen om Gronland Series, Bind XXXIX and XL, Copenhagen: C. A. Reitzel, 1914, pp. 86–89.

_____. "Legends and Tales from Angmagsalik." In *The Ammasalik Eskimo: Contributions to the Ethnology of the East Greenland Natives*, edited by William Thalbitzer and translated by Johan Petersen. Meddeleser om Gronland series, Bind XXXIX and XL. Copenhagen: C. A. Reitzel, 1914, pp. 298–300.

Howitt, Alfred W. *The Native Tribes of South-East Australia*. London: Macmillan, 1904.

Jochelson, Waldemar. *Religion and Myths of the Koryak*. Jesup North Pacific Expedition. Vol. 6. (AMNH Memoirs, 10, pts. 1 and 2) Leiden, N.Y.: 1905–1908.

Ksenofontov, Gauriil V. *Legendy i rasskazy o shamanach u yakutov, buryat i tungusov*. Izdanie vtoroe. S predisloviem S.A. Tokareva. Moscow: Izdatel'stvo Bezbozhnik, 1930. Translated by Adolf Friedrich and Georg Buddruss, *Schaman geschichten aws Sibirien*, Munich: Otto Wilhelm Barth-Velag, 1955.

La Barre, Weston. *The Ghost Dance*. New York: Dell, 1972.

Lamb, F. Bruce. *Wizard of the Upper Amazon*. 2d ed. Boston: Houghton Mifflin, 1975.

Lame Deer, and Erdoes, Richard. *Lame Deer: Seeker of Visions*. New York: Simon and Schuster, 1972.

Larsen, Stephen. *The Shaman's Doorway*. New York: Harper & Row, 1976.

Linderman, Frank B. *Plenty-coups*. Lincoln, Nebr.: University of Nebraska Press, 1962.

Lommel, Andreas. *Shamanism*. New York: McGraw-Hill, 1967.

Myerhoff, Barbara G. *Peyote Hunt*. Ithaca, N.Y.: Cornell University Press, 1974.

_____. "Shamanic Equilibrium: Balance and Mediation in Known and Unknown Worlds." In *American Folk Medicine: A Symposium*, edited by Wayland D. Hand, pp. 99–108. Berkeley: University of California Press, 1976.

Munn, Henry. "The Mushrooms of Language." In *Hallucinogens and Shamanism*, edited by Michael J. Harner, pp. 86–122. Oxford: Oxford University Press, 1973.

Neihardt, John G. *Black Elk Speaks*. Lincoln, Nebr.: University of Nebraska Press, 1961.

Park, Willard Z. *Shamanism in Western North America*. New York: Cooper Square, 1975.

Popov, Andrei A. "How Sereptie Djarvoskin of the Nganasans (Tavgi Samoyeds) Became a Shaman." In *Popular Beliefs and Folklore Tradition in Siberia*, edited by Vilmos Diószegi. Translated by Stephen P. Dunn, pp. 137–146. Bloomington, Ind.: Indiana University Press, 1968.

_____. *Tavgijcy: Materialy po etnografii avamskich i vedeerskich targicev*. Trudy instituta antropologii i etnographi, t. 5, vyp. 5. Leningrad, Akademiya anu SSR, 1936.

Prem Das [Paul Adams]. "Huichol Nieríkaya: Journey to the Realm of the Gods." Unpublished, 1977.

Radin, Paul. *Crashing Thunder.* New York: Prentice-Hall, 1926.

Rasmussen, Knud. *Across Arctic America, Narrative of the Fifth Thule Expedition.* Translated by W. E. Calvert, ed. from *Fra Grøland till Stillehavet* (Copenhagen, 1925). New York: Greenwood Press, 1969. Reprint. New York: Putnam, 1927.

―――. *The Alaskan Eskimos, as Described in the Posthumous Notes of Dr. Knud Rasmussen.* Edited by H. Ostermann with E. Holtved. Translated by W. E. Calvert. Report of the Fifth Thule Expedition, 1921–1924. Vol. 10, no. 3. Copenhagen: Gyldendal, 1952.

―――. *Intellectual Culture of the Hudson Bay Eskimos.* Translated by W. E. Calvert. Report of the Fifth Thule Expedition, 1921–1924. Vol. 7. Copenhagen: Gyldendal, 1930.

―――. *Intellectual Culture of the Iglulik Eskimos.* Translated by William Worster. Report of the Fifth Thule Expedition 1921–1924. Vol. 7, Part I. Copenhagen: Gyldendal, 1930.

―――. *The Netsilik Eskimos: Social Life and Spiritual Culture.* Translated by W. E. Calvert. Report of the Fifth Thule Expedition, 1921–1924. Vol. 8. Copenhagen: Gyldendal, 1931.

―――. *The People of the Polar North, A Record.* Compiled and edited by G. Herring. Philadelphia: Lippincott, 1908.

―――. *Rasmussens Thulefahrt: 2 Jahre im Schlitten durchunerforschtes Eskimoland.* Edited by Friedrich Sieburg. Frankfurt: Frankfurter Societäts, 1926.

Reichel-Dolmatoff, Gerardo. *The Shaman and the Jaguar.* Philadelphia: Temple University Press, 1975.

Rothenberg, Jerome, (ed.). *Technicians of the Sacred: A Range of Poetries from Africa, America, Asia and Oceania.* Garden City, N.Y.: Doubleday, 1968.

Rubenstein, Carol. *Poems of Indigenous Peoples of Sarawak: Some of the Songs and Chants.* Parts 1 and 2. Special Monograph no. 2. Sarawak Museum Journal Series. vol. 21, no. 42 Sarawak, 1973.

Sieroszewski, Wenceslas. "Du chamanisme d'après les croyances des Yakoutes, Mémoire présente au Congrès International d'Histoire des Religions, en séance de section, le 3 septembre 1900." In *Revue de l'Histoire des Religions* (Annales du Musée Guimet) 46 (1902): 204–233 and 299–338.

Spier, Leslie. *Klamath Ethnology,* University of California Publications in Archaeology and Ethnology, no 30. Berkeley, Calif.: University of California, 1930.

Shternberg, Lev Iakovlevich. "Divine election in primitive religion (including material on different tribes of N. E. Asia and America)." In *Congrès international des americanistes: Compte-Rendu de la XXIe session, 2ème partie,* tenue a Göteborg en 1924. Nendeln (Liechtenstein): Kraus Reprint (Kraus-Thomson Organization Ltd.), 1968.

―――. "Shamanism and Religious Election." In *Introduction to Soviet Ethnology.* Vol. 1. Edited by Stephen P. Dunn and Ethel Dunn. Berkeley, Calif: Highgate Road Social Science Research Station, 1974.

Strachan, Alan. *Paths of Transformation.* Honors Thesis, University of California, Santa Cruz, 1977.

Underhill, Ruth Murray. *Singing for Power.* Berkeley: University of California, 1976.

Warner, W. Lloyd. *A Black Civilization*. Rev. ed. New York: Harper & Row, 1937.

Wasson, R. Gordon. *The Wonderous Mushroom*, forthcoming.

_____; Cowan, George; Cowan, Florence; and Rhodes, Willard. *María Sabina and Her Mazatec Velada*. New York: Harcourt Brace Jovanovich, 1974.

Watts, Alan W. *The Two Hands of God*. Toronto: Collier, 1969.

Wilbert, Johannes. "The Calabash of the Ruffled Feathers." *artcanada* special issues nos. 184–187: *Stones, Bones and Skin: Ritual and Shamanic Art*, Toronto: Society for Art Publications, December 1973–January 1974.

FOR THE BEST IN PAPERBACKS, LOOK FOR THE